THE PEOPLES OF THE
SOVIET FAR EAST

THE PEOPLES OF THE
SOVIET FAR EAST

BY

WALTER KOLARZ

ARCHON BOOKS
1969

First Published 1954
Reprinted 1969 with permission
in an unaltered and unabridged edition

SBN: 208 00701 6
Library of Congress Catalog Card Number: 69-12416
Printed in the United States of America

PREFACE

This book, though self-contained, is the continuation of *Russia and her Colonies*. It deals with Russian colonization and Soviet nationalities (colonial) policy in a vast territory which I have described, for lack of a better term, as the 'Soviet Far East'. From the official Soviet point of view, the Soviet Far East comprises all territories of the U.S.S.R. situated to the east of Lake Baikal. It covers the Autonomous Republics of Yakutia and Buryat-Mongolia as well as the whole expansive Pacific coastal areas of the Soviet Union reaching from the Bering Straits down to Vladivostok. On the whole, I have accepted this official definition of the 'Soviet Far East' but I have added to it the Mongol People's Republic, the former People's Republic of Tuva, and a number of small nationalities which are closely connected with the latter.

Few foreigners have visited the Soviet Far Eastern territories during the last fifteen or twenty years and most of these few were not exactly 'visitors' but were inmates of Far Eastern forced labour camps. Some of them, like Mrs. Elinor Lipper, have written moving and revealing accounts of their experience, but naturally they could not deal with the problems of Soviet colonial policy in the Far East except in a few casual though valuable remarks. The only group of foreigners given a chance to travel extensively as tourists in the Soviet Far East and to visit even such normally prohibited places as Magadan and Irkutsk consisted of the former United States Vice-President, Henry Wallace and his entourage. The Wallace trip took place under the close supervision of the Soviet Police Ministry. This fact alone made it impossible for Mr. Wallace and the members of his mission to get access to the more essential relevant material on Soviet colonial policy in the Far East.

The isolation of the Soviet Far East from the outside world was completed in the second half of 1948. In August of that year the only Western diplomatic representation in the whole of Soviet Asia, the American Consulate-General in Vladivostok, was closed down at the request of the Soviet authorities. On September 30th, 1948, the Soviet Ministry of Foreign Affairs issued a circular which listed as forbidden areas practically all administrative units of the Far East from Irkutsk to Vladivostok.

In these circumstances, for any study of the problems of the Soviet Far East one has to rely almost exclusively on published Soviet material, and even there one faces considerable difficulties. The Moscow Press contains only scanty and sporadic information about the problems of the Soviet Far Eastern territories and the literature which the central state publishing houses produce about them is poor. From the Soviet Far East, itself, books, pamphlets and journals have reached the non-communist world only on a few occasions and it is usually a question of luck or coincidence whether a given book or pamphlet on the Soviet Far East becomes available abroad or whether it can be obtained in a particular country.

As every student of Soviet affairs knows, the term 'Soviet sources' includes not only positive statements but also omissions. The silence observed in official Soviet quarters and in their press about a previously much advertised institution, a prominent personality, or even an entire people, has often had historical significance. Experience has shown that such 'negative' evidence though not ideal from the point of view of the historian is usually reliable. I have used it in this book in a number of instances, particularly when trying to disentangle the story of Marshal Blyukher's downfall and in describing the fate of the Korean and Chinese minorities in the Soviet Far East.

In view of the scarcity of straightforward documentary material I have also drawn on a number of Soviet novels, plays and poems which touch upon the problems of the Far East. By force of circumstance Soviet writers are, as a rule, highly responsive to the wishes of the political leaders of the Soviet State. It is therefore legitimate to consider Soviet *belles-lettres* as a fairly accurate reflection of the official communist approach towards the nationalities question and other aspects of the Soviet Far East. The gaps in my sources are nevertheless colossal and there is little hope that they can be filled as long as Soviet Russia and its sphere of influence remain virtually sealed off from the rest of the globe.

My sincere gratitude goes to those friends who have sacrificed much time to read either the manuscript or the proofs of this book which owes a great deal to their frank criticism and valuable suggestions.

September 21st, 1953   WALTER KOLARZ

CONTENTS

CONTENTS

CONTENTS

MAPS

ILLUSTRATION

SEA OF OKHOTSK

U. S. S. R.

G G

130 140

G Okha

Nikolaevsk

G G

G

Svobodny Aleksandrovsk Former
Soviet-
Japanese
Komsomolsk Border
Blagoveshchensk 50

50 Uglegorsk
Makarov

Birobidzhan Chekhov Yuzhno-
Jewish Khabarovsk Kholmsk Sakhalinsk
Autonomous Nevelsk
Province Korsakov
MANCHURIA
Border

G

SEA

Voroshilov OF JAPAN
Suchan 140
Vladivostok JAPAN
Poset

Former Korean Coal Deposits
National District G Gold Mines
0 Miles 200 Oil Wells

130

Copyright

1. THE SOUTH-EASTERN PART OF THE SOVIET FAR EAST

I

THE RUSSIANS OF THE SOVIET FAR EAST

Outwardly there is no great difference between the Russian Far East and the rest of the Soviet Russian Empire. The Communist Party seems to rule in Vladivostok and Khabarovsk as firmly as in Moscow and Leningrad. Nevertheless, the Russian Far East has an individuality of its own and has its special problems. Vladivostok lies as far away from Moscow as London does from Winnipeg, Capetown or Calcutta. Such a gigantic distance must have political consequences even in an autocratic or totalitarian state. In territories where Russia borders on China, Korea, Japan and the United States, the outlook of the local Russian inhabitants is bound to differ from that prevailing on the banks of the Don or the Volga. Geographical circumstances force the Russians of Vladivostok, Blagoveshchensk or Khabarovsk to feel themselves 'Far Easterners' ('Dalnevostochniki'), pioneers who have a special political and historic mission, incomparably more complicated than the tasks confronting the population of Central or Western Russia.

In Czarist Russia it was generally understood that the Far East was a 'special case'. Until Russia suffered defeat in the war against Japan in 1905 she looked upon her Far East as a base for the conquest of wide Asiatic territories – Manchuria, Korea, China and Tibet. There seemed to be no limit to her imperialistic ambitions. Japan's victory completely changed this situation. Russian expansion in the Far East met with a serious setback, and many Russians even doubted whether Vladivostok and other Far Eastern possessions of the Czarist Empire could be held for any length of time. Russia, it is true, was connected with the Pacific coastal areas by the Trans-Siberian Railway, but there was widespread fear that this link might not prove solid enough. In 1909 the well-known liberal monthly journal of St. Petersburg, *Vestnik Evropy*, warned the government that the Russian Far East might act towards Russia in the same way as New England had acted towards the English crown. The separation of the Pacific possessions from the Russian Empire appeared as a real danger which could be averted only by a policy of concessions and economic privileges. The writer of the article in *Vestnik Evropy* reminded his readers that the revolt of Britain's former North American colonies occurred over a question of customs

1

duties and that this should be a lesson to Russia in dealing with her distant Far Eastern colonies.[1] A democratic and liberal Russia might well have granted special rights to the Russian Far East and perpetuated the freedom of customs duties which the ports of Vladivostok and Nikolayevsk enjoyed at the beginning of the century.* The Russian Far East might have achieved, within the Russian Empire, something approaching a dominion status. The democratic régime which was ready to open Russia's windows into the world collapsed in 1917 after only a few months' existence. But even the Soviet régime, which succeeded it, could not escape from the geographical peculiarities of the Far East and from the special mentality of the Russian 'Far Easterners'.

I. THE POLITICAL FRAMEWORK

THE FAR EASTERN REPUBLIC

In the early years of Soviet rule the special communist approach towards the Russian Far East found expression in the establishment of the 'Far Eastern Republic' (F.E.R.). This buffer state was set up by a decision of the Central Committee of the All-Russian Communist Party. The Republic was to appeal to the patriotism and to the anti-Japanese animosities of the Far Eastern Russians, but not to their sympathies for an international communism. It was to have a 'bourgeois democratic character'. Its constitution did not include any provisions about the setting-up of Soviets, but provided for a National Assembly to be elected by universal direct and secret ballot. The national flag of the Republic was red and blue and its coat of arms discarded the communist symbols, hammer and sickle. Instead, it showed an anchor and a pickaxe crossed over a wheat-sheaf. There were no 'People's Commissars' in the Far Eastern Republic, only ministers, and there was no 'Red Army', only a 'Revolutionary People's Army'.

Although the F.E.R. was founded by the Kremlin for mere tactical reasons some of its leaders took it very seriously and they wanted to transform the Republic into a living political reality. They demanded that the F.E.R., which reached in the west as far as Lake Baikal, should extend its territory to the Yenisey River, and they also pleaded for greater independence from Moscow than the Bolshevik Central Committee was willing to grant. Some quarters of the F.E.R. even toyed with

---

* Complete freedom from customs duties existed in the Russian Far East between 1862 and 1888. In 1888 customs duties were introduced for sugar, matches and kerosene and after 1901 duty had to be paid on industrial articles but not on agricultural produce (except for flour) nor on capital goods. Only Sakhalin and Kamchatka remained exempt. To attract more settlers freedom from customs duties was restored in 1904, but was finally abolished again in 1909.

2

the idea of an American orientation and conducted a great deal of propaganda in the United States. A dispute broke out also among the Far Eastern communists as to the selection of the Republican capital. Those who stood for greater independence suggested that the capital should be established there where contact with the non-Russian world was most intimate, in Vladivostok. The Bolshevik Central Committee, on the other hand, realized the dangers inherent in such a move. It ruled that the headquarters of the Far Eastern government should be in the Russian city of Chita and not in the cosmopolitan port of Vladivostok.

Throughout its existence the F.E.R. had a very difficult time. Parts of the Republic were occupied by Japanese troops and others were the scene of white guard activities. Accordingly, the government of the F.E.R. exercised only a nominal sovereignty over certain of its provinces. Paradoxically enough, the Japanese occupation of the F.E.R. was not only the chief source of its weakness but also its principal *raison d'être*. The setting-up of the F.E.R. enabled the Russian Far Easterners, particularly the peasant colonists, to support Soviet foreign policy and the Soviet fight against foreign intervention without identifying themselves with the Communist Party and its economic aspirations. On October 25th, 1922, the last Japanese soldier left the Russian mainland and the need for a 'Far Eastern Republic' ceased automatically. The Constituent Assembly of the F.E.R., in which the communists had four-fifths of all seats, decided to hand over its powers to a 'Far Eastern Revolutionary Committee', the *Dalrevkom*, which was already a direct organ of the Soviet Government.

The decision of the Far Eastern Constituent Assembly did not mean that the Russians of the Far East were in any way united behind the Communist Party. The communists constituted a minority in the Far East even smaller than anywhere else in Soviet Russia. Early in 1922 they had only 7,000 members in the whole of the F.E.R., and this was on the eve of a purge which aimed at a reduction of the membership by 15 to 18 per cent.[2] The Party relied on the support of a section of the 'Far Eastern Trades Union Congress' (D.V.S.P.S.) which had 40,000 members; but how many of them really sympathized with the communists it is impossible to say. In view of its numerical weakness and isolation the communist movement in the Far East had to go carefully and had to make some concessions to regionalist tendencies. Many people in the Russian Far East continued to favour a special status for their homeland and hoped that after the abolition of the F.E.R. it would not become just another Soviet Russian province. At the beginning their hopes were not entirely betrayed.

3

THE FAR EASTERN TERRITORY

During the whole period from 1922 to 1937–38 the Soviet Far East enjoyed a special position within the Soviet Union. From the administrative point of view the Soviet Far East formed one large unit, the 'Far Eastern Territory' (F.E.T.). It covered roughly one-eighth of the entire surface of the U.S.S.R. The F.E.T. existed from January 1926 until October 1938, but there was a slight amputation of the territory in 1930, when the districts of Sreten and Chita were detached. Militarily, too, the Soviet Far East had a semi-independent existence by the establishment, in August 1929, of the Special Far Eastern Army ('Osobaya Dalnevostochnaya Armiya') usually referred to by its initials as ODVA and a year after its foundation as OKDVA (Osobaya Krasnoznamyonnaya Dalnevostochnaya Armiya', meaning 'Special Far Eastern Army decorated with the Order of the Red Banner').

Both army commanders and administrators in the Far East showed a considerable degree of independence, which, in some cases, even expressed itself in open opposition to the régime. This is true, in particular of the party leaders of Vladivostok, a city which, like that other opposition centre, Leningrad, was a window into the world. The radical course, aiming at the liquidation of the remnants of private property, which the Bolshevik Party took after its Fifteenth Congress (1927) did not meet with approval in a trading centre like Vladivostok. Both Vladivostok and Chita became, in the late twenties, strongholds of a right-wing opposition and the Central Committee in Moscow had to dismiss the local party chiefs.[3]

Difficulties between the centre and the Far Eastern communists continued after the suppression of the right-wing deviation. Problems connected with the implementation of the First and Second Five-Year Plans were an almost inexhaustible source of disagreements. Already during the first Five-Year Plan period the State Planning Commission in Moscow had worked out big development schemes for the Far East, providing for the building of additional railways, an increase of coal and oil production, and far-reaching industrialization. When it became clear that many of the envisaged projects could not be carried out neither Moscow nor Khabarovsk wanted to take the blame for the failure. The central authorities complained about the inefficiency of the 'Far Easterners' and the latter denounced the lack of understanding of the officials at the centre. At the Sixteenth Party Congress, which was held in 1930, the spokesman of the F.E.T., Perepechko, referred to the 'hideous attitude of various central organizations' towards the economic problems of the Far East.[4] If it were not for this negligence, Perepechko asserted, the F.E.T. would carry out the basic tasks of the Five-Year

Plan in three years. The later development showed that it took not three but ten years to reach the target figures which the first Five-Year Plan had fixed for the coal and oil production of the Far East. * The Central Government refused to admit that the shortcomings in the Far East resulted from deficiencies of all-Union planning, and tried to put the blame on local scapegoats who were charged with committing deliberate sabotage. More than that, the Central Government alleged that the Far Eastern administrators were 'Japanese spies', although they were, presumably, no more connected with Japan than the Leningrad opposition was linked with Germany. The Far Eastern communists, it is true, had shown great eagerness to establish commercial relations with other Pacific countries including Japan, but this had been done with the agreement of the centre.

THE PURGE OF THE 'CIVILIANS'

Although there was no evidence for charges of high treason the Soviet Government carried out a purge on a vast scale throughout the Soviet Far East. It would be incorrect to say that there was one big purge. There were at least two purges, one directed primarily against 'civilian' communists, and another aimed mainly at the army. The first purge, which was closely connected with economic shortcomings, started in the first months of 1937 and led to the disappearance of the head of the administration of the F.E.T., Krutov, and of the party secretary, Lavrentev. At the same time administrative heads and party officials were sacked all over the Soviet Far East. For many months there were no 'first secretaries' in many city committees and district committees of the Communist Party.

There is one aspect of the purge of the 'civilians' in the Far East which deserves special mention, the purge of the railwaymen. The railwaymen of the Far East were traditionally the backbone of the Communist Party in that distant part of the Soviet Union, and the solidity of Moscow's connection with the Pacific coastal areas depended largely on their efficiency. In the 'thirties' their job became increasingly difficult. Between 1933 and 1936 the freight turnover of the Far Eastern railways had increased three times. This was more than they could stand. The Far Eastern railway system broke down. A great many accidents occurred. The Government asserted that they were all engineered 'on instructions of the Japanese intelligence service.' The supreme responsibility for the wrecking of trains was officially attributed to Trotsky and to the

* Production of oil was to reach 464,000 tons by the end of the first Five-Year Plan in 1932. In 1933 output was 196,000 tons; in 1936, 308,000 tons, and in 1938, 360,000 tons. The coal target for 1932 was 4,000,000 tons. In 1933 output had reached 2,020,000 tons, and in 1936, 3,617,000 tons. The target for 1937 was 5,000,000 tons, but actual production in 1938 was only 4,750,000 tons.

various members of the so-called 'Anti-Soviet Bloc of Rights and Trotskyites' which was allegedly led by Bukharin. In the Far East itself the Soviet Government staged a big trial of leading railway officials working on the Amur railway line, a sector of the Trans-Siberian railway. The trial took place in the town of Svobodny. All forty-four defendants were sentenced to death as 'Japanese spies'. They included the deputy head of the Amur railway line, the head of its planning department, the deputy head of the locomotive service and many other people of similar standing in the Far Eastern railway transport.[5] The sentence of Svobodny had considerable repercussions throughout the F.E.T. Sweeping changes took place not only in the top leadership of the Far Eastern railways but also among the rank and file of the railwaymen. Demobilized soldiers were rapidly trained for the railway and called upon to fill the gaps opened by the purges.

The man who, in 1937, carried out the purge in the Soviet Far East was a complete newcomer to the territory. His name was Vareikis, he was Lithuanian-born and had occupied various important positions in European Russia, as party secretary first of Voronezh and later of Stalingrad. He was also a member of the Central Committee of the Bolshevik Party. When he arrived in Khabarovsk in the spring of 1937 he seemed to possess the full confidence of Stalin, but by the end of the year he had lost it. He was charged with surrounding himself with spies and white guardists. A case in point was the editor of the largest Far Eastern newspaper *Tikhookeanskaya Zvezda* (Far Eastern Star), Shver, who was expelled from the party by a special decision of the Central Committee taken at the beginning of October.[6] Vareikis survived his friend only by a few days.

THE PURGE OF THE FAR EASTERN ARMY

The disgrace of Vareikis and his supporters carried the disintegration of the party apparatus in the Far East a step further. Only one important force continued to exist in the F.E.T., the Special Far Eastern Army and its commander, Marshal Vasily Konstantinovich Blyukher. But it was clear that this last bulwark of Far Eastern 'autonomism' would, sooner or later, be affected by the big Stalinist clean up of Russia's military leadership. One of the defendants of the Tukhachevsky trial of June 1937, the commander of the Byelorussian Military District, Uborevich, had had important connections with the Far East. In 1922 he had been the liberator of Vladivostok and he had stayed in the F.E.T. for several years. There was another military person who was closely linked with Stalin's Far Eastern opponents, Gamarnik, the chief of the Political Administration of the Red Army and an Assistant People's Commissar for Defence. Had he not committed suicide he would most

6

certainly have appeared in the Tukhachevsky trial. Gamarnik's presence in the Far East was frequently mentioned in the Soviet Press, the last time late in 1936, when he attended the autumn manœuvres of the OKDVA.[7] One of the last pictures which Soviet newspapers published of Gamarnik showed him with the Far Eastern deputies to the Eighth Congress of Soviets.[8] So there is no doubt that Gamarnik stood in close personal contact with some of the leading personalities of the F.E.T. It is possible that he had closer contacts with the civilian than with the military opposition in the Far East. This might explain why his fall from favour did not harm the Special Far Eastern Army directly, except for its political departments which were under Gamarnik's orders.[9] At any rate, the Tukhachevsky-Gamarnik *affaire* did not affect Blyukher's prestige immediately. Blyukher was even one of the judges who sent Tukhachevsky and his associates to the gallows: these judges, who also included Marshal Timoshenko and Marshal Budyonny, were officially referred to as 'the flower of our glorious army'.[10] In the months after the Tukhachevsky trial they served Bolshevik propaganda as examples that Stalin had not wiped out Russia'a entire military leadership.

It seems that in the winter of 1937–38, Blyukher and his army reached the culminating point of their power in the Far Eastern Territory. The influence of Blyukher and his army was particularly visible in the elections which took place in December 1937 for the Supreme Soviet of the U.S.S.R., the first to be held under the new Stalin Constitution. Out of the nine deputies which the F.E.T. sent to the Soviet of the Union four belonged to the OKDVA, including Blyukher himself and his deputy, Mikhail Karpovich Levandovsky, who commanded the troops of the maritime region around Vladivostok. The fifth deputy, a submarine commander, represented the Pacific Fleet.* The party, the administration and the N.K.V.D.† had one deputy each. Only the ninth deputy represented the common people. He was a Stakhanovite worker in the timber industry.

When the Soviet parliament met in January 1938 Blyukher was elected a member of its presidium. In the following month, on Red Army Day, he was awarded the 'Order of Lenin'. At the end of May a meeting of 6,500 workers and peasants nominated him as a candidate for the elections to the Supreme Soviet of the R.S.F.S.R.[11] Until the

* The Soviet Pacific Fleet was built up between 1932 and 1937. In the first years of the Soviet régime a Russian Pacific Fleet was as good as non-existent; until 1932 it included but one single gun-boat. Describing the situation at the time of the arrival in Vladivostok of the first Red Navy commander in the Pacific, M. V. Viktorov, *Pravda* said pointedly 'There was a commander, there was also a Pacific, but no Pacific Fleet' (*Pravda*, March 29th, 1937.) It was Viktorov's achievement to create a Soviet Pacific Fleet in a matter of four to five years. He too was eliminated in the big clean-up of 1937-38.
† The N.K.V.D., the People's Commissariat for Internal Affairs, later Ministry for Internal Affairs (M.V.D.) is the ministry responsible for the Soviet police.

end of July, Blyukher still appeared in public and was still in command in the Soviet Far East, but two rather strange things had happened. First, a carefully prepared party conference of the OKDVA, which was scheduled for the beginning of June, was cancelled at the last minute; and secondly, the OKDVA itself was suddenly renamed 'Far Eastern Front' ('Dalnevostochnii Krasnoznamyonnii Front'). The change occurred between July 5th and 6th, and must have greatly puzzled the Soviet public, which was as familiar with the initials 'OKDVA' as with U.S.S.R., N.K.V.D. and R.S.F.S.R.

The actual disappearance of Blyukher coincides with some major border incidents which the Japanese provoked on Lake Khasan during the last days of July and the beginning of August. The Soviet armed forces remained in control of the situation and killed over 400 Japanese. On the whole the incident on Lake Khasan was rather welcome to the Kremlin, for it gave the government the opportunity to prove that the efficiency of the army was not impaired by the purge. Moreover, the 'defeat of the samurais', as official propaganda styled the historic episode on the Manchurian border, supplied the pretext for a big campaign to strengthen the morale of the Soviet rear. All over the Soviet Union meetings were held in factories, collective farms and offices protesting against the Japanese aggression and sending greetings to the Soviet armed forces who were watching over the security of the Far Eastern borders. None of the resolutions adopted at these meetings contained the slightest reference to the once so popular Marshal Blyukher. The press gave all the credit for the speedy liquidation of the Khasan Lake incident to rank and file soldiers and junior officers, as if no general had been connected with the operation. Only considerably later was the new commander in the Far East mentioned – Grigory Mikhailovich Shtern.[12]

What happened to Blyukher and why it happened was never officially stated, except, perhaps, for some general cryptic remarks made by the Head of the Political Administration of the Red Army, Mekhlis, and by Blyukher's successor. The former told the party conference of the 'First Separate Army',* in September 1938, that the plotters among the party members of the Far Eastern Army had been 'smashed and destroyed'. Shtern was a little more explicit when, in addressing the Eighteenth Party Congress, he referred to 'traitors, spies and monsters' who had infiltrated into responsible positions in the Far Eastern armies.

The disgrace of the Marshal was not a local event of the Soviet Far East, but one of national importance for Soviet Russia. Blyukher was a potential Russian Bonaparte, more dangerous to Stalin than even

* The 'First Separate Army' ('Pervaya Otdelnaya Krasnoznamyonnaya Armiya') was a new name for the purged OKDVA, the term 'Far Eastern Front' being used for a few weeks only.

Marshal Tukhachevsky. The latter was primarily a soldier, but Blyukher was both soldier and political leader. Unlike Tukhachevsky, Blyukher was of proletarian origin – he had started life as a shop-assistant in St. Petersburg and had later become a metalworker – and his popularity with the Russian working class was secure. Unlike Tukhachevsky, Blyukher had suffered under the Czarist régime. He had joined the Bolshevik Party a whole year before the October Revolution, early enough to lay claim to the once so honourable title of 'Old Bolshevik'. Although only a private in the Czarist army in which Tukhachevsky had served as an officer, Blyukher emerged as one of the great military commanders of the young Soviet State during the Civil War. In 1918, by his remarkable expedition across the Ural mountains, he secured the victory of the Revolution on what was then the 'Eastern Front'. For this outstanding feat he was awarded the Order of the Red Banner. He was the first person to receive this decoration.[13]

Blyukher's association with the Soviet Far East, which became the main reason for his prominence, started in 1921. He commanded that heroic march to the Pacific Ocean which included such momentous events of the Russian Civil War as the storming of the heavily fortified white-guard stronghold, Volochayevka, the capture of Khabarovsk, and the final liquidation of Japanese intervention.

For Russia as a whole the elimination of Blyukher meant that Stalin's last potential competitor, a man who might have easily become more popular than he, had gone. For the Soviet Far East it meant the end of a historic period and it also resulted in a rewriting of its past history. Naturally, Blyukher's real historic feats remained unchanged, but the régime did its best to strike his name from history as it lives on in the minds of the people, particularly in the minds of the rising generation. It is difficult to write the history of the Soviet Far East up to 1938 without mentioning Blyukher, but Stalin's historians have achieved this task. Blyukher's name is now left out of all accounts of the Russian Civil War. The first edition of the *Large Soviet Encyclopedia*, in its volume, Number 6, which was published in 1930, described Blyukher as 'one of the outstanding personalities of the Red Army'. The second edition of the *Large Soviet Encyclopedia*, which was published after the Second World War, did not mention him at all.

THE TRIUMPH OF THE N.K.V.D.

The reorganization of the 'Special Far Eastern Army' and the disgrace of its commander were followed by the abolition of the Far Eastern Territory. It may be argued that this latter measure was not especially prompted by the peculiarities of the situation in the Far East. The Soviet Government had gradually abolished all the original large administrative units, such as, for instance, the West Siberian Territory, the East Siberian Territory and the North Caucasus Territory. The Far Eastern Territory was, however, the last to be affected by these administrative reforms, and then only after the purges there had been completed. On October 20th, 1938, it was decreed that the Far Eastern Territory would cease to exist and that two new 'Territories' would take its place, the Khabarovsk Territory, which still included the bulk of the former F.E.T., and the Maritime Territory, with Vladivostok as the capital. After the war the administrative splitting up of the Soviet Far East was carried further. In the west, the Khabarovsk Territory lost the Amur Province (administrative centre: Blagoveshchensk) and, in the east, Sakhalin was removed from its jurisdiction and made a self-contained province.

To consolidate the position of the party in the two new 'Territories', a position so badly shaken by the purges, the government saw it necessary to strengthen the powers of the N.K.V.D., particularly the control which the latter exercised over several vital branches of Soviet Far Eastern economy. The full extent of the N.K.V.D. rule in the Far East was disclosed by the Soviet Economic Plan for 1941, a secret document produced for inter-departmental use, but not intended for the Soviet public and still less for foreigners.* It showed that the People's Commissariat for Internal Affairs was a much more important organizer of certain industrial activities than the ministries nominally responsible for them. The plan revealed, for instance, that the N.K.V.D. controlled nearly 83 per cent of the coal output of the Khabarovsk Territory. Only 13 per cent of it was in the hands of the People's Commissariat for Coal (*Narkomugol*) and the remaining 4 per cent was split up between other ministries. In the field of timber production the N.K.V.D. did not hold the same monopoly. It provided 'only' one-third of the entire timber supply of the territory, slightly more than the quota allocated to the People's Commissariat for the Timber Industry (*Narkomles*). Another important sector of N.K.V.D. work was production of building material. Over one-fifth of the bricks produced in the Khabarovsk Territory in 1941 was to come from the Chief Administration of Corrective Labour Camps, one of the specialized agencies of the N.K.V.D. In the much smaller Maritime Territory the N.K.V.D. has little importance as an economic factor, except for the timber industry, where it tackled over 20 per cent of the whole production. But

* The full title of the document is 'Gosudarstvenny Plan Razvitiya Narodnogo Khozyaistva S.S.S.R. na 1941 god (Prilozheniya k Postanovleniyu S.N.K. S.S.S.R. i TsK VKP (b) Nr.' 127 ot 17 Yanvarya 1941 g.) – State Plan for the Development of the National Economy of the U.S.S.R. for 1941 (Appendices to the Decree of the Council of People's Commissars and of the Central Committee of the All-Union Communist Party (Bolsheviks), Nr 127 of January 17th, 1941.) The material on the economy of the Soviet Far East is contained in the appendices 371, 372 and 373, pp. 324–336.

even where the N.K.V.D.-M.V.D. has no direct economic power it is the decisive political force, above all, in border areas like the Maritime Territory of the Soviet Far East.

There are indications, however, that the police ministry has encountered certain difficulties among the Far Eastern Russians during the war and post-war period. Conditions were certainly favourable to a re-emergence of that Far Eastern regionalism which Soviet power has tried so hard to eliminate. The people of Vladivostok, in particular, must have felt once more that the natural destiny of their city was that of a window into the world. They saw the many American lend-lease shipments arriving in their harbour and were bound to draw certain conclusions about the desirability of international trade and Soviet-American co-operation. More than people in other parts of the Soviet Union must the Russian inhabitants of the Pacific coastal areas have resented the policy of rigid isolationism which the Soviet Government has pursued particularly since 1947.

This frame of mind of the 'Far Easterners' makes it understandable that the very existence of an American consulate in Vladivostok was a matter of concern to the Soviet Government. The building of the consulate was put under constant supervision and for long periods it was floodlit at night. In 1948, the Soviet Government used a flimsy pretext to demand from the United States that they should withdraw their consular personnel from the Pacific port. The measure had little importance for the Americans as the activities of the four American consular officials were extremely limited, but it had a certain symbolic significance. The closing down of the consulate was a way of telling the people of Vladivostok that their hopes of their city becoming a link between Russia and the West were once more doomed. Some years later the charge was made that the consulate had been the centre of a spy-ring. This accusation was first put forward in the short story *In a Seaside Town* ('V Primorskom Gorode') which the popular Soviet illustrated *Ogonyok* published in 1950. In the daily press the 'plot' was mentioned for the first time on February 8th, 1953, when *Izvestiya* wrote : 'In 1947, the organs of the state security service liquidated a spy-nest organized by the assistant naval attaché at the American consulate general of Vladivostok, Richard'. *Izvestiya* produced no further details nor any evidence to support its disclosure which it simply quoted from a book *The Secret Weapon of the Doomed*. This latter work had come out under the auspices of the Komsomol organization. The absurdity of the Vladivostok spy story does not preclude the possibility that many Russian Far Easterners in the late 'forties' and early 'fifties' were persecuted for pro-Western sentiments just as others had been victimized for alleged pro-Japanese leanings in the late 'thirties.'

The particular sensitiveness which the Soviet authorities have shown

11

with regard to the Far Eastern Russians since the Second World War can also be illustrated by another fact. Soviet jamming of Western broadcasts started in the Far Eastern territories of the Soviet Union several months before it came into operation in other parts of Russia.

II. THE PROBLEM OF COLONIZATION

THE HISTORICAL BACKGROUND

The great decisive problem which had confronted both Czarist and Russian authorities in the Far East was that of the colonization of the territory. Under the Czarist régime Russian colonization could be roughly subdivided into three periods. The first ran from the annexation of the Amur and Pacific coastal regions in 1858–60 to 1883, the second from 1883 to about 1900, and the third from 1900 until the First World War.

Until 1883, the only way of reaching the Far East from European Russia was to cross the whole of Siberia on horseback, and this meant two to four years' travel. The formidable journey, under very primitive conditions, resulted in complete physical exhaustion which, in a number of cases, compelled the prospective Amur colonists to abandon their original aim and settle down somewhere in Siberia. Those who eventually reached the end of their journey were appallingly weak from starvation, hardship, and the diseases which they had contracted during the journey. To make things worse there was no proper settlers' organization to help them when they arrived. It is not surprising, therefore, that in such circumstances the colonization of the Russian Far East made little progress, and the yearly average number of newcomers in these parts did not exceed 1,000.

The year 1883 saw the opening of the sea route for the use of prospective settlers. Despite the fact that the sea route reduced the journey to a few weeks only, it never became really popular with Russian and Ukrainian colonists, since travelling by sea was alien to their mentality. Nevertheless, several thousands of would-be settlers let themselves be persuaded to board ships in Odessa for Vladivostok, where they received a much better welcome than those who had arrived earlier by the land route; they were fed and housed, given medical attention and provided with farming equipment.

It was only after 1900, with the opening of direct rail communication between Russia and the Far East, that Russian colonization did enter a more active phase. In the initial stage the Trans-Siberian railway line cut the duration of the journey to approximately thirty days. While the first Russian colonists in the Far East had come chiefly from the over-populated gubernii (provinces) of Kiev, Chernigòv and Poltava, the inhabitants of over forty-five European Russian gubernii participated in the colonization after the hardships of a long and complicated journey had been alleviated.[14] Migration to the Far East assumed a real mass character, particularly after the Russo-Japanese War, when numbers reached the record height of 76,637 in 1907.

The boom of the migration to the Far East in the last years of the Czarist régime made little difference to the magnitude of the task which the Soviet power had to face. This can be gathered from the fact that in 1926 the total number of inhabitants in the F.E.T. was still below the two million mark, and this included both Asiatics and Europeans. The number of Europeans alone did not exceed 1,600,000, including 1,531,000 representatives of the three main Slavonic peoples of the U.S.S.R. – Great Russians, Ukrainians* and Byelorussians. Thus, the Europeans of the Russian Far East were an insignificant factor compared with the masses of China and Japan living at Russia's doorstep. We shall see now by what means the Soviet Government tried to change the situation and what success it achieved in its endeavours.

COLONIZATION BY CONVICTS

Colonization by convicts is neither a Soviet nor a Russian invention. It has been practised elsewhere, for instance, in Australia, but there it came to an end in 1838. In Russia, more particularly in the Russian Far East, colonization by convicts is not only flourishing at the present time, but it may not even have reached its maximum expansion. Certain remote Soviet Far Eastern territories have absorbed especially high numbers of forced labourers. Consequently, the colonization of the vast area which forms the hinterland of the Okhotsk Sea is almost exclusively due to convicts working under the supervision of the M.V.D.

* According to the 1926 census the Ukrainians in the Far Eastern Territory numbered 315,000 and the Byelorussians 41,000. There are particularly important Ukrainian settlements near the town of Blagoveshchensk, as well as at several points along the railway line running from Khabarovsk to Vladivostok, parallel to the Chinese-Soviet border. The Soviet régime provided Ukrainian language schools for the Ukrainian settlers and founded as many as seventeen Ukrainian 'National Districts' in various parts of the F.E.T.

Ukrainian nationalists refer to the entire Soviet Pacific coastal area as the 'Green Wedge' (Zeleny Klin) as distinct from the 'Grey Wedge', which is the Ukrainian settlers' area in Northern Kirghizistan and Southern Kazakhstan. These nationalists are inclined to consider the Soviet Pacific region a Ukrainian and not a Russian national possession. Indeed, the *Ukrainian Encyclopedia*, published by Ukrainian scholars of Eastern Galicia during the inter-war period, described the 'Green Wedge' as a 'Ukrainian colony on the Pacific Ocean'. The *Encyclopedia* estimated that 30 per cent of the population of the 'Green Wedge' were Ukrainians, against 52 per cent 'Muscovites', i.e., Great Russians. (*Ukrainska Zagalna Entsiklopedia*. Lviv-Stanislaviv-Kolomiya, 1935, vol, ii, pp. 42–3.) The importance of the 'Ukrainian problem' in the Soviet Far East must not, however, be overestimated. The dividing line in the Far East does not run between the various groups of European colonists but between Europeans and Asiatics.

(previously N.K.V.D.). Under the general direction of the latter a powerful state enterprise called 'Dalstroy' has come into being in the Soviet Far East. It has taken over many functions that are usually carried out by local government organs. Dalstroy is primarily a mining trust for the development of gold mining on the upper reaches of the Kolyma River. Similar to some mining companies in the colonies of other powers, such as the Société Minière du Haut Katanga in the Belgian Congo, the Dalstroy rules almost as sovereign master over the territory where it exploits the underground riches. Although administrative authorities do exist in the land of the Dalstroy they are completely dependent on the directorate of this enterprise.

The activities of the Dalstroy are many-sided. The 'Mining Administration' ('Gornoe Upravlenie') is only one of several big departments over which the Dalstroy director and his two deputy directors rule. In addition to the 'Political Administration', there is an 'Administration for Agriculture' supervising the work of the local collective farms and state farms, and an 'Administration for Road Building'. There are also a fair number of subsidiary trusts and enterprises which take their orders from the Dalstroy director. There are, for instance, the supply organizations 'Dalstroysnab' and 'Kolymsnab', the coal-mining trust 'Dalugol', a building trust, the state trading firm 'Magadantorg' and a special fleet which connects the Dalstroy with Vladivostok. This entire huge organization is kept together by a small army of M.V.D. men and by a whole network of 'political departments', the activity of which extends to the most distant parts of the Kolyma mining district. The bulk of the workers, technicians and officials of the Dalstroy consists of actual convicts, or of ex-convicts who have been set free because of 'good behaviour'. A list of over 400 Dalstroy officials and workers who were awarded orders and medals at the beginning of 1941 shows that the Dalstroy is a microcosm of the Soviet Union. Indeed, a list of people decorated with the medal 'For Excellency of Labour' starts rather significantly with the following three names:

1. Abdulgasimov, Nazhim, miner;
2. Akopyan, Amayak Avanesovich, newspaper editor;
3. Aksenov, Vladimir Mikhailovich, driver. . . .[15]

Of these three the first is a Moslem, the second an Armenian and the third a Russian. The order is perhaps not very characteristic since the Russian element predominates by far among the more prominent Dalstroy people, but there are also Ukrainians, Georgians, Armenians, Jews and Moslems among them.

The colonization activities of Dalstroy have changed the character of the hinterland of the Okhotsk Sea, which, until 1931, was still virtually uninhabited. The most palpable achievement has been the foundation of the town of Magadan, the post-war population of which has been estimated at 50,000–70,000 inhabitants. Official Soviet sources, while glossing over the strange origin of Magadan, have described it as an important cultural centre, including several houses of culture, dozens of clubs, cinemas, libraries, and two theatres, one for drama, the other for musical comedy. Former prisoners who passed through Magadan have asserted that the actors of the drama theatre were convicts, but Soviet sources of more recent date declare that they were recruited from Moscow drama schools. By December 1952, Magadan had grown large enough to deserve administrative promotion. A decree of the Presidium of the Supreme Soviet transformed it from a district town into a provincial town.[16]

Magadan is the largest locality which owes its existence to Dalstroy, but there are others further inland. One of them is Atka – a name which, at the first glance, seems to have an exotic Asiatic flavour, but is in reality an expression of the unromantic technological mind of Soviet Russia. It is simply an abbreviation of 'Avtotraktornaya Kolonna' (Motor Tractor Column), a tribute to the pioneer role of motorized transport in a territory without a railway. Even in 1946 Atka had large garages and automobile repair works where work never stopped, 'not even for a single minute'. Moreover, Atka produces electrical equipment for the purposes of Dalstroy.[17]

MILITARY COLONIZATION

Another interesting and unusual form of colonization introduced in the Soviet Far East is what might be described as 'military colonization'. Discharged soldiers of the Red Army, artillery and cavalrymen, infantry and members of the signal corps, as well as sailors of the Red Fleet, settled down with their families in the fertile border regions on the Ussuri River. These military colonists formed a kind of peasant militia ready to be called up at any time for the defence of the 'socialist fatherland'. The first 'Red Army' and 'Red Fleet' collective farms were formed in 1931. They soon became the pride of the entire Soviet Far East and the head of the administration of the F.E.T., Krutov, described them as a shining example for the entire Far Eastern peasantry.

Not all demobilized soldiers became agriculturists; some of them remained in the Far East as lumbermen and fishermen and many also worked on the Far Eastern railways, as has already been mentioned. At the beginning of 1938, 5,000 demobilized Red Army men were accepted into the service of railways. They were all provided with houses and small plots, and each of them received a government grant for the purchase of a cow.[18]

This last point is particularly characteristic of Soviet colonization policy in the Far East. To increase its defence potential in the Far

Eastern border areas the government made concessions even in the economic sphere. In European Russia only collective farmers were at that time allowed to own a cow as their own personal possession, never industrial or transport workers.

KOMSOMOL COLONIZATION

The military colonization largely overlaps with another special form of colonization in the Soviet Far East, which is carried out with the help of the Communist Youth League, the Komsomol. The Youth League is the backbone of the Far Eastern units of the Soviet Army. Towards the end of the inter-war period 60 to 70 per cent of the soldiers in the Far East were Komsomol members. Hence among the demobilized soldiers, too, there must have been a good deal of 'Komsomol spirit'. The Komsomol influence in the Far East is, however, by no means confined to the army. The entire Soviet Far East has been described as a 'Komsomol Territory'. This is true both in the figurative and in the literal sense. The Soviet Far East is 'komsomolsky' because it is a young pioneer country, but the Komsomol, the Communist Youth League, is also directly connected with the Soviet Far East as one of the principal promoters of its colonization.

Many Communist Youth League members went to the Far East as individuals out of a spirit of adventure and also out of a feeling of patriotic duty. The Komsomol, as an organization, was responsible for two big spectacular actions. One was the foundation of the town Komsomolsk-on-Amur, the other was the movement initiated by Madame Khetagurova.

The history of Komsomolsk goes back to the spring of 1932 when the Central Committee of the Communist Youth League chartered two steamers, *Kolumb* and *Komintern*, which sailed with 400 young people, including a number of Civil War orphans, to the village of Permskoe on the Lower Amur. (The village had been founded as early as 1858 by Russian peasant colonists hailing from the region of Perm in the eastern part of European Russia.) Even the first small party of Komsomol members outnumbered the local population of 160 inhabitants. In the second half of 1932 many more young people arrived, and in December of the same year the All-Russian Executive Committee published a decree which transformed Permskoe into the town of Komsomolsk. The decree read well in the Moscow newspapers, but to the young builders of Komsomolsk it must have appeared utterly unrealistic. At the time when the decree was published they were in a state of despair. The building of the town had had to be interrupted in view of the harshness of the Russian Far Eastern winter, and the inexperience of the new settlers had resulted in great complications. During this early period of construction Komsomolsk had a street with the characteristic nickname of 'Street of Accidents', and a whole quarter was known as the 'Fire Settlement' ('Pozharny Posyolok').

Things in Komsomolsk went wrong for several years, and in 1937, when the city celebrated its fifth anniversary, the party authorities thought that the time had come to carry out a large-scale purge among the builders of the 'City of Youth'. One of the most distinguished citizens of the new town, the director of its metallurgical plant, then declared bluntly, 'We are mercilessly rooting out this scum of wreckers'.[19] 'This scum of wreckers' were people whom official Soviet propaganda had previously included among the selfless enthusiastic patriots engaged in self-sacrificing, heroic construction work. To justify the purge the party leadership alleged that 'agents of foreign intelligence services, bandits and diversionists' had penetrated into the ranks of workers and technicians of Komsomolsk, thanks to the complacency of certain leading personalities. According to the official version the 'enemies of the people' at work in Komsomolsk were very active and ingenious. They mixed concrete with sugar so that the degree of its cohesion was lowered, they put glass into ball-bearings to provoke accidents and destroyed vital blue-prints to delay the growth of local industry.

The real reason for the chaos in Komsomolsk was not the criminal activity of wreckers, but the lack of co-ordination between the various state trusts which owned the industrial enterprises in the town-to-be. Each of these trusts constructed a workers' settlement around its plant, and until 1940 there was no over-all building plan for the much advertised town of the Communist Youth League. This explains why sanitary conditions and municipal services were still practically non-existent, even by the outbreak of the Second World War.

The over-all building plan of Komsomolsk which came into being in 1940 provided for a population of 500,000.[20] Although the fulfilment of this aim is still far off, Komsomolsk has become an economic and cultural factor in the Far East. In 1947 the town had 100,000 inhabitants and was the proud owner of two undertakings of all-Union importance, the Iron and Steel Works, 'Amurstal', and a shipyard.[21] Cultural life, too, had developed greatly. The number of schools reached thirty-four in 1947 and forty-five in 1952. In addition, Komsomolsk has a Palace of Culture, a theatre, thirty libraries, a training college for teachers of secondary schools, a music school and four 'parks of culture and rest'.[22] It has tried to keep up its reputation as a 'City of Youth' and is still recruiting young workers from European Russia, particularly from among war orphans.

The second big Komsomol initiative for the settlement of the Far East, the Khetagurova movement, has its roots in the lack of women in the Far East and the necessity to remedy the situation. The well-known Soviet writer Pavlenko has referred to this problem in one of his novels in the following words, 'From the polar tundra down to Korea everybody dreams of women. Nowhere else do people get married as quickly as there. Widows do not exist in the Far East. Only the oldest women overcome by senility remain single'. There is a lot of truth in what Pavlenko said. The proportion of women in the population of the Far East diminishes the further one goes east. The 1926 census showed that for every 1,000 men there were 962 women in the area just east of Lake Baikal, 918 in the Amur region, 704 in the Pacific coastal region and 689 on Sakhalin island. This is an abnormal situation, though characteristic of the pioneer stage of colonization activities all over the world.

To make the balance between the two sexes more even, a movement was created designed to bring young girls to the F.E.T. It was associated with the name of an ordinary Soviet citizen, a young woman of twenty-two years of age, Valentina Khetagurova-Zarubina. Khetagurova was the wife of a major serving with the 'Special Far Eastern Army'. Her claim to fame was a letter which she addressed to the girls of the Soviet Union. The letter was published on February 5th, 1937, and is an extremely interesting document.[23] Official inspiration had certainly a lot to do with it, but the letter nevertheless had a personal touch, and in some passages the Russian woman triumphed over the communist official. The needs of the Far East, Khetagurova said, were great. 'We need fitters and turners, teachers and draftswomen, typists and account-ants – all to the same degree'. In the event of a war Khetagurova promised different kinds of jobs. Women would then be employed as nurses, radio operators and even as machine gunners. She appealed to the personal pride of would-be migrants to the Far East; 'We want only bold, determined people, not afraid of difficulties'. She described the Far East as an exotic dreamland 'where still a short time ago there were only deer, tigers and lions' and where 'wonderful work, wonderful people and a wonderful future' would meet the girls.

More important than all this was the assurance which Khetagurova gave, not expressly, but by implication, namely, that every girl would find a husband in the Far East and possibly even one holding com-missioned rank in the army. She told the girls of Soviet Russia her own personal success story: 'In the autumn I made the acquaintance of Major Khetagurov. My life became fuller and brighter when I became married to him. . . .' The Russian girls could not be told more clearly why they should follow the example of Valentina Khetagurova.

The Khetagurova letter had considerable success. By the end of 1937 as many as 70,000 Soviet girls had registered with the authorities as volunteers for the Far East, and many actually went there. They were called 'Khetagurovki' – Khetagurova girls.

THE 'NORMAL' COLONIZATION

So far only those forms of colonization in the Far East have been mentioned which might be described as typically 'Soviet', ranging from the terror exercised by the N.K.V.D. to the exuberant enthusiasm of the Komsomol.* In addition, the Soviet Government has continued the normal, ordinary colonization which went on in Czarist times. The Soviet Government has provided a number of genuine incentives to make it worth while for Russian peasants and workers to go to the Pacific coastal areas.

The first important special measure for the encouragement of voluntary migration to the Far East was a decree which the government issued on December 11th, 1933. It freed the collective farmers of the Far Eastern Territory for the duration of ten years from all compulsory grain and rice deliveries to the state. It reduced by 50 per cent the compulsory deliveries of meat, vegetables, milk and wool, and in certain distant areas such as Sakhalin and Kamchatka these deliveries were abolished altogether. To the workers and technicians of the Far East the decree of December 11th, 1933, brought higher wages and salaries. The personnel of the Far Eastern mining industry received an automatic rise of 30 per cent, and all other categories of workers and technicians one of 20 per cent. On the same occasion the pay of soldiers of the Special Far Eastern Army was increased by 50 per cent, and that of officers by 20 per cent.

It seems that these 'Stalin Privileges' as they were called were not quite sufficient to attract settlers to the Far East. Another decree was, therefore, published on November 17th, 1937, which aimed chiefly at the encouragement of agricultural colonization. On the strength of that decree, groups of collective farmers going to the Far East were to be exempt from taxation for six years and to obtain state credits for fifteen years. The decree further pledged the state to pay 50 per cent of the costs of all buildings erected by the colonists.

So much for the legislation passed for the encouragement of colonization in the Far East. In practice, things proceeded very often on lines that are reminiscent of Gogol's *Dead Souls*. Each Soviet state authority or building organization in need of manpower for the Far East had its own small recruiting office in Moscow. Special recruiting agents were employed who were paid a fixed sum for every person whom they persuaded to take up work at a Far Eastern building site or factory. The usual tariff was thirty roubles per person, but occasionally the fee was

---

* Another special form of Soviet colonization in the Far East was the mobilization of Jews for the settlement of Birobidzhan. The author has described the failure of this experiment in *Russia and her Colonies* (London, George Philip and Son, Ltd., pp. 173–8).

higher. Since the agents were remunerated on a 'piece rate basis', they were naturally interested in enlisting the largest possible number of people. One can well imagine that the recruiters made use of all sorts of glittering promises and also that they paid little attention to the character and abilities of the prospective Far Eastern colonists. The afore-mentioned Madame Khetagurova who exposed in a Moscow journal this 'recruitment racket', concluded her account laconically: 'And so it happened that quite a lot of scum was sent to the Far East'.[24]

Those consenting to go to the Far East as free workers received upon leaving Moscow or another city of European Russia a special bonus and a maintenance allowance covering the entire long journey from European Russia to their final place of destination. The total amount of bonuses and allowances thus earned might not have meant a great deal to a Western worker, but it was a considerable sum for the impoverished Soviet citizen of the 'thirties.' It was tempting and led to abuses. Quite a number of people cashed the special remuneration, went to the Far East, worked there for a while and got themselves discharged for reasons of health. Having returned to Moscow they let themselves be recruited once more for the Far East by another state trust and the whole game started again from the beginning.

The majority of the voluntary colonists who, up to the end of the Second Five-Year Plan, came to the Soviet Far East established themselves in towns. The two largest cities of the Soviet Far East, Vladivostok and Khabarovsk, therefore grew considerably. Between 1926 and 1939 the population of Khabarovsk increased from 52,000 to 199,000, and that of Vladivostok from 108,000 to 206,000.

As a consequence of the growth of the existing towns and the foundation of new ones such as Komsomolsk, Magadan and Birobidzhan City, the relation between the urban and rural population in the Far East changed to the detriment of the villages. In 1926 only 24 per cent of the population of the Far East lived in towns, but by 1939 over half of all 'Far Easterners' could be classified as 'urban'.

The encouragement of the urban population in the Far Eastern provinces led to neglect of agriculture. During the period of the First and Second Five-Year Plans the area under cultivation in the Soviet Far East diminished by over 20 per cent, from 2,848,000 acres in 1928 to 2,223,000 acres in 1938. Consequently, instead of providing more for the newcomers, the food supply for the Soviet Far East became more dependent on deliveries from areas thousands of miles away. This created an unsatisfactory situation not only from the narrow economic point of view but also from the military which demanded complete self-sufficiency in fuel, raw materials and food. Molotov himself proclaimed the principal of self-sufficiency for the Soviet Far East at the Eighteenth Congress of the Bolshevik Party, in March 1939, and demanded, in particular, 'full liquidation' of all shortcomings in Far Eastern agriculture. The Third Five-Year Plan, therefore, aimed at an increase of the agricultural population of the Far East. About 100,000 new collective farmers were to settle down in the Khabarovsk Territory[25] alone.

The outbreak of the war prevented the full implementation of the resettlement plan, but it was, at least, successfully started. Russian peasants went to the Far East mainly from the Provinces of Kursk, Oryol, Voronezh, Ryazan, Stalingrad, Tambov and Penza. Kursk and Oryol seem to have led the migration movement. There was a great deal of propaganda for the resettlement plan and during a certain period almost every single issue of the Moscow newspapers carried a news-item showing how well those farmers had fared who had consented to go to the Far East, and how heartily they had been received there by the old-timers. The big All-Union Agricultural Exhibition which was opened in Moscow on the eve of the Second World War was likewise put into the service of the resettlement campaign. The Far Eastern pavilion of the exhibition illustrated, with the help of statistics and pictures, all the delights of peasant life east of Lake Baikal. In addition, the pavilion served as a convenient place for officially organized meet-ings at which collective farmers of the Chita Province, and the Khabarovsk and Maritime Territories talked to peasants of European Russia about the advantages of Far Eastern agriculture.[26] These propa-ganda efforts were not in vain. In fact, the resettlement plan for 1940 was already fulfilled by October of that year,[27] and numerous peasant settlers also went to the Far East in the first half of 1941, continuing to do so almost until the Hitlerite invasion of the Soviet Union.

Peasant colonization in the Far East was resumed after the war. Its precise extent is not known. Official Soviet sources have shrouded it in mystery and apparently consider it a military secret. In the absence of reliable statistics a rough, and not necessarily accurate, estimate about the increase in the population of the Soviet Far East can only be made by a comparison of the numbers of constituencies which were created for the elections of 1937, 1946 and 1950. There was hardly any change between 1937 and 1946. For the Supreme Soviet elections in 1937 the F.E.T. was subdivided into nine constituencies, each of them represent-ing a theoretical population of 300,000. The total population of the Far East in the narrower sense (including Sakhalin) was, thus, 2,700,000. In 1946 the Khabarovsk and Maritime Territories comprised nine con-stituencies on the Asiatic mainland, whilst a tenth constituency was formed by Sakhalin and the Kurile archipelago. The total population of the Soviet Far East at the beginning of 1946 could, therefore, hardly have exceeded 2,700,000 on the Asiatic continent or 3,000,000, including the Soviet island possessions in the Pacific.

A decree of January 9th, 1950, giving a new list of constituencies for the Supreme Soviet elections established four new constituencies in the Far East. The constituency of Khabarovsk was divided into a town and a country constituency, another new constituency was formed around the Okhotsk Sea and two more constituencies were created on Sakhalin. The total population of the Soviet Far East would accordingly have been, in 1950, in the neighbourhood of 4,200,000. It is, however, unlikely that this figure was really reached. The population of each of the three Sakhalin constituencies, in particular, may be considerably below the 300,000 mark.

III. THE SOVIET FAR EASTERN MYSTIQUE

The Soviet régime worked for the strengthening of the Russian Far East not only by mobilizing manpower for its colonization, but also by building up a Far Eastern 'mystique', a nationalistic ideology which flattered national pride to the utmost degree. After the end of the Second World War the Soviet Government, with the help of a large army of historians, writers and poets, promoted a cult of Russian heroes of the Pacific. The object of the new propaganda campaign was to show that Russians had played an outstanding part in the discovery of the Pacific and that, by their past records, they were entitled to much more influence in decisions concerning Pacific affairs than the 'imperialist powers' were ready to grant them. The campaign was also intended to prove that Czarist Russia had failed to grasp the opportunities offered to her in the North-West Pacific and that the Soviet Union defended energetically those national Russian interests in the Far East which the old régime had neglected.

RUSSIAN COLUMBUSES

To proceed in a strict chronological order the first 'Russian hero of the Pacific' to be mentioned is Semen Dezhnev. Soviet propaganda popularized him particularly in connection with the tercentenary in 1948 of the discovery of the Behring Strait, which separates Asia from America. The Danish explorer, Vitus Behring, after whom the strait is called, may only have rediscovered it one hundred years after Dezhnev had sailed around the 'nose of Asia', the north-eastern tip of Siberia. As late as the nineteenth century, some outstanding Russian scholars still doubted whether Dezhnev could really be credited with this daring feat. Soviet writers, however, are quite positive about Dezhnev's pioneer role. In 1945 the Chief Administration of the Northern Sea Route issued a popular book on Dezhnev, which waived aside all doubts as to Dezhnev's voyage, and described Dezhnev himself as 'a glorious representative of the all-enduring Russian people'.[28]

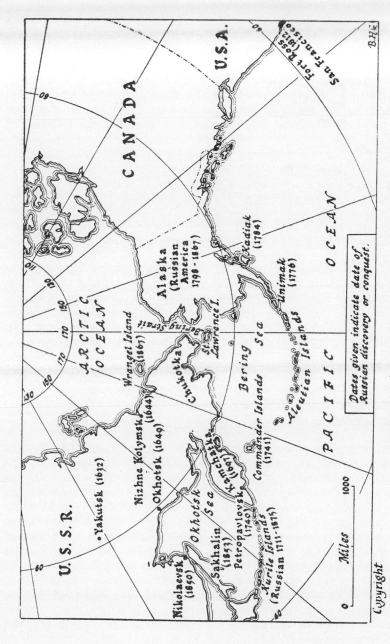

Dates given indicate date of
Russian discovery or conquest.

2. THE RUSSIAN EMPIRE IN THE NORTH PACIFIC

23

The next 'Soviet hero' operated on the other side of the Behring Strait, in what, until 1867, was called 'Russian America'. He was the Russian merchant, Grigory Ivanovich Shelikhov, who, in 1784, founded the first permanent Russian settlements in Alaska. Shelikhov's contemporary, the great poet Derzhavin, called him the 'Russian Columbus'. This description, 'Russian Columbus', plays a great part in Soviet propaganda. Because of a feeling of inferiority, *vis-à-vis* the Western World, the Soviet Union has claimed a large number of inventions and geographical discoveries for the Russians, including the discovery of America. Columbus discovered only the American East coast. North-West America was a Russian discovery for which the credit goes in the first place to Shelikhov. It is obvious that the Russians of the Soviet Far East and of Eastern Siberia are most easily attracted by the idea of a 'Russian Columbus'. The Mayor of Irkutsk and the head of the Irkutsk provincial administration have been in the forefront of those who have advocated a systematic publicity campaign for extolling Shelikhov's memory. These two, together with seven other distinguished Soviet citizens, demanded in a letter to the Moscow *Literary Gazette* in October 1950, that Shelikhov should be honoured lavishly on the 155th anniversary of his birthday. In the centre of Irkutsk a Shelikhov monument ought to be erected, they recommended. The Ministry for Cinematography was to produce a film on the 'Russian Columbus', the All-Union Society for the Dissemination of Scientific and Political Knowledge to organize lectures throughout the country about his life and deeds, and the State Publishing House for Geographical Literature was to publish his biography.[29] Since then many of these demands have probably been carried out.

Shelikhov's epithet, 'Russian Columbus', has frequently been challenged. Russian historians of the nineteenth and twentieth centuries considered Shelikhov a braggart who greatly exaggerated his Alaskan exploits, and in particular, the number of Alaskan natives converted to Christianity, so as to get larger subsidies for his trading firm. This poor view of Shelikhov was taken by the pre-revolutionary *Russian Encyclopedia*, and the first edition of the *Soviet Encyclopedia* has not corrected it. According to the latter, Shelikhov was just a 'representative of merchant capitalism' not worthy of major attention. Nevertheless, Shelikhov was a man of vision. He conceived the bold plan of a Russian Empire in the North-West Pacific which would have its granary in California and its naval base in the Hawaiian Islands. Shelikhov also wanted to encourage trade relations with China, Japan and India, and he dreamt of voyages to the Philippines, and even to the North Pole.

Shelikhov's successor, Aleksandr Andreevich Baranov, who started a more systematic exploitation of Russian America by founding the 'Russian-American Company', has also his place in the Soviet pantheon.

Baranov is venerated as a 'self-sacrificing patriot', and a manual for Soviet teachers gives the following appraisal of him: 'Baranov, this outstanding personality, during twenty-eight years kept the administration of Russian America firmly in his hands. Thanks to his personal courage and keen intelligence he opened up and explored its vast spaces. In a hard struggle with privations, the hostility of militant tribes and the mean intrigues of foreign merchants, he established Russian rule over the huge territories of Alaska and Northern California'.[30] Baranov has also become the hero of an historical novel. The author of the novel, Ivan Kratt, described Baranov and his associates as modest and just people, without prejudice against natives, and loved by everybody with the exception of a few villains.[31]

'RUSSIAN AMERICA'

Among Baranov's collaborators there is one whom the Soviet régime has particularly singled out for posthumous glorification, Ivan Kuskov. Until the beginning of 1948, Kuskov's name was unknown even to many well-educated Russians. The Soviet Government rescued it from oblivion by a propaganda campaign on a large scale, which started in Torma, a small town in the Northern Russian Province of Vologda. The town council of Torma met and decided to erect a monument to Kuskov. The importance of this gesture might have escaped the peoples of the Soviet Union had not the Russian Press explained and advertised it all over the country. Kuskov appeared as the man who, acting under Baranov's general orders, had extended Russian America from Alaska to California. It was he, who, in 1812, had hoisted the Russian flag at the entrance of San Francisco Bay and founded 'Fort Ross', the southernmost Russian-occupied point on the American continent.

Not only the biographies of people like Shelikhov, Baranov and Kuskov have been reinterpreted, but the entire history of 'Russian America'. Alaska is not a conquest of Russian Czarism and imperialism, but belongs to 'democratic Russia', to 'people's Russia'. 'The settlement of Alaska by Russians', said the *Literary Gazette*, 'bore a clearly expressed labouring and democratic character dissimilar to the trade-plundering colonization by the Anglo-Saxons, who recruited their agents from among tramps, adventurists and criminals'.[32] The same point is elaborated in greater detail in what is purported to be a popular scientific booklet on the history, geography and economic conditions of Alaska. There, it is said that the colonization of Alaska was progressive because most of the Russian settlers were peasants, eager to shake off the arbitrary rule of the estate owners. Many people went to Alaska because they found the oppressive atmosphere of the Czarist régime unbearable. Others were sent there because of their political convictions. Not only was the colonization of Alaska itself 'progressive' and 'democratic', the management of the Russian-American Company also was. One of its chief executives, K. F. Ryleev, was executed for his part in the December rising of 1825, and there were other prominent 'Decembrists' among the officials of the Company.[33]

Soviet propaganda has tried to show that Baranov and Kuskov conducted a progressive policy towards the natives of North America, totally different from the Anglo-Saxon or Spanish policy towards Red Indians. This is untrue and has been contradicted by Russian sources themselves. A Russian naval officer, who visited Alaska at the time of Russian occupation, has given the following eloquent description of Baranov's policy towards Eskimos and Aleuts: 'Woe to those who resisted him. He destroyed them mercilessly, deported them to uninhabited islands, deprived them of all means of contact with each other, and mixed people of various tribes so that there could be no malicious conspiracy against the Russians. He was feared by the savages, they considered him as the scourge of heaven. Since they had no chance to revolt they were forced to become his slaves and to forget all about their previous freedom'.[34] As a matter of fact, the Aleuts revolted against Russian rule, as the Russian historian, Shashkov, pointed out in his book on the Russian-American Company, and these revolts led to the extermination of a large part of 'this restless people'. How many Aleuts have perished altogether in the years of Russian rule it is impossible to say. According to the official data of the Russian-American Company there were 8,405 Aleuts in Alaska in 1824, but only 4,363 were recorded in 1859. It would be true to say, therefore, that Russian colonization of Alaska was, from the humanitarian point of view, by no means better than, say, British colonization of Australia in its initial stage.

Nevertheless, Russian policy towards the native peoples of Russian America did have its brighter aspects. Those responsible for it, however, were not Shelikhov, Baranov and the other newly discovered national heroes of Soviet Russia, but people whom the Soviet régime is not very keen on publicizing, the Christian missionaries. It was they who founded the first schools in Alaska, educated a fair number of natives, and even translated religious books into the Aleut language. The most important Russian churchman working in Alaska was Ivan Veniaminov (1797–1879). He was the author of a grammar of the Aleutian language which was published in St. Petersburg in 1846. The 'apostle of Alaska', as the Russian historian, Zernov, calls him, became later, under the name of Innokentii, Metropolitan of Moscow.[35]

The scope of these Russian church activities was, however, very small and one cannot say that the end of Russian rule in Alaska, in 1867, meant in any way a major loss to the native peoples; but of course it was, historically speaking, a great loss for the Russian State. Soviet Russia was more conscious of this loss than Czarist Russia had ever been. In Soviet political literature published after the Second World War the abandonment of the Russian outposts in California in the 'forties' and the sale of Alaska to the United States appear not only as regrettable blunders, but almost as acts of treason on the parts of the Czarist Government.

THE RUSSIAN PACIFIC

Russian traditions in the Pacific, as presented by Soviet propaganda, are by no means confined to Russian rule over Alaska and 'Fort Ross'. Quite a number of Russian naval expeditions took place throughout the nineteenth century in various parts of the Pacific Ocean. The public, and particularly Soviet youth, has been acquainted with them since 1945 in various ways. Stories about these expeditions have been written anew, in the form of historical novels or of straightforward descriptions, with the obvious object of stimulating national pride.

From this patriotic Soviet Russian literature centring on the Pacific one can learn a great deal – for instance, that the Russians discovered as many as 400 small Pacific islands, more particularly those belonging to the Paumotu Archipelago in the South-East Pacific, and some of the Marshall Islands. All these islands had been named after Russian generals in the war against Napoleon, and other famous Russian historical figures. Some of the Russian names still persist. Thus the, Lisiansky Island, a possession of the U.S.A., east of Midway Island, bears the name of a well-known Russian seafarer, and east of Samoa there still exists a Suvorov Island belonging to Britain. Also, the big island of New Guinea has important Russian associations. Russians are not credited with its discovery, it is true, but it was a Russian scholar to whom was due the first detailed description of the Papuan people. The Russian explorer, Miklukho-Maklay (1846–88), spent some time with the Papuans. The result of his observations was included in his diaries, which were not published until the Soviet régime came to power. As the Russian geographer, L. S. Berg, puts it, Miklukho-Maklay died before he succeeded in writing his fundamental scholarly works, but, even so, he is highly honoured in the Soviet Union. After all, he was the first Russian to demand that Russia should have a colony in the Pacific.[36] The Institute of Ethnography of the Academy of Sciences has been called after him and a play 'White Friend' has been produced in which he is the central figure. He appears there as the 'champion of black and coloured peoples enslaved by the colonizers of the West'.[37]

'NEVELSKOY'S IMMORTAL FEAT'

For Soviet patriotic ideology one historic personality is more important than all those mentioned so far, Admiral Gennady Ivanovich Nevelskoy (1813–76). The entire modern Russian Far Eastern policy goes back to his geographical discoveries. They resulted in the Russian annexation of the entire Lower Amur region up to the Ussuri confluence, as well as in the Russian seizure of Sakhalin. Until Nevelskoy's expedition, the Amur was not recognized as a 'useful' river and a channel of Russian expansion, nor was it known that Sakhalin was an island and not a peninsula. Nevelskoy, who had sailed from Kronstadt across the Atlantic and the Pacific, on August 13th, 1850, hoisted the Russian flag at the point of the Amur estuary which later became known as the town Nikolayevsk Amursky. Hence, the Amur region became the only part of Russia which was annexed by a naval expedition. Nevelskoy's 'immortal feat' enabled the Russian Empire to concentrate in its Far Eastern policy on areas close to the Chinese border, instead of using up its efforts in the distant Kamchatka or even Alaska. On the one-hundredth anniversary of Nevelskoy's appearance in the Amur estuary, the Soviet régime expressed its appreciation of the courageous seafarer in no unmistakable terms. A monument was erected in his honour in the town of Nikolayevsk and a number of popular books were published on the occasion. The Publishing House of the Central Committee of the Communist Youth League, 'Molodaya Gvardiya', brought out an historical novel largely dealing with Nevelskoy, and the State Publishing House for Cultural and Educational Literature produced a biography of the admiral.[38]

PORT ARTHUR

The gallery of heroes of the Russian Far East would be incomplete without mentioning the defenders of the Russian fortress Port Arthur during the Russo-Japanese War. When Port Arthur fell, Lenin wrote that the Russian proletariat had every reason to rejoice at 'progressive and advanced Asia inflicting an irreparable blow on backward and reactionary Europe'. When looking back on the defence and doom of Port Arthur, Stalin's Russia, however, takes no guidance from Lenin, but from the son of a Czarist officer, Stepanov, who, in 1905, belonged to the garrison of the besieged fortress. This man published, in 1944, an historical novel on Port Arthur which earned highest praise in the most authoritative Soviet circles. The book, which also served as the basis of a play, was, in the first place, a tribute to two great Russian patriots, Admiral Makarov, Commander of the Russian Pacific fleet and General Kondratenko, the main embodiment of the spirit of resistance in Port Arthur. Stepanov did not consider that the defence of Russia's naval base in the Pacific was merely an imperialistic affair. For him there existed the most intimate link between Port Arthur and the entire Russian people. This he expressed by letting General Kondratenko make the following appeal to his soldiers: 'Behind us has been left but a narrow strip of Russian land with the town of Port Arthur. *This is our Russian town*: for its construction we have spent millions of our national income and invested a great amount of work. You yourselves have worked to build up the fortifications and batteries. And besides, in Port Arthur is our Fleet. We have to defend stubbornly our positions. The whole fatherland is following the course of the war and the defence of Port Arthur with breathless attention. Let us give all our forces, and if necessary, our lives in order to uphold in dignity the glory of the Russian arms in the Far East'. The book from which these lines are quoted was an ideological preparation for the re-establishment, in 1945, of a Russian naval base in Port Arthur, 'the town of Russian glory', as it is usually referred to.

SERGEY LAZO

The Soviet régime itself has not been able to make any substantial addition to the impressive gallery of heroes of the Russian Far East from Dezhnev to Admiral Makarov. Such 'heroes' as there emerged under Soviet rule, Marshal Blyukher in particular, were liquidated by the Cheka-G.P.U.-N.K.V.D. There is only one important exception to this rule the guerilla leader of the Civil War in the Far East – Sergey Lazo. Lazo was an officer of the Czarist army who went over to the revolutionary camp and joined the Bolshevik Party in the middle of 1918. He fought courageously against the White Guards and the Japanese in the Pacific coastal areas. In 1920 the latter burnt him alive in Vladivostok when he was only twenty-eight years old.

The way in which Lazo died predestined him to become not only a hero of the Soviet Far East, but also a symbol of Russian resistance to Japanese militarism and imperialism. Whenever the name of Lazo was mentioned – in newspaper articles and history books, in songs and in plays – it was meant as a challenge to Japan. But as history in the Soviet Union is always rewritten and reinterpreted in accordance with the propaganda interests of the moment, the personality of Lazo has undergone a revaluation. After the Second World War he became an anti-American figure as well as being an anti-Japanese one. According to an up-to-date version of Lazo's biography, the responsibility for his death lay jointly with the Japanese and the Americans. He was killed 'with the knowledge and agreement' of the American interventionists.[39] A book which prominently featured Lazo's part in the political and military events that took place in the Russian Far East in 1918, N. Kolbin's *Partisans* (*Partizany*), was rewritten with the express purpose of denouncing American intervention. The first edition of the book, which the Far Eastern state publishing house 'Dalgiz' brought out in

1948, had only been anti-Japanese. In response to criticism in the official press the author produced, in 1951, a second edition of the same book into which a number of anti-American passages had been inserted.[40]

The interpretation of the personality of Lazo underwent a change in another direction also. Originally, Lazo appeared in Soviet propaganda as an international communist fighting for the victory of the World Revolution in the Far East. As time went on this international aspect was pushed into the background, and Lazo was transformed into a patriotic Russian, although, being a Moldavian of Swiss extraction, he had not a drop of Russian blood in his veins.[41] The favourite quotation which Soviet propagandists of the later period picked out of Lazo's statements reflects indeed a most patriotic frame of mind: 'We shall fight with our lives for the homeland against foreign invaders. For this Russian land on which I am standing now we shall die and shall not give it up to anyone'.[42] It must be admitted that the Russian patriot, Lazo, appeals much more than the communist guerilla leader. A man like Lazo would have become a national hero anywhere in the world, for a person who is killed by foreign invaders under dramatic circumstances always occupies an honourable place in the history of his nation.

These few examples may suffice to characterize the new Pacific 'mystique' which the Soviet régime has created. The whole Russian people is to be indoctrinated with the new Pacific ideology, but in the first place, this ideology is intended as a moral equipment for the Russian settlers on the Pacific coast. They are to be made more sure of themselves, and more ready to overcome difficulties by instilling into them the proud feeling that they are the successors of Dezhnev and Shelikhov, of Kuskov and Nevelskoy, and also, of course, of Sergey Lazo.

BIBLIOGRAPHICAL NOTES TO CHAPTER I

1. *Vestnik Evropy*, vol. 255, January 1909, p. 437.

2. *Zhizn Natsionalnostei*, March 22nd, 1922.

3. *Large Soviet Encyclopedia*, vol. 20, Moscow 1930, p. 289

4. *Pravda*, July 1st, 1930.

5. *Pravda*, May 22nd, 1937.

6. *Pravda*, October 6th, 1937.

7. *Pravda*, November 11th, 1936.

8. *Pravda*, November 28th, 1936.

9. *Pravda*, April 3rd, 1937.

10. *Pravda*, June 11th, 1937.

11. *Krasnaya Zvezda*, May 28th, 1938.

12. *Pravda*, October 26th, 1938.

13. *Novy Mir*, February 1938, p. 218.

14. *Vestnik Evropy*, vol. 233, 1905, p. 233.

15. *Pravda*, January 12th, 1941.

16. *Vedomosti Verkhovnogo Soveta S.S.S.R.*, Nr 1, 1953.

17. *Komsomolskaya Pravda*, December 12th, 1946.

18. *Pravda*, February 1st, 1938.

19. *Komsomolskaya Pravda*, June 12th, 1937.

20. *Pravda*, May 17th, 1940.

21. *Pravda*, June 19th, 1947.

22. *Ogonyok*, Nr 24, June 1952, p. 27.

23. *Komsomolskaya Pravda*, February 5th, 1937.

24. *Novy Mir*, March 1938, pp. 202–3.

25. S. K. GERASIMOV, *Patrioty Dalnego Vostoka* – Patriots of the Soviet Far East, Moscow 1946, p. 105.

26. *Pravda*, August 4th, 1939.

27. *Pravda*, October 30th, 1940.

28. V. A. SAMOILOV, *Semen Dezhnev i ego Vremya* – Semen Dezhnev and his Time, Moscow 1945, p. 114.

29. *Literaturnaya Gazeta*, October 24th, 1950.

30. A. ADAMOV, *Pervye Russkie Issledovateli Alasky* – The First Russian Explorers of Alaska, Moscow 1950, p. 13.

31. IVAN KRATT, *Ostrov Baranova* – Baranov's Island, Moscow 1946.

32. *Literary Gazette*, Nr 3, 1951.

33. V. P. KOVALEVSKY, *Alyaska* – Alaska, Moscow 1952, p. 27.

34. MARKOV, *Russkie na Vostochnom Okeane* – The Russians on the Eastern Ocean, Moscow 1849, p. 53.

35. ZERNOV, The Russians and their Church, London 1945, pp. 138–9.

36. *Small Soviet Encyclopedia*, second edition, vol. 6, Moscow 1937, p. 893.

37. *Komsomolskaya Pravda*, February 2nd, 1952.

38. N. ZADORNOV, *Dalyoky Kray* – Distant Country, Leningrad 1950, and I. VINOKUROV and F. FLORICH, *Podvig Admirala Nevelskogo* – The Feat of Admiral Nevelskoy, Moscow 1951.

39. *Zvezda*, Nr 9, September 1951, p. 165.

40. *Zvezda*, Nr 9, September 1951, p. 166.

41. *Sergey Lazo*, Moscow 1938, p. 215.

42. *Dalny Vostok*, Nr 3, 1952, p. 154.

II

THE POLICY OF THE WHITE SOVIET FAR EAST

The encouragement of European colonization is the positive side of Soviet policy in the Far East. Theoretically, this European colonization had no exclusive character; it could be supplemented by an Asiatic colonization. Indeed, both the Czarist Government and the Soviet régime, in its initial stage, admitted Asiatic immigrants to the Russian Far East, and made use of them. In the latter part of the 'thirties', this policy was reversed. The Soviet Government ceased to be interested in mere colonization of the Russian Far East; it wanted European colonization only. However eager communist Russia might be to assist the victory of communism in China, Korea and Japan, she would not like to see her Chinese, Korean and Japanese friends appearing as worker and peasant colonists in the Pacific coastal areas of the U.S.S.R.

Soviet policy in relation to Chinese, Korean and Japanese immigrants has become very similar in substance to the 'White Australia policy', or, as it is now called less provocatively, 'immigration restrictive policy'.* It may be argued that the non-admission of permanent Asiatic settlers implies no particular bias against Asiatics on the grounds that the territory of the Soviet Union has been sealed off against immigrants from non-Soviet European territories as well. This is certainly true, but in the case of the Asiatics the Soviet Government went a step further. It made the policy of the White Soviet Far East retroactive and eliminated those groups of immigrants who had settled there at a time when Russian and Soviet policy had been less narrow-minded.

I. THE 'RUSSIAN' KOREANS

UNDER THE CZARIST RÉGIME

A Korean problem has existed in Russia ever since Russian frontier guards appeared on the Korean frontier. The Korean immigration into

* The Communist Party is the only Australian party which fights against the White Australia policy. The official pamphlet of the Australian communists, 'Australia's Part in the World Revolution', which was issued in 1930, stated: 'The White Australia policy is a capitalist measure for stirring up racial antagonism between the workers, and preparing for imperialist and colonial wars.'

32

Russia started in 1861, the same year in which the first Russians settled down in the area of the Bay of Poset. As the first Korean colonists in the Russian Far East received good treatment, more and more Koreans crossed the border. The Korean authorities viewed this migration with some uneasiness and put every possible obstacle into the way of people who wanted to leave the country. Would-be emigrants were frequently killed, or robbed of all their belongings. Nevertheless, Korean emigration to Russia continued despite all difficulties. By 1868 four large Korean villages existed in Russian territory. The total number of Koreans in the Ussuri region then exceeded 1,800, whilst the Russian peasant settlers and Cossacks in the same area numbered 6,200.

From the Russian point of view the Korean immigration was all the more valuable because the Korean peasant settlers showed great willingness to assimilate themselves, to accept the Russian language and the Russian Orthodox faith. Even in the very early stage of the immigration quite a number of the 'Russian Koreans' became Christians. The famous Russian traveller, Przhevalsky, who in the years 1867–69 made a journey to the Ussuri region, gave a characteristic example of the speedy process of assimilation undergone by the new Korean subjects of the Czars. Przhevalsky mentioned the case of the headman of the village Tyzen-Khe (Ryazanovka), the largest of the first four Korean settlements in Russia. This headman had not only become a Christian; he had also acquired some knowledge of Russian, was clad in the Russian peasant fashion, and had abandoned his Korean name, calling himself Peter Semyonov after his godfather, a Russian officer.[1]

Przhevalsky, whom the Soviet régime still considers as a great authority on the Russian Far East, viewed the progress of Korean immigration with mixed feelings. He was the first Russian to see that the immigration, while helping to open up the new Pacific territories, might involve certain dangers. He openly declared that the settlement of Koreans so near the border was no minor mistake and he suggested that the Koreans should be settled along the middle reaches of the Amur, a measure which in Przhevalsky's view, would facilitate their russification. Przhevalsky's warning was not entirely disregarded by the authorities. A new big party of Korean immigrants which reached Russia in 1871 was not used for the colonization of the Russian-Korean border area but directed, instead, to a point 217 miles west of Khabarovsk where its members founded the village of Blagoslovennoye 'the Blessed'. The village was frequently mentioned as a prosperous, well administered community. Thirty years after the foundation of the village, the official Guide of the Great Siberian Railway stressed that it made a very good impression and that the love of work and order of its inhabitants was visible in the way in which they built their houses and tilled their fields.[2] Under the Soviet

33

régime Blagoslovennoye was incorporated into the Jewish Autonomous Province.*

Despite the successful experiment conducted in Blagoslovennoye the bulk of the Korean immigrants continued to settle down near the Korean border in the region of Vladivostok. Until the beginning of the twentieth century this Korean immigration was prompted mainly by economic reasons, but the Japanese occupation of Korea provided new political incentives for the trek into the Russian Far East. The number of Koreans in the Russian Pacific coastal areas, which had reached 23,000 in 1898, went up to 46,000 in 1907, and to 52,000 in 1910. In the First World War the 'Russian Koreans' proved themselves loyal subjects of the Czars. Four thousand of them served in the Russian Army, including one hundred and fifty as officers.

DURING AND AFTER THE CIVIL WAR

The February Revolution of 1917 led to a great upsurge of social and political activities among the Korean population of the Russian Far East. Korean societies and peasant leagues were founded, and in May 1917 the First Congress of Korean Revolutionary Organizations was held in the town Nikolsk-Ussuriisky (now 'Voroshilov'). The large majority of the delegates supported the Russian Provisional Government, to which a telegram of greetings was sent. The Congress took a stand against russification, demanded a Korean seat in the future Russian Constituent Assembly, and advocated certain improvements for the existing Korean schools. The latter demands were made by Korean teachers, who played a leading part in the Congress and in the Korean National Union, the representative body of the Russian Koreans. Even after the October Revolution, the spokesmen of the Korean people in Russia showed little enthusiasm for the Bolshevik cause, and continued to support the party of the Socialist Revolutionaries. The Second Congress of Korean Revolutionary Organizations, which was held in May 1918, proclaimed the neutrality of the Koreans in the Russian Civil War. In reality the Central Executive Committee of the Korean National Union (renamed, early in 1919, All-Korean National Council) was anything but neutral. It took up a 'counter-revolutionary' attitude, boycotting the Soviets, but participating in the work of the regular local government organs, the 'zemstva'.

* Until 1930 there were still more Koreans than Jews in what later became the Jewish Autonomous Province. The territory then included 3,200 Koreans and 2,700 Jews. The Koreans had four and the Jews three 'National Village Soviets'. The other ethnic groups then represented in Birobidzhan were Russians (27,350), Ukrainians (3,000), Far Eastern natives (700) and Chinese (500). The second edition of the *Large Soviet Encyclopedia* published in 1952, however, mentions only Jews, Russians and Ukrainians as inhabitants of the Province.

Throughout the whole period of Civil War and foreign intervention in the Far East the communists formed only a small minority among the 'Russian Koreans'. The Bolshevik Party tried to gain some influence among the Koreans by playing up the more recent immigrants, who had not yet been granted Russian nationality, against the old immigrants. Consequently, the Korean members of the communist guerilla detachments were recruited primarily from the new immigrants who expected from the Soviet régime improvements in their material and legal status.

The more communist rule consolidated in the Far East the less freely could the All-Korean National Council express its views. In September 1920, when it had moved from Nikolsk Ussuriisky to Blagoveshchensk, it issued a statement in favour of the Soviet Government which the Communist Party authorities themselves refused to take seriously. For them it was a hypocritical opportunistic document.[3]

The statement seems to have been the swan song of the All-Korean National Council. The organization was dissolved and a communist-directed 'Union of Koreans' came into existence with its headquarters in Moscow and branch organizations in Leningrad and other important Soviet cities. This organization, which was likewise disbanded after a few years' existence, appears to have been concerned only with the Korean diaspora in Russia proper. In the Soviet Far East the Communist Party and the Communist Youth League had the monopoly for the representation of Korean interests. During a short period there were even special Korean sections inside the Communist Party of the Soviet Far East, but they proved to be inexpedient and were dissolved in 1923, having existed for six months only. At the same time 750 Korean party members, out of a total of about 1,000 were expelled, presumably for nationalist leanings.[4]

Soon after the purge of 1923 both the Communist Party and the Communist Youth League recruited new members from the Korean minority. In Vladivostok, for instance, the Communist Youth League had, in 1927, 7,409 Russian and 5,885 Korean members.

There are no absolutely reliable data available as to the numerical strength of the Korean element in Soviet Russia after 1917. Many Koreans emigrated to Russia in the years of the revolutionary confusion in the hope that the Russian Far East would become more and more internationalized. According to the Ministry of Nationality Affairs of the Far Eastern Republic the Koreans numbered 300,000 in the buffer state, and were, after Russians and Ukrainians, its third largest ethnical group. In 1927 there were only 170,000 Koreans in the Soviet Union according to official data, but unofficially there were 'at least 250,000'.[5]

LITTLE SOVIET KOREA

The large majority of the Koreans of the Soviet Far East remained concentrated in the Vladivostok area (okrug) where they formed, in 1926, about one quarter of the entire population. The largest Korean communities lived in the Suchansk district, to the east of Vladivostok, and in the area of Poset, to the west of Vladivostok, in the immediate neighbourhood of the Korean and Manchurian borders. Several dozens of Korean villages in that area were united into a 'Korean National District'.[6] Ninety-five per cent of the population of the District were Koreans. Their main occupations were rice-growing, fishing and timber cutting.

Relations between Russians and Koreans in the Vladivostok region left much to be desired under the Soviet régime. The collectivization of agriculture in particular led to considerable difficulties. When the first collective farms were founded in the Pacific coastal areas near Vladivostok, the local authorities gave privileged treatment to the Russian farmers at the expense of the Koreans. The Russian collective farms received more land and were better provided with agricultural machinery and even with credits. An article which the organ of the Soviet of Nationalities *Revolyutsiya i Natsionalnosti* published early in 1931 stated bluntly that this discrimination was prompted by 'great power chauvinism' on the part of the District Executive Committees ('Rayispolkomy') of the Vladivostok region as well as on the part of the regional agricultural authorities.

Revolyutsiya i Natsionalnosti illustrated this anti-Korean discrimination by the example of two new adjoining *kolkhozy*. The first was the Russian kolkhoz 'OKDVA', the second the Korean collective farm 'Tikhookeanets Revolyutsioner' ('The Revolutionary on the Pacific'). These two collective farms differed from each other not only in their ethnic composition but also in regard to the amount of land allotted to them. In the Russian kolkhoz, 'OKDVA', there was an average of 59 acres per household, against 20 acres per household in the Korean 'Revolutionary on the Pacific'. This state of inequality induced the Koreans to complain to the authorities about 'Russian chauvinism'. The complaint made things worse. It enraged the local Russians against their Korean neighbours. A number of violent clashes occurred between Russians and Koreans almost at the gates of Vladivostok. The organ of the Soviet of Nationalities asserted that the fault was with the Russians who had assaulted Korean collective farmers. The blame for the incidents could not be put on 'kulaks' and 'class enemies' as was done in similar circumstances in other parts of the Soviet Union. The Communist Youth League participated in beating up the Koreans. The latter aired their indignation against the outrages committed by Russian collective farmers by turning against the collective farm system itself. As an expression of protest Korean peasants took the initiative in disbanding a number of collective farms in the Vladivostok countryside.[7]

The worst aspect, from the point of view of the theory of Soviet nationalities policy, was that the local authorities in the Soviet Far East did not see the political implications of the Russian-Korean incidents but considered them as mere acts of 'hooliganism'. As the district and area (okrug) committees of the Party failed to remedy the situation, the Party leadership in Khabarovsk had to take things in hand. In a special meeting, held in the winter of 1930–31, the Communist Party Committee of the F.E.T. decided to take measures against 'Great Russian chauvinism' in the areas with a mixed Russian-Korean population, and it can be assumed that conditions improved after this intervention. Nevertheless, the events which marked the initial period of collectivization in the Vladivostok area constitute an essential part of the background, explaining those drastic measures which the Soviet Government took a few years later against the Koreans and other Asiatic minorities.

In the cultural field the Soviet régime advanced greatly the Korean minority in the Russian Far East. The Soviet Koreans were well provided with educational facilities which had been almost completely lacking under the Czarist régime. The number of Korean schools in the F.E.T. increased with every year and reached the figure of 300 in 1937, of which fifty-three were in the National District. The Korean minority owned three secondary schools, two technical colleges, two teachers' training colleges (including one in the Korean National District), and a Korean Pedagogical Institute in Vladivostok. The Soviet Korean intelligentsia had also the opportunity to study either in that city, at the Far Eastern University, or at the Sun Yat Sen University in Moscow.

There were several Korean communist newspapers, of which the largest, *Vanguard*, was published in Vladivostok, 10,000 copies being printed. From 1930 a special Korean newspaper was published for the Korean fishermen of the maritime region. The Committee of the Communist Party of the Korean National District also had an organ of its own, *Along the Path of Lenin*.[8]

KOREANS AS 'SPIES' AND 'DIVERSIONISTS'

In 1937 the policy of building up a little Soviet Korea was completely abandoned. The Soviet nationalities policy adopted a new objective instead, the liquidation of the Korean minority in the Soviet Far East. The Soviet Government had suddenly become aware of the dangerous sides of the Korean immigration to which Przhevalsky had already drawn attention, particularly their presence in strategically important areas near the Russian borders. In addition, the Soviet régime felt some doubts about the loyalty of the Koreans in a case of emergency. Whilst the Koreans of Korea proper were solidly anti-Japanese, the Soviet régime had no guarantee that the bulk of the Koreans of the Soviet Union would not support the Japanese invader. They had, after all, their grievances, such as forcible collectivization and suppression of local nationalism by the Soviet régime. It must be said in fairness to the régime that in the years 1936–38 incidents on the Soviet-Manchurian border practically never ceased, and the Soviet State had good reasons to feel its security in the Far East threatened. But in their fear of spies, wreckers and diversionists, the Soviet authorities went so far as to suspect every Korean and Chinese of being a Japanese accomplice, and to seek safety in the wholesale transfer of all Asiatics from the Soviet Far East.

This measure, which is a heavy blot on Soviet nationalities policy, was never publicly announced, but it is not too difficult to reconstruct it from indirect hints and omissions in the Soviet Press. The first indirect intimation of extraordinary measures taken, or about to be taken, against Koreans and Chinese was contained in an article about 'Foreign Espionage in the Soviet Far East', which *Pravda* published on April 23rd, 1937. The article stated that the Japanese secret service made use of a large number of Koreans and Chinese as agents in the Soviet Far East. These agents, said *Pravda*, were camouflaging themselves as inhabitants of those districts of the Soviet Far East where they were supposed to carry out their activities. The Japanese intelligence, therefore, closely studied the national composition of every given Soviet district and posted, accordingly, Korean or Chinese or Russian white guards. Not only was primitive 'spying' going on in the F.E.T.; agents were also infiltrating into institutions of military importance, with the aim of creating groups of spies, saboteurs and diversionists. As a rule these agents penetrated into the party as well as the Communist Youth League. Of course, there was, in the view of *Pravda*, a close contact between these direct agents and all local elements hostile to the Soviet power, i.e., 'Trotzkyites and other double-dealers'.[9]*

* It is quite likely that the Japanese intelligence service did infiltrate into the ranks of the Korean and Chinese minorities in the Far East. On the other hand, it is certain that the same method was applied by the Soviet counter-espionage *vis à vis* the Russian emigrés in Manchuria and China proper. In 1940 there were 70,000 Russians in Manchuria (including 40,000 in Kharbin), 20,000 in Shanghai and 10,000 in Tientsin. Many of these Russians were pro-Soviet. Thus four-fifths of the Shanghai Russians acquired Soviet citizenship many months before the city was taken by Mao Tse-tung. The pro-Soviet elements among the Russian colonies in China were naturally of great use to the N.K.V.D. but the primary concern of the latter was to penetrate into the leading strata of the white emigration which collaborated with the Japanese authorities. A popular Soviet play, 'On the other Side', by A. Baryanov shows the cunning way in which Soviet intelligence operated in Manchuria. The hero of the play is a Soviet intelligence officer who poses in Kharbin as the son of a white guard general assassinated by the Bolsheviks. Before going on his mission he learns by heart all the more important prayers of the Orthodox Church, a knowledge which greatly assists him in deceiving the emigrés.

On the basis of this story, which bore all the hallmarks of a typical plot hatched by the N.K.V.D., everybody, and in particular every Korean and Chinese, could, in future, be suspected of working for the Japanese intelligence. Membership of the party, or of the Komsomol, was no evidence of loyalty; on the contrary it could well serve as an additional evidence of treason, since a spy had every interest in becoming a member of such respectable organizations.

Having made its fantastic accusations against the Koreans and Chinese of the Soviet Far East, *Pravda* mentioned these two minorities no more.* On June 28th, 1937, when the new party secretary of the F.E.T. reviewed, in the columns of *Pravda*, the achievements of the Soviet Power in the Far East, he dwelt in some detail on the Jewish immigration into Birobidzhan, but ignored the Koreans. This might have been an oversight on his part. It was more characteristic that the Korean contribution to the victory of the Soviet régime in the Far East, previously so loudly advertised, was not mentioned at all in the many articles which the Soviet Press published at the end of October 1937, in connection with the fifteenth anniversary of the liberation of Vladivostok.

A more important and more direct clue to the transplantation of the Russian Koreans was, however, contained in a cryptic governmental announcement which *Pravda* published on its back page on December 20th, 1937. It said: 'The Council of People's Commissars of the U.S.S.R. and the Central Committee of the All-Union Communist Party (Bolsheviks) have expressed their gratitude for exemplary and precise fulfilment of a Government assignment in the field of transport to the chief of the N.K.V.D. administration in the Far Eastern Territory, G. S. Lyushkov, to the whole staff of the N.K.V.D. of the F.E.T. and to the personnel of the Far Eastern Railway which participated in the implementation of the assignment.'[10] The announcement, it is true, did not mention the nature of the 'government assignment in the field of transport', but there can be no doubt that only a matter of great importance could have warranted this special expression of thanks to the N.K.V.D. and the railways. It was not a military matter since, in this case, the Special Far Eastern Army would also have been mentioned. A large scale shifting of population would be a plausible explanation.

---

* An article in *Izvestiya* of September 24th, 1937, dealing at length with Japanese spying contained an implicit general warning against Japanese agents in Korean disguise without referring to their activities in the Soviet Far East. The article warned that Japanese spies might have both Soviet and Japanese (Korean) nationality. It mentioned the case of the Korean, Kim Zaen, who headed a 'spying diversionist organization' which was discovered in Moscow in 1934. This Korean had taken on Soviet nationality in 1929 but when he got into trouble the Japanese interceded in his favour and claimed him as their subject.

THE AFTERMATH OF THE 'LIQUIDATION' MEASURES

From a nationalist and imperialist Russian point of view, the measures against the Koreans were amply justified by the border incidents which took place in August – September 1938 in the former Korean National District of Poset. The area in question was, as has been seen, the scene of unpleasant events between Russian and Korean collective farmers, which must have left rather bitter memories. It may have been fortunate for the Soviet Union, therefore, that the Korean population was already evacuated at the time when the Russian-Japanese skirmishes took place.

From a political and international angle, the action against the Koreans did not damage Soviet prestige, owing to the discretion with which it was carried out. Neither the Western democratic camp nor the German-Japanese Anti-Comintern block showed any interest in the problem. Strangely enough, the 'Little Soviet Korea' around Vladivostok had never, except perhaps in the early 'twenties,' had any real export value as far as Korea proper was concerned. Communism in Korea struggled throughout the inter-war period against almost insurmountable difficulties. It remained a small sect without any influence on the popular masses, always an easy prey to all sorts of nationalistic and petty bourgeois deviations.*

It does not seem that the Korean communists have ever made use, in their propaganda, of the Korean National District in the Soviet Union and its achievements in the economic and cultural sphere. Such statements of the Korean Communist Party as are known do not mention the 'District' at all.

From the economic point of view the anti-Korean measures resulted in a clear disadvantage for the Soviet Far East, though not for the U.S.S.R. as a whole. One of the main tasks of the Korean minority in the economic field consisted in developing the cultivation of rice. Under the Czarist régime, rice-planting in the Russian Far East had only an experimental character. It did not assume major proportions until after 1917. This was not the merit of the Soviet authorities, but of the Japan-

---

* The following passage from a resolution which the political secretariat of the Comintern Executive Committee passed in December 1928 might illustrate this point: 'The ranks of the Communist Party of Korea have in the past consisted almost exclusively of intellectuals and students. A Communist Party built on such foundations cannot be a consistently bolshevik and organizationally sound Party. The first task of the communist movement of Korea is therefore to strengthen its own ranks. The problem of improving the social structure of the Party is confronting us in its full scope. The petty-bourgeois intellectual composition of the Party, and the lack of contact with the workers have hitherto constituted one of the main causes of the permanent crisis in the communist movement of Korea. The frequent failures of the Korean communists show that the Party was unable to organize its conspiratorial work properly.' (Resolution of the E.C.C.I. on the Korean Question, International Press Correspondence, February 15th, 1929, p. 132.)

ese occupants, who had made a close study of the economic potentialities of the Russian Pacific coastal regions during the period of
intervention. Japanese experts had estimated that between twenty and
twenty-five million acres of Russian land in the Far East could be used
for rice plantations.[11] But the Japanese did not approach the problem
from a theoretical angle alone; they also encouraged rice-growing in
practice. In 1918 only 674 acres of land in the Russian Far East grew
rice, against 6,476 acres in 1920, and 21,590 acres in 1921.[12] Encouraged
by these successes, the Soviet authorities drew up a 'Ten-Year Plan for
Rice Cultivation'. It foresaw that the area to be planted with rice was to
reach 232,000 acres in 1936, which was a modest target but meant,
nevertheless, a sevenfold increase as compared to the rice-growing area
at the beginning of the plan period. It does not seem that the target was
ever reached. The departure of the Koreans from the Soviet Far East
put a stop to the further development of rice cultivation there. For
future reference it is worthwhile to remember that the cultivation of
rice, the staple food of the Far Eastern peoples, is possible on a vast
scale in the Soviet Pacific coastal areas. This possibility might stimulate
future waves of Asiatic immigrants to the Russian Far East, if and when
circumstances allow.

THE SOVIET KOREAN DIASPORA

The economic losses which the departure of the Koreans caused to the
Soviet Far East were compensated by the benefits which they brought to
those areas of the U.S.S.R. to which they were directed by the authorities. The Koreans of the F.E.T. provided very valuable colonists for
Uzbekistan. There they were resettled particularly in the Lower, Central
and Upper Chirchik Districts of the Tashkent Province, and in the
Gurlen District of the Khorezm Province. Many of the Korean colonists
have shown a high degree of efficiency, and since the end of the Second
World War the Soviet Press has frequently published lists of Korean rice-
and cotton-growers who were awarded Orders and Medals for outstanding achievements on the labour front. In one case as many as 31 Koreans
of the Tashkent Province were awarded the title 'Hero of Socialist
Toil'.[13] Several of the Koreans in question had Russian Christian names
or even both Russian Christian names and Russian patronymics, a sure
sign that their families had settled in Russia before the coming to
power of the Bolshevik Party.

A particularly important piece of pioneering was accomplished by the
Koreans who had been sent to the Khorezm Province. Before their
arrival there, only steppe grass grew on what are now very fertile rice-
fields. In formerly uninhabited territory the Koreans founded, through

41

'selfless work', a big 'Stalin Collective Farm', which, every year, increases its rice deliveries to the State.[14]

In addition to the Korean settlements in the Tashkent and Khorezm Provinces, there are Korean groups in other parts of the Soviet Union which came into existence independently of the mass evacuation of the Korean minority from the Far East. The most important of them have lived as rice planters in the Kzyl Orda Province of Kazakhstan since 1928. The Kazakhstan Koreans have not only prosperous collective farms, but also a remarkable cultural institution, the Korean State Theatre, which has repeatedly received honourable mention.

Other Korean communities have been less fortunate, for instance, those transferred to the Don area have disappeared without trace after fulfilling a purpose which was as immoral as it was useful from the point of view of the Soviet régime. The functions of these isolated Korean groups might be illustrated by the example of the Korean communal farm, ('kommuna') 'Don-Ris', which was set up near the Don Cossack village Sinyavskaya in the Taganrog District. The Koreans arrived in that village at a time when collectivization of agriculture was still in its beginning, and the very fact that they at once founded a 'kommuna', a particularly advanced type of collective farm was bound to be felt as a provocation by the local people. The unpopularity of the Korean newcomers increased further when a number of them (including several Korean members of the Communist Party) took an active part in so-called 'economic-political campaigns' ('khozpolitkampanii') which aimed at terrorizing the 'kulaks' and confiscating their property. This created the impression among the local Russian peasants that there existed a close connection between the arrival of destitute Koreans in the area, and the de-kulakization measures. A class conflict which the Soviet Government provoked all over the Soviet Union thus appeared locally as a national conflict. The discontent of the peasants was diverted from the Soviet Government to the unfortunate Korean settlers, who had allowed themselves to be used as shock-troops by the régime, and who indeed had hoped to get a share in the spoils taken from the 'kulaks'. All in all the 'Don-Ris' experiment was a typical example of the 'divide and rule' aspect of Soviet nationalities policy.[15]

II. THE CHINESE MINORITY IN RUSSIA

It cannot be said with certainty when the Chinese started to live in what is today the Soviet Far East. An outstanding Russian authority on the Ussuri and Amur territories, Vladimir K. Arsenev, stated that the Chinese arrived there only thirty years prior to the Russian annexation, i.e., about 1830. When the Chinese Government ceded the Ussuri Provinces to Russia, by the treaty concluded in Peking on November 2nd,

1860, it did not know for certain whether there were Chinese subjects in that area. Article One of the Treaty used the tentative phrase 'should there be any Chinese subjects in the Ussuri territory . . .' In such a case the Russian Government pledged itself to leave the Chinese at their places of residence, and to allow them to continue fishing and hunting.[16]

Przhevalsky, the first Russian traveller in the Ussuri region, who has already been quoted, believed however, that the presence of Chinese in the Ussuri area could be traced back to the middle of the seventeenth century. Since then, the country has been used as a place of exile by the authorities of Northern China. At the time of the final Russian occupation the Ussuri region contained, according to Przhevalsky, both a Chinese brigand element and a Chinese sedentary agricultural population. The local Chinese, said Przhevalsky, had developed agriculture to a high degree of perfection and variety. They were growing beans, maize, oats, wheat, melons, red pepper, tobacco, cabbage, garlic and onions.[17]

However divergent may be the opinions about the history of the Chinese prior to the establishment of Russian sovereignty in the Ussuri region, there is general agreement that they constituted a very important factor, at least during the first 60 years of Russian rule in that area. The inefficiency of the Russian administration was the great chance of the Chinese. The absence of generous grants to Russian peasants indirectly favoured the Chinese farmer. The insufficient supply of goods from the Russian hinterland made the Chinese trader a necessity. The lack of an energetic political leadership on the part of the Russians enabled the Chinese to form a state within the state, to live according to their own laws, to have their own private courts, and to rule in many places over the aborigines.

Chinese influence was strong, not only in the forest areas situated some distance from the Russian administrative centres, but also within these centres themselves, particularly in the towns of Nikolsk Ussuriisky, Khabarovsk and Vladivostok. In each of these three towns there were not only thousands of Chinese but also well organized and powerful Chinese societies which worked under the supervision of the Ministry of Labour, Commerce and Agriculture in Peking. The Vladivostok Chinese Society had existed since 1881, that of Khabarovsk since 1889, that of Nikolsk Ussuriisky since 1908. These Societies were frequently frowned upon by the Czarist Government, and there were times when they had to work under conditions of illegality, but it was the Soviet régime which did away with them altogether. The Chinese Societies in these three towns of the Russian Far East were only the most prominent of an entire network of Chinese organizations, which had sprung up in all areas of the Russian Pacific Province where Chinese used to live.

Last but not least the Czarist régime attracted a large number of

Chinese labourers to the Russian Far East. Until 1910, Chinese man-power was almost exclusively used for all public works commissioned by the Czarist authorities either in the Russian Far Eastern territories proper or in Manchuria. These included in the first place the port and fortress of Vladivostok and the Ussuri and Eastern Chinese railway lines. Most of the time, the Czarist authorities showed benevolence to Chinese labourers and preferred them to Russians both for their readiness to accept very low wages and for their lack of interest in politics. In 1903 the military governor of the Amur district expressed himself against the despatch of Russian workers to the Far East who he said would only swell the ranks of the discontented, whilst the Chinese workers were placid and caused no difficulties. Legal restrictions against employment of Chinese and other foreign workers did exist during the last few years of Czarist rule; but how little effective these restrictions were is shown from the example of the Far Eastern gold-mining industry. In 1902 it was almost entirely staffed by Russians. In 1916 the share of the Russian element among the goldminers in the Far East was only 7 per cent, practically all others being Chinese.[18]

VLADIVOSTOK OR KAI SHEN VEI?

If it is generally true to say that the Soviet régime prevented the Chinese from dominating the Ussuri and Amur region, nowhere has this Russian mission of the Soviet Government found such a clear expression as in Vladivostok, Russia's principal port on the Pacific Ocean.

As long as the Czarist régime lasted, and even in the first years of the Soviet régime, Vladivostok showed every sign of becoming a big inter-national trading centre, a kind of northern Shanghai, instead of being a Russian bulwark on the Pacific Ocean. The big trade of Vladivostok was primarily in the hands of the German and British firms, the most important of all being the Hamburg merchants, 'Kunst and Albers', with roughly the same importance in the Russian Far East which the United Africa Company or John Holt have on the African West Coast. The Chinese supplied the masses of the civilian population of the town for which its Chinese name, 'Kai-Shen-Vei', would have been more appropriate than 'Vladivostok' which means 'Ruler of the East', a term which, at that time, was misleading.

The official statistical data give a good picture of the importance of the Chinese factor in Vladivostok. In 1879, seven years after the town had been proclaimed principal Russian port on the Pacific, the popula-tion of Vladivostok included about 600 Russian civilians against 3,470 Chinese and 500 Koreans. Russian predominance was artificially main-tained by the presence in the town of a military personnel, 4,088 strong.[19] By the beginning of the century the situation had not greatly altered.

The Vladivostok Chinese population was still considerably larger than the Russian civilian population in the city. In 1902 the population of Vladivostok included 15,000 Chinese, 2,300 Koreans, 2,400 Japanese, 11,500 Russians and a garrison of 13,000 men. In the first years of the century the number of Chinese in Vladivostok went on increasing; it reached 23,600 in 1911, and 26,780 in 1912, not including illegal immigrants who were not registered with the Russian police. According to information from Chinese quarters they numbered several thousand.[20] During the first years of the Soviet régime the Chinese element was still very much in evidence in Vladivostok. The census of 1926, it is true, showed a clear preponderance of the Russians, who numbered over 65,500. The Chinese numbering 22,000, ranked second, followed by Koreans (6,900), Ukrainians (6,000), Poles (1,720), Jews (1,180), Latvians (665) and Japanese (582). To the traveller who went from European Russia to Vladivostok the town offered a different picture from the one conveyed by the official population statistics. For example, a reporter of the communist German newspaper *Deutsche Zentral-Zeitung*, which was published in Moscow, gave the following description: 'When entering the waiting room of the Vladivostok railway station, one notices at once that one is in the East. One even thinks one is in China – so many Chinese! Yes, Vladivostok is very largely a Chinese city. . .'[21]

With its large Chinese population Soviet Vladivostok retained in its initial stage, the character of a northern Shanghai. Although the main streets of the city were called after Lenin, Marx, and October 25 (the day of the final establishment of Soviet rule in the Far East), foreign, in particular Asiatic, capitalism had by no means abdicated. It was even favoured by the official 'New Economic Policy'. Vladivostok still had its Japanese banks, it retained its Japanese shipping lines, its Chinese and Japanese hotels. Chinese and Japanese newspapers were published side by side with the Russian communist organ *Krasnoye Znamya*.[22]

The first Five-Year-Plan brought about the doom of the Chinese traders in the Soviet Far East but Chinese could still exist there as hardworking labourers and dockers, particularly in Vladivostok. A communist traveller from Central Europe, Otto Heller, who visited Vladivostok on the eve of the tenth anniversary of its inclusion into Soviet Russia described it as an international workers' town, primarily a town of Russian and Chinese workers. This is what Heller said about the Vladivostok Chinese: 'The Chinese dockworkers who are working in hundreds not only in the transit docks but also in the timber and bunker docks are exceedingly active. Socialist competition, shock-brigades, training courses, abolition of illiteracy – one finds all these to an equal extent among the European and Asiatic workers'.[23] Heller mentioned the building by the Soviet authorities of a new Chinese quarter including clubs, dining halls and a mechanical laundry, but what impressed him even more was the 'International Seamen's Club' of Vladivostok. He said, significantly, that the influence of the club was felt in all the ports of East Asia. Heller may have overestimated tl importance of the club but it is true that both the Comintern and the Profintern, the international Communist trade union organization, had considered Vladivostok as an important base for revolutionary activities in the Far East. The former had founded a short-lived 'Far Eastern Secretariat' in Vladivostok, the latter had convened to that city the Second Congress of its Pan-Pacific Secretariat. This body was intended to foster unrest in all countries bordering on the Pacific and to encourage the foundation of communist trade unions there. The Vladivostok Congress (it was called a 'Conference' when the attendance turned out to be poorer than expected) was a failure and its decisions had no political repercussions in the Far East.

Vladivostok's inability to become a centre of revolution in the Far East was presumably one of the considerations which determined the Soviet Government finally to do away with the 'northern Shanghai', even a proletarian Shanghai, and to transform the city into a Russian bulwark on the Pacific Ocean.

SOVIET RUSSIA AND THE LATINIZATION
OF THE CHINESE SCRIPT

Not only the Chinese population of Vladivostok, but the entire Chinese minority of the U.S.S.R. was, until 1937, and particularly around 1930, expected to play an outstanding part in revolutionizing China. If not to promote the political revolution, the Soviet Chinese were at least intended to bring about a cultural revolution. The latter was to consist in the abolition of the Chinese 'hieroglyphs' and the introduction of the Latin alphabet. Between 1929 and 1937 a number of Soviet personalities, both politicians and scholars, concentrated a great deal of energy on the latinization of the Chinese script. The sequence of events was roughly as follows. A learned Chinese communist, whom the Soviet Press usually referred to under the pseudonym 'Strakhov', worked out a Latin alphabet for the Chinese language. In 1929 and 1930 Chinese workers and students in Moscow, Leningrad, Khabarovsk and Vladivostok held meetings welcoming Strakhov's initiative. Then the Soviet Academy of Sciences took control of operations. A 'Latinization Brigade' was set up within the Chinese section of the Oriental Institute of the Academy. In May 1931, the All-Union Executive Committee for the New Alphabet approved the Chinese latinized alphabet. The 'Latinization Brigade' then went to the Far East, summoned a 'First Conference for Latinization', and organized a permanent 'Far Eastern Committee for the New Alphabet'. Between 1932 and 1934 the new alphabet was introduced in the few Chinese schools of the Soviet Union whereby the teaching of the 'hieroglyphs' remained a special subject from the second class on. The Chinese newspapers of Vladivostok were also printed in Latin characters. In addition, an entire literature in the new script came into being. By January 1st, 1935, as many as fifty books and pamphlets had been published in the 'Latinghua', as the Chinese Latin script was also called.[24]

The Soviet initiative did stir up considerable interest in China itself, particularly when the first pamphlets in the new script started to reach Chinese intellectual circles. Inspired by the Soviet example, an entire movement promoting the latinization of the script emerged in China which had many supporters. No doubt the penetration into China of the Soviet-invented Latinghua was one of the major successes of the Soviet nationalities policy. But, whilst the Latinghua became an export article, it was suppressed in Russia itself, for no Chinese books, pamphlets and newspapers in Latin characters seem to have been printed in the U.S.S.R. after 1937.[25] The absence of such literature is connected not only with the general measures taken against the Chinese minority in the U.S.S.R. but also with the fact that the Soviet Government had, in the later 'thirties', changed its attitude towards latinization. In 1937 the Soviet Government already had grave doubts as to the wisdom of the introduction of the Latin alphabet for non-Russian peoples. As by that time the Chinese minority in Russia was no longer a recognized factor, it was spared the experiment of a Chinese script in Cyrillic letters.

CHINESE AND RUSSIAN 'PROLETARIAT'

Up to now it would appear that Russian-Chinese relations in the Soviet Far East had been fairly idyllic until the turning point of 1937. In reality there was a great deal of tension between Russians and Chinese, much more than between Russians and Koreans. The ordinary Russian Far Easterner often held the local Chinese minority responsible for the anti-Russian policy pursued by Chinese war-lords in Manchuria, particularly their aggressive actions against the Chinese Eastern Railway which was under joint Soviet-Chinese management. The Chinese-Soviet conflict over this vital railway line reached its climax in 1929, and it was only natural that it should have provoked a wave of chauvinism in the Russian Far East, to which the local Chinese fell victims. Already then the Russians of the Far East would have welcomed the expulsion of the Chinese. However this was not yet official Soviet policy, and the Soviet Government shielded the Chinese minority against Russian hostility as well as it could. But many of the local authorities pursued a policy of their own. In one district, the gold-mining region of Zeya, north of Blagoveshchensk, they embarked on an open persecution of the Chinese, and arrested them in large numbers. This injustice was later redressed, and the Soviet officials guilty of this excess were punished by imprisonment from two to five years.

With the connivance of Soviet officials there were also anti-Chinese outrages in Nikolsk Ussuriisky where twelve Russians including the deputy commander of the local militia had to be arrested for 'chauvinism'. Most of the Far Eastern Russians put on trial for chauvinistic activities belonged to the working class. The chief bulwarks of anti-Chinese agitation apart from the goldmines of the Soyuzzoloto trust were the 'Dalzavod', the big shipbuilding yard of Vladivostok and the 'Dalselmash', a plant in Khabarovsk producing agricultural machinery. Russians working in these enterprises frequently assaulted Chinese workmen and used against them such terms of abuse as 'Fazan', 'Kitayeza' and 'Chan-Kai-shi', the last named being the Russian version of Chang Kai-shek.

The Party headquarters in Moscow were continually admonishing the Far Eastern trade union and Party organizations to put an end to the anti-Chinese manifestations. Their laxity in fighting the chauvinists, particularly those of proletarian origin, was notorious. The communist city secretary of Vladivostok, for instance, did his best to stop an investigation by a *Pravda* correspondent into the treatment of the local Chinese.[26]

Notwithstanding all the unpleasant incidents in the Soviet Far East, people in European Russia were persistently told that there was harmonious co-operation between the Chinese proletariat and the Russian working class. A representative of that Chinese proletariat, a shockworker of the Suchan coalmines, was even sent to Moscow to address the Sixth Congress of Soviets which was held in March 1931. He brought greetings from his Chinese fellow-workers, and drew attention to the increased participation of Chinese in local government bodies of the F.E.T. At the Seventh Congress of Soviets, which was held in March 1935, no Chinese representative attended, but the head of the provincial administration of the F.E.T., Krutov, mentioned, in an address to the Congress, several positive facts about the Chinese minority, particularly the existence of Chinese schools, and of a Chinese theatre in Vladivostok. At the Eighth Congress of Soviets which met in November 1936, to adopt the new Stalin Constitution, there was again a Chinese delegate, the famous Stakhanovite of the fishing industry, Li Un Kho.[27] Other Chinese Stakhanovites who had distinguished themselves in coalmining and agriculture were frequently praised in the Soviet Press thoughout the year of 1936, when the Stakhanov movement was still young.

The Chinese proletariat did indeed play an important part in the economy of the Soviet Far East. In 1926 the Chinese and other 'oriental workers' supplied 50 per cent of all manpower employed in Far Eastern coalmining and 35 per cent of the labour force of the timber industry. So the anti-Asiatic measures of 1937 hit first and foremost the ordinary Chinese workers and not any Chinese upper class. Chinese coalminers, for instance, were removed from the Suchan coalmines in connection with official Soviet statements that 'acts of sabotage' had been committed in the pits in conformity with Japanese instructions.[28]

The second edition of the *Large Soviet Encyclopedia* indirectly confirms the elimination of the Chinese minority of the Soviet Far East. A short article on Vladivostok in the *Small Soviet Encyclopedia* published in 1934 still referred to a 'considerable number of Chinese and Koreans'.[29] The *Large Soviet Encyclopedia* published in 1952, on the other hand, ignores these two peoples when devoting to the city a much more detailed description. The new edition of the standard Soviet reference book has also shown by omission that all institutions of the large Russian port which were the pride of Soviet nationalities policy before the Second World War have gone. The Chinese theatre which, incidentally, was not founded by the Soviets but the Chinese merchants at the end of the nineteenth century, has been abolished. The only four theatres now existing in the city are the Russian Gorky Theatre, the Theatre of the Pacific Fleet, the puppet theatre and the youth theatre. *[30] Also the Chinese newspaper of Vladivostok has disappeared, whereas the number of Russian papers in the city has increased. Even the 'Far Eastern University' with its Chinese and Korean departments was disbanded. It is the only university in the U.S.S.R. which has met such a fate.

After the purge in the Far East, groups of Chinese continued to live in other parts of the Soviet Union, in Moscow, Leningrad and other industrial centres of European Russia, as well as in Soviet Central Asia. The 1939 census, however, indicated a great decrease in the number of Chinese living in the U.S.S.R. As compared with the 1926 census their number was reduced by two-thirds, from 92,000 to 29,000, but these figures may not give an absolutely reliable picture as to the strength of the Chinese element in Soviet Russia, for the 1939 figure seems to include only Soviet citizens of Chinese origin, and not people who retained Chinese nationality.

There is sufficient, though unofficial, evidence available to show that

* There is positive evidence that the theatre was still in existence in March 1937 (*Pravda*, March 22nd, 1937), but it must have been closed down soon afterwards. Foundation and abolition of theatres for national minorities has always been symbolic of the trends of Soviet policy towards the nationalities concerned. In 1931 the Soviet Government founded the 'First Polish Theatre' in Kiev as an encouragement to the Polish minority to build up a Polish national culture independent of the culture of 'bourgeois Poland'. Later, when this attempt was abandoned, the Polish theatre was abolished. In 1949 the Soviet Government closed down the Jewish theatre in Moscow as part of a whole series of repressive measures against Jewish nationalism.

the Chinese in Soviet Russia fared badly in the late 'thirties' not only in the Far East but in every part of the Union in which they lived. F. Beck and W. Godin in their book on the Russian purge[31] mention mass arrests of Chinese, which occurred, apparently, in 1937. The authors themselves had met many Chinese in the prison of Kharkov; they were all charged with espionage in favour of Japan and some even with preparing terror acts against the members of the Soviet Government. Most of them were very humble laundrymen and absolutely incapable of committing the crimes of which they were accused.

III. THE SOVIET EMPIRE VERSUS THE JAPANESE PEOPLE

Soviet Russian policy towards the Japanese suffers from duplicity. As communists, the Soviet leaders are interested in the establishment of a communist régime in Japan, and, as Russians, they want to expand the Russian Empire at the expense of the Japanese people. The internationalist-communist approach towards the Japanese problem has largely remained theoretical whilst the nationalist Russian trend has prevailed in practice.

Soviet Russia's theoretical approach towards the Japanese people has been expressed not only in various pronouncements of the Communist International, but also in novels of Soviet writers dealing with problems of the Far East. The best example of the latter category is Peter Pavlenko's novel *Na Vostoke*, translated into English as 'Red Planes Fly East'. Pavlenko's book, which was written in the early 'thirties', anticipated a Russo-Japanese War. The author predicted that it would end with a communist victory and with mass fraternization between Russian, Chinese, Korean and Japanese communists. The final chapter of the book deals with the building of a new international city in the Soviet Far East situated near the Korean frontier. Most of the inhabitants of the new city are Japanese prisoners of war, reason enough to give the city a Japanese name, 'Sen Katayama', after a famous Japanese communist.[32]

The Russo-Japanese War came, but it resulted in quite a different relationship between Soviet communists and Japanese from that which Pavlenko had predicted. Soviet policy towards the Japanese people after the Second World War transformed the 'City of Sen Katayama' into a utopian dream. Soviet Russia's attitude was uncompromisingly imperialistic and nationalistic, not only towards the small Japanese groups living within the pre-1945 frontiers of the U.S.S.R.,* but also

* The number of Japanese living permanently in the territory of the Russian Empire has always been very small. Nevertheless, at the beginning of the century more and more Japanese settled in the Vladivostok region. Their number increased from 2,061 in 1897 to

towards the hundreds of thousands of Japanese colonists in the new Soviet territories – Karafuto and the Kurile Islands. Soviet practice in these territories showed that the Soviet Government did not believe in peaceful co-operation and co-existence between Russian colonists on the one hand and Japanese workmen, peasant settlers and fishermen on the other. The actions taken by the Soviet Government on Sakhalin and the Kurile Islands also proved that Soviet Russia was not guided solely by opposition to Japanese militarism and imperialism; her measures were those of a ruthless European colonial power against an Asiatic people.

The annexation of Southern Sakhalin and the Kurile Islands differed in character from most of the other territorial aggrandizements which Russia carried out during and after the Second World War. In the case of Eastern Poland, the Transcarpathian Ukraine, Bessarabia and the Baltic States, Russia claimed to have liberated the peoples of these territories from fascist, capitalist and landlord oppression. No such argument was advanced about the territories which Soviet Russia took from Japan. Moscow simply invoked the Treaty of Yalta and the historic rights of Russia, making it quite clear that the latter were much more important than the former. There is probably no other instance in which the Union of Socialist Soviet Republics has appeared with such cynical frankness as the heir and successor of the Empire of the Czars. This is how the official organ of the Law Institute of the All-Union Academy of Sciences formulated the 'legal side' of the annexation of the Japanese possessions:

'The Yalta and Potsdam decisions providing for the return to Soviet Russia of Southern Sakhalin and the Kurile Islands were no more than the re-establishment of historic justice which was trampled down by aggressive Japanese policy. Southern Sakhalin and the Kurile Islands are genuinely Soviet territories. The historic rights of the Soviet Union on them are based, above all, on the indisputable fact that they were first discovered and developed by Russian sea-farers and explorers. . . The fact that Russian seafarers and explorers were the first to discover and develop the Kurile Islands and Sakhalin gave the Russian Government the right to consider these territories as integral parts of the Russian State.'[33]

over 3,000 in 1907, and to over 4,000 in 1909. After the establishment of Soviet rule the Japanese colony in the Russian Far East was all but completely liquidated. At the end of 1925 there were only 600 left. (Academy of Sciences of the U.S.S.R., *Obyasnitelnaya Zapiska k Etnograficheskoi Karte Sibiri* – Explanation of the Ethnographic Map of Siberia, Leningrad 1929, p. 94).

SAKHALIN

When, in August of 1945, the Soviet Government belatedly entered the war in the Far East it pursued one aim above all, to decide the struggle for the island of Sakhalin once and for all in Russia's favour.

Russians and Japanese have disputed the possession of the island ever since the middle of the nineteenth century. The first diplomatic document which reflects both Japanese and Russian interest in Sakhalin was the Treaty of Shimoda, which was concluded in 1855. It established a Russo-Japanese condominium. The condominium status was confirmed by a convention which Russia and Japan signed in 1867, but it was abolished in 1875 by the Treaty of St. Petersburg, which made Sakhalin an undivided Russian possession. In 1905 a radical change occurred. The Treaty of Portsmouth cut Sakhalin in two. Russia lost to Japan the part of Sakhalin south of the Fiftieth Parallel, a territory to which the Japanese refer as 'Karafuto'.

Russia and Japan may have been equally eager to own Sakhalin, but the island was of very unequal value to the two Powers. For Russia, Sakhalin was a question of prestige, a strategic outpost and an accessory which rounded off her gigantic Asiatic possessions but which the Russian people did not really need. For Japan, Sakhalin was an outlet for its population surplus and an organic part of its island Empire. Until 1905 the Czarist authorities of Sakhalin had achieved little of which to be proud. The island had then about 40,000 inhabitants or one per square mile. Most of the population consisted of convicts, exiles and their families. Officials and soldiers constituted the second largest group, and there were only a few hundred voluntary settlers who were without any family ties on the island. When Russia lost Southern Sakhalin she naturally withdrew her subjects and Japan had to start from the very beginning to colonize the territory. The Japanese shouldered this task without delay and devoted a great deal of energy to it. In 1910, Karafuto already had over 10,000 inhabitants, and, by the outbreak of the First World War, over 60,000. The Czarist authorities did not succeed in meeting the challenge of the Japanese. After the defeat of 1905 they paid little attention to the part of the island which had remained in Russian hands. Colonization by convicts was stopped, but no free colonization took its place. Many of the former convicts and exiles left the island and there was a marked decline of population. In 1910 only 10,500 people lived in Northern Sakhalin.

The successful start of Japanese colonization in Karafuto stirred up Japanese desire for the possession of the whole of Sakhalin, and in 1920 Japan took advantage of the Russian Civil War to occupy the territory north of the Fiftieth Parallel. The conduct of the Japanese occupation authorities in Northern Sakhalin from 1920 to 1925 left no doubt as to Japan's intention to stay there for good. The Japanese commander banned all Russian political activities, Japanese civil and penal law replaced Russian legislation, and even the streets of Alexandrovsk, the chief town of Northern Sakhalin, were given Japanese names.[34] It was not so much the progressing consolidation of the young Soviet state which in the end prompted Japan to leave Northern Sakhalin, but rather American insistence on Japanese withdrawal from all Russian territories occupied during the Civil War. Northern Sakhalin was the last Russian territory to be freed from the military forces of the intervention powers.

Though liberated from the Japanese military occupation, Sakhalin still remained partly within the Japanese economic sphere. By the treaty concluded in Peking in 1924, Russia granted Japan coal and oil deposits in Northern Sakhalin for a period of 45 years. The Japanese coal concessions were situated on the west coast of the island and covered an area of 13,600 acres. Between 1927 and 1935 between 100,000 and 125,000 tons of coal were exported to Japan from the concession area. The areas of the oil concessions were much larger, and stretched along the entire east coast of the island. By the beginning of the Second Five-Year Plan almost half of all Sakhalin oil was produced by oil wells belonging to a Japanese company.[35] Japanese oil and coal concessions survived the general liquidation of foreign concessions in the Soviet Union which took place during the Second Five-Year Plan. In 1941, when the Japanese Foreign Minister, Matsuoka, signed the Japanese-Soviet Neutrality Pact, he gave a written undertaking that the liquidation of the Northern Sakhalin concessions would follow 'within several months'. However, the actual abandonment of the concessions was carried out only as the result of a Japanese-Soviet agreement of March 1944.

The Soviet régime did its best to learn from the mistakes which from a Russian imperialist standpoint Czarist policy had committed in the handling of the Sakhalin question. It realised that a large number of Russians had to be brought into Northern Sakhalin if the territory were to remain a safe Russian possession, and if its coal and oil riches were to be properly exploited. Soviet experts considered that Northern Sakhalin could, as a fuel base, become the backbone of the entire Soviet Far Eastern economy. They estimated that the Northern Sakhalin coal deposits exceeded two thousand million tons, and the oil deposits one hundred million tons. Bearing all this in mind Soviet Russia entered into a race with Japan for the development of Sakhalin. The Soviet authorities devoted their particular attention to the consolidation of two localities, the 'socialist oil town' of Okha, and the mining town of Due, which absorbed colonists from practically every Russian mining centre.[36] From a purely statistical point of view Soviet Northern

Sakhalin proved unable to equal Japanese Karafuto. Throughout the inter-war period the population of Karafuto grew from 106,000 in 1920 to 339,000 in 1938. By the outbreak of the Second World War the population of Karafuto was roughly three times that of Northern Sakhalin, and in 1945 it had more than 400,000 inhabitants. There was, however, a considerable difference of quality between the settlements built north and south of the Fiftieth Parallel. Those constructed on the Russian side were usually more solid and more suitable to withstand the harshness of the climate than most of the housing in Karafuto. But the Japanese did a great deal to develop the fishing and timber industry and to increase coal mining and in the later stages they also encouraged agricultural settlement. The cultural progress in Karafuto was also remarkable. In 1940 the territory had 253 schools with 56,000 pupils (as against 17,500 schoolchildren in Northern Sakhalin in 1945). There were also three secondary schools for boys and three for girls and one commercial college.[37]

The necessity for further peaceful competition between Russians and Japanese on Sakhalin ended in August 1945 when, a few days before the end of the war in the Far East, Soviet forces moved into Karafuto. The Soviet troops found themselves in a comparatively densely populated Japanese country where only a few solid block-houses reminded them of the Russian rule before 1905. Everything else they saw in Karafuto was the work of the Japanese administration and of the Japanese people.

On the morrow of the occupation the embarrassing question of what to do with the Japanese faced the Russian administrators. The revolutionary Soviet nationalities policy of the 'twenties' would have had a simple answer to the problem: the transformation of Karafuto into a Japanese Autonomous Soviet Socialist Republic as a base for communist infiltration into Japan proper. As the Soviet régime had long ago dispensed with its original concept of internationalism it chose quite a different approach. The Karafuto Japanese were treated as a conquered people who, although not enjoying political rights, were, nevertheless, during a transition period expected to work for the Soviet state under the supervision of Russian civilian and military authorities. The Soviet High Command issued, indeed, a proclamation to the Karafuto Japanese which stated : ' The Red Army has brought you peaceful work and order. It has no intention of interfering with your life. It brings you freedom and happiness. The High Command of the Soviet Armed Forces requests you to stay where you are and to work honestly in factories and workshops, in offices, trading establishments and in agriculture.'

The proclamation of the Soviet High Command was only a manœuvre designed to prevent chaos in Karafuto pending the arrival of the first Russian colonists : it did not reflect the real intentions of the Soviet

Government, which was determined from the outset not only that Japanese rule should come to an end but also that Japanese settlers should leave the island to make room for Russians. Soviet Russia could not afford the luxury of a Japanese national minority accounting for roughly 10 per cent of the entire population of the Soviet Far East.

The reunited Sakhalin was to be a Slav bastion as well as a communist outpost in the Pacific. It was natural, therefore, that Russia should have demanded the evacuation of the majority of Japanese to Japan proper. A small group of Japanese remained in Karafuto, but they were told that the country in which they were allowed to continue to live was a Russian territory from which all traces of Japanese civilization and Japanese traditions were to be eradicated. In 1946 a Ukase of the Presidium of the Supreme Soviet stipulated that the towns of Sakhalin were to receive new names which were to bear witness to the Russian contribution towards the opening up of Pacific territories in general, and of Sakhalin in particular. The first Russians to be honoured by having towns named after them were Admiral Nevelskoy and the officers under his command who, in September 1852, had hoisted the Russian flag in Sakhalin. The port of Honto was called 'Nevelsk' and several smaller places were named after other members of the Nevelskoy expedition, for instance Tonnai became 'Boshnyakovo' and Ushiro 'Orlovo'. The largest port of Karafuto – Otomari – was given the name of 'Korsakov' in memory of Captain Rimsky-Korsakov who, in 1853, had taken possession of that place. The town of Shirutoru on the East coast of Karafuto is now called 'Makarov', after another Russian admiral. Another town in Southern Sakhalin was named after the Russian writer Chekhov who had visited the island and given a vivid description of its backwardness under Czarist rule. There are other new names with which nothing of historical interest is associated. Esutoru, the centre of the coalmining region of Southern Sakhalin, is now known as 'Uglegorsk' which is derived from the Russian word 'ugol' (coal). The capital of Karafuto, Toyohara, which had had 50,000 inhabitants under Japanese rule was simply renamed 'Yuzhno-Sakhalinsk' – town of Southern Sakhalin.

These new Russian names were symbols of the victorious entry of Russian culture into Karafuto, expressed in the foundation of Russian schools, by a Russian theatre in 'Yuzhno-Sakhalinsk', and particularly by the arrival of a large stream of Russian colonists. They came, as a Soviet reporter said, 'from the most distant places of the homeland'. They included 'oil workers from Baku, miners from the Donbass and Kuzbass and fishermen of the White, Caspian and Azov Seas'.[38] Collective farmers came to Sakhalin chiefly from the provinces of Tambov, Ryazan, Kirov, Bryansk, Gorky, Kursk, Smolensk, Kaluga and Kostroma, i.e., from Great Russian areas. Ukrainians do not seem to have participated in the colonization of Sakhalin to any great extent. Was this resettlement action purely voluntary? It was voluntary in the sense that the collective farmers who travelled to their new homes were neither deportees nor victims of the N.K.V.D., as those 'kulaks' sent to distant Far Northern places in the 'thirties' had been. On the other hand, it would be wrong to think that a peasant of Ryazan or Kursk was as free to go or not to go to Southern Sakhalin as an Englishman is when deciding to emigrate to Australia or to New Zealand. The available evidence shows that 'operation Southern Sakhalin' was connected with a certain amount of moral pressure. It was carried out roughly as follows. The Resettlement Administration, which is an agency of the Government of the Russian Federation, first fixed the number of settlers which Southern Sakhalin was to absorb during a certain period. Having done this, the Administration sent out instructions to the various 'Executive Committees' of the provinces of Central Russia to recruit peasant colonists. These instructions were then passed on to the village councils and the individual collective farms. The riches of Southern Sakhalin, its forests, hunting grounds and the excellency of its agricultural soil, were portrayed to the peasants in vivid colours. But the peasants were also told that emigration to the new Soviet land was a patriotic duty. This was reflected in the slogan which was chalked on the railway trucks carrying the first settlers to the distant land. It said 'The Homeland has sent us to Southern Sakhalin'.[39] However, there were quite a number of material incentives which prompted people to go to the island. Each collective farmer ready to settle down in Sakhalin received from the State a loan of 20,000 roubles only half of which was to be repaid in instalments spread over ten years.

Even more important than the development of agricultural colonization was the recruitment of personnel for the fishing industry of Southern Sakhalin. The fishing industry of the reunited island yields about one-seventh of the catch of fish of the U.S.S.R., and about one-quarter of the world's production of canned crab. A large number of demobilized soldiers were, therefore, encouraged to take up residence in the territories reconquered from the Japanese. This part of the Russian colonization of Karafuto took place under the supervision of one of the foremost leaders of the Soviet state, Anastas Mikoyan.

Sakhalin and the Kurile Islands have such a high priority as resettlement areas that they are being colonized even at the expense of the 'old' Soviet Far East. A Government decree of March 1st, 1946, stipulated that wages and salaries in Sakhalin were to be fifty per cent higher than on the Far Eastern mainland, and on the Kurile Archipelago, even 100 per cent higher.

To maintain the stream of colonists to Southern Sakhalin, Soviet propaganda extolled the achievements of Russian reconstruction work there in enthusiastic terms which were similar to those previously used about the building of Komsomolsk. Poets, songwriters and novelists were mobilized to tell the Russian people that 'there are no distant islands but only one great powerful Russia', that Sakhalin must remain Russian for ever, and that 'no smell, no breath' must be left over from the Japanese, as the poet Feoktisov said in his poem 'Fiftieth Parallel'.[40]

KURILE ISLANDS

Soviet occupation of the Kurile archipelago at the end of the Second World War was different in character from the establishment of Russian sovereignty over Southern Sakhalin. The occupation of the Kurile Islands meant the replacement of an Asiatic by a European imperialism. It cannot possibly be described as a blow to the Japanese people. Only the two southernmost islands of the Kurile chain, Kunashiri and Jeterofu Shima, were an exception in this respect since Japanese colonists had there established themselves and founded ten and five villages respectively.

The northern Kurile Islands, though unsuitable for colonization for climatic reasons, proved to be of the utmost strategic importance to Japan. The northernmost island of the archipelago, Shimoshuto, forms an ideal jumping board in the direction of Soviet Kamchatka, from which it is separated by a distance of less than seven miles. The second northernmost Kurile island, Paramushiro, proved to be a valuable Japanese naval base, being closer to the westernmost Aleutian Islands, Attu and Kiska, than the nearest American naval base of Dutch Harbour. For Soviet Russia, too, the strategic value of the Kurile Islands is paramount. In Soviet hands the Kurile Islands form a dagger pointed toward the Japanese island of Hokkaido, as well as improving Russia's strategic position *vis-à-vis* the United States.

Ever since Russian sovereignty over the Kurile Islands was re-established in 1945, the Soviet Government has tried to consolidate its position there by the encouragement of Russian colonization. Soviet propaganda has frequently commented sneeringly on the inability of the Japanese to colonize the archipelago – there were never more than 15,000 Japanese in the islands – and has predicted that Russians would do their job more efficiently and put the Japanese to shame. Only young and enthusiastic Soviet citizens, such as Communist Youth League members imbued with a high spirit of adventure and patriotism, were considered fit for the difficult task of colonizing the Kurile Islands.

Konstantin Badigin, a 'Hero of the Soviet Union', after visiting the Kurile Islands, told the Soviet youth in the newspaper *Komsomolskaya Pravda*: 'Here (in the islands) a wide field is opening for the constructive energetic activity of our youth. May our boys and girls remember their distant ancestors, those fearless seafarers and untiring explorers who, centuries ago, did so much to make the Kurile Islands ours, and may they give their strength to the rebirth of these far-off genuinely Russian lands.'[41]

A few thousand Russians have responded to this and other similar appeals. Among the new Russian settlers of the Kurile Islands there are many young demobilized soldiers as well as fishermen from Archangel, Astrakhan and the Far Eastern mainland. The Russian colonizers paid particular attention to the three islands in which the Japanese had been interested, Kunashiri and Jeterofu Shima in the south, and Paramushiri in the north. The administrative headquarters of the 'Kurile District' were set up on Jeterofu Shima or Iturup. One of the Japanese villages of the island was transformed into the Russian settlement 'Kurilsk', and serves now as a Soviet district centre. Another 'economic and cultural centre', Yuzhnekurilsk, was erected on Kunashiri which because of its nearness to Japan exercises particular attraction on the new colonizers. A third Russian township, Severokurilsk came into being on Paramushiri, the former Japanese fortress island.

To encourage further settlers to go to the Kurile Islands official propaganda tries to create the impression that sport, culture and medical and economic conditions in the new Soviet colony are little different from those prevailing in the most civilized parts of the U.S.S.R. The following is a typical news item trying to 'catch' colonists from among the young generation:

'A stadium for 3,000 spectators has been built in the youngest Soviet town – Severokurilsk on the Kurile Islands. Although this town is little more than one year old, sports have already made considerable progress in it. The Dynamo, Spartak and other sports societies have set up branches there. Football is especially popular. Severokurilsk football teams will participate in the match for the championship of the Soviet Far East'.[42]

Another news item, published from 'Kurilsk', announced the publication of a newspaper the *Red Lighthouse*, the foundation of three clubs, of a 'House of Culture' and of three hospitals.[43] A third item claimed that a circle of young writers and poets had been organized in Yuzhnekurilsk.[44] The photographs which have been published about the new Soviet settlements on rare occasions have somewhat contradicted the optimistic picture of the Press reports; they show a rather primitive state of affairs.

It is doubtful whether the official propaganda campaign has made the Kurile Islands in any way more attractive to the average Soviet citizen. In the popular mind they are tantamount to the end of the world and people are afraid of being sent there.

KAMCHATKA

In Kamchatka, too, the Soviet régime was able to inflict a heavy defeat on Japan and make up for a certain 'neglect' of Russian national interests by the Czarist régime. Being unable to exploit fully the waters off Kamchatka and of the Okhotsk Sea, Czarist Russia had granted equal fishing rights to the Japanese in a Fishing Convention signed in 1907. The Convention resulted in a peaceful Japanese invasion of the Kamchatka peninsula. In 1910 as many as 6,869 Japanese were engaged in the fishing industry of Kamchatka, whilst its total population was 9,500. In the following years the number of Japanese steadily increased, and, in 1914, 8,886 Japanese were working in the fishing industry of Western Kamchatka, as against 1,569 Russians, some of whom were employed by Japanese firms.[45]

During the Russian Civil War, Japan contrived to consolidate her predominant position on the peninsula. Between 1917 and 1922 she raised the number of fishing lots in Kamchatka from 200 to roughly 400. All but one of the twenty-four canneries which existed in Kamchatka in 1923 were in Japanese hands.

When Russian sovereignty over the Far Eastern territories of the Russian Empire had been fully restored, Soviet leaders deemed it advisable to tolerate Japanese presence on the peninsula for a certain period. At the same time, everything was done to consolidate the Russian position in Kamchatka without openly provoking Japanese hostility. This consolidation was achieved by the planned increase of the population of Southern Kamchatka, which, between 1927 and 1934 alone, grew from 9,700 to 28,300. The immigration of Russians into the economically vital areas of the peninsula enabled the Soviet authorities to replace Japanese workers by Russians fairly rapidly. As late as 1928 Kamchatka's fishing industry relied on 52 per cent Japanese manpower. Four years later that percentage was reduced to 4, and in 1933 there were no longer any Japanese workers in the peninsula's fishing industry. In the same year the number of Russian canneries in Kamchatka reached 21 while there still existed 25 Japanese canneries. Despite all the progress made by the Russians, Japan, in the middle of the 'thirties', was still in control of two-thirds of Kamchatka's catch, including the most valuable salmon catch. In 1936 between 10 and 12 per cent of the entire Japanese fish production and 40 per cent of Japanese crab fishing were supplied by the Kamchatka catch.

During the Second World War Japan was allowed to maintain her canneries in the peninsula. On March 10th, 1944, the Soviet-Japanese Fishing Convention was extended until the end of 1948. The Allied victory over Japan, however, made the Convention null and void long before the date of its expiration, and so did away with the last foreign 'concession' in Soviet territory. So it was that the Soviet Union won the 'Battle of Kamchatka', a keen contest for the first place among the fishing powers of the world. It was a battle without bloodshed, but it may prove to have been more costly to the Japanese in the long run than the battles of Okinawa and Iwojima, provided that the Russians are able to exploit to the full the advantages they have gained. The establishment of a Russian fishing monopoly in the north-western Pacific, which Japan's defeat made possible, meant that the Soviet régime could broaden considerably the food supply base of her north-eastern possessions and extend Russian colonization in Kamchatka and the areas around the Okhotsk Sea. It seems, however, that the Soviet régime took more away from the Japanese than it could digest. It has never been able to fulfil the fishing part of the Five-Year Plan in the Far East.

* * *

Soviet policy towards Eastern immigrants compares unfavourably with the treatment which the United States and Canada meted out to the 313,000 Japanese of Hawaii and North America (160,000 in Hawaii, 129,000 in the United States proper and 24,000 in Canada) even after the Pearl Harbour attack. The differences between the Soviet and the North American approach can be summarised as follows:

1. Canada and the United States evacuated the Japanese from certain strategically exposed territories at a time when the two countries were at war with Japan. Every attempt was made not to remove them too far away from their original homes. Most of Canada's Japanese, for instance, were allowed to remain within the 'Canadian Far West'. Soviet Russia deported her oriental immigrants from border areas both before the beginning of hostilities and after their termination. The immigrants had either to leave the Soviet Union altogether, as was the case with the Japanese, or take up residence in areas a great distance from their original places of residence as in the case of the Koreans and Chinese of the Soviet Pacific coastal province.

2. In Hawaii the United States have succeeded in Americanizing the Japanese community and rendering it largely immune against Japan even in time of war. Less than 1 per cent of the entire Japanese population of Hawaii were interned, and only 981 Japanese were deported to North America. These were mostly Shinto and Buddhist priests, teachers, and other persons known for their sympathies with the Japanese cause. All the rest were able to continue their work as shop-keepers, farmers and clerical workers throughout the war. Some of the younger Japanese even served in the American army. After the war only one hundred Hawaiian Japanese returned to Japan. From Canada not more than one-sixth or four thousand of the whole Japanese community went to their country

of origin after 1945. Communist Russia, on the other hand, showed by the wholesale evacuation measures in the Soviet Far East that she did not believe in a successful future 'sovietization' of the Japanese of Sakhalin and the Kurile Islands, or even of the Vladivostok Chinese and Koreans.
3. In North America even the Japanese evacuees enjoyed the benefits of democratic institutions. The Japanese of California took their case, though unsuccessfully, to the Supreme Court of the United States and there was freedom of speech in the Japanese 'relocation centres' that existed in California, Arkansas, Utah and Idaho. Japanese Americans found champions among Americans of Anglo-saxon stock and a comprehensive book which took up their case with great insistence saw as many as five reprints during the war. The Canadian Japanese too were not helpless. They had associations and a newspaper *The New Canadian* to defend their interests. The case of the Canadian Japanese was amply discussed in parliament and in the Press. Nothing of all this is possible under Soviet conditions.
4. All negative measures taken against the Japanese in Canada and the United States took place under the full control of public opinion. The administration had to render account for every single evacuated Japanese, for housing and health conditions in the reception areas, and even for the school attendance of the evacuated Japanese children. In the Soviet Union the evacuation of Chinese and Koreans took place under conditions of the greatest secrecy and is not traceable in any accessible official records. It was the arbitrary action of a police state.[46]

BIBLIOGRAPHICAL NOTES TO CHAPTER II

1. N. PRZHEVALSKY, *Puteshestvie v Ussuriiskom krae*, 1867–69. Travel in the Ussuri Region, 1867–69. St. Petersburg, p. 111.

2. *Guide to the Great Siberian Railway*, published by the Ministry of Ways of Communication, St. Petersburg 1900, pp. 416–17.

3. The statement is reproduced in an official work on the revolution in the Far East, *Kommissiya po istorii Oktyabrskoy Revolyutsii i R.K.P. (Bolshevikov), Revolyutsiya na Dalnom Vostoke* – Commission for the History of the October Revolution and of the Russian Communist Party (Bolsheviks), The Revolution in the Far East, Moscow-Leningrad 1923, pp. 359–74.

4. S. D. ANOSOV, *Koreitsy v Ussuriiskom krae* – The Koreans in the Ussuri Region, Khabarovsk. Vladivostok 1928, pp. 24–5. Quoted by John N. Washburn 'Soviet Russia and the Korean Communist Party', *Pacific Affairs*, March 1950, vol. xxii, Nr 1, p. 61.

5. *Sovetskaya Aziya*, 1929, Nr 25, p. 45.

6. *Tikhy Okean*, 1937, Nr 11, p. 579.

7. *Revolyutsiya i Natsionalnosti,* February–March 1931, Nr 11–12, p. 80.

8. F. SHABSHINA, *Velikaya Oktyabrskaya Sotsialisticheskaya Revolyutsiya i Krestyanskoe Dvizhenie v Koree* – The Great October Socialist Revolution and the Peasant Movement in Korea, Voprosy Istorii, June 1949, p. 12. This article is the only one published in a Soviet periodical after the Second World War which throws some light on the history of the Soviet Koreans. Its purpose was to stress the impact of the October Revolution on the anti-Japanese peasant movement in Korea. In this connection the author of the article could not avoid mentioning the Koreans of the U.S.S.R. but she seemed to consider them as temporary immigrants and not as a permanent ethnic minority of the Soviet Union. The Korean National District is not mentioned in the article.

9. I. VOLODIN, *Inostranny Shpionazh na Sovetskom Dalnom Vostoke* – Foreign Espionage in the Soviet Far East, *Pravda,* April 23rd, 1937.

10. *Pravda,* December 20th, 1937.

11. *Sovetskaya Aziya,* Nr 25, 1929, p. 47.

12. *Novy Vostok,* Nr 29, 1930, p. 173.

13. *Izvestiya,* May 24th and May 25th, 1951.

14. *Pravda Vostoka,* May 30th, 1951.

15. *Sovetskaya Yustitsiya,* July 10th, 1931, pp. 18–19.

16. WLADIMIR K. ARSENJEW, *Russen und Chinesen in Ostsibirien,* Berlin 1926, p. 43.

17. PRZHEVALSKY, op. cit., p. 79.

18. N. V. ARKHIPOV, *Dalnevostochny Kray* – The Far Eastern Territory, Moscow-Leningrad 1929, pp. 34–7.

19. *Zhivopisnaya Rossiya* – Picturesque Russia, vol. xii, second part, Moscow-Leningrad 1895, p. 448.

20. ARSENJEW, op. cit., p. 56.

21. FRIESEN, *Der Ferne Osten,* Moscow 1927, p. 17.

22. A. RADO, *Fuehrer durch die Sowjetunion,* Berlin 1928, p. 641.

23. OTTO HELLER, *The Port of Vladivostok, Once and Now,* International Press Correspondence, October 13th, 1932, p. 962.

24. *Zvezda,* Nr 2, 1946, pp. 242–7.

25. JOHN DE FRANCIS, *Nationalism and Language Reform in China,* Princeton University Press, 1950, p. 106.

26. *Pravda,* January 31st, 1931. For other material about anti-Chinese agitation, see *Pravda,* August 4th, 1929, *Pravda,* January 6th, 1931, and *Sovetskaya Yustitsiya,* January 20th, 1931, pp. 29–31.

27. *Pravda,* December 5th, 1936.

28. People's Commissariat of Justice of the U.S.S.R. Report on Court Proceedings in the case of the Anti-Soviet Bloc of Rights and Trotzkyites, etc., Moscow 1938, p. 15.

29. *Small Soviet Encyclopedia*, second edition, vol. 2, Moscow 1934, p. 531.

30. *Large Soviet Encyclopedia*, second edition, vol. 8, Moscow 1952, p. 228. See also *Ogonyok* 1947, Nr 43, p. 24.

31. *The Russian Purge and the Extraction of Confession*, Hurst and Blackett Ltd., London 1951, p. 110.

32. P. PAVLENKO, *Red Planes Fly East*, George Routledge and Sons Ltd., London 1938, pp. 500–504.

33. *Sovetskoe Gosudarstvo i Pravo*, Nr 5, 1952, p. 68.

34. *Krasny Arkhiv*, 1937, vol. 83, p. 94.

35. KONSTANTIN POPOV, *Ekonomika Yaponii* – The Economics of Japan, Moscow 1936, p. 500.

36. J. OSIPOV, *Sakhalinskie Zapiski* – Sakhalin Notebook, Moscow 1946, p. 53.

37. MARTIN SCHWIND, *Die Gestaltung Karafutos im Japanischen Raum*, Justus Perthes, Gotha 1942, p. 185.

38. *Science and Life*, February 20th, 1951.

39. *Ogonyok*, September 1946, Nr 35–36, p. 19.

40. *Oktyabr*, Nr 6, June 1950, pp. 123–4.

41. *Komsomolskaya Pravda*, July 25th, 1946.

42. *Soviet Monitor*, January 1st, 1948.

43. *Trud*, July 23rd, 1948.

44. *Literaturnaya Gazeta*, July 28th, 1946.

45. M. A. SERGEEV, *Narodnoe Khozyaistvo Kamchatskogo Kraya* – The National Economy of the Kamchatka Territory, Moscow 1936, p. 222.

46. The factual material about the Japanese in Canada, the United States and Hawaii is taken from the following works: Andrew W. Lind, *Hawaii's Japanese, An Experiment in Democracy*, Princeton University Press 1946; Carey McWilliams, *Prejudice, Japanese-Americans: Symbol of Racial Intolerance*, Little, Brown and Cie, Boston 1945; Forrest E. La Violette, *The Canadian Japanese and World War II, A sociological and psychological account*, University of Toronto Press 1948.

Main areas of
Russian Settlement

ARCTIC OCEAN

Bering Strait

ESKIMOS

CHUKCHI

ESKIMOS

YUKAGIRS

KORYAKS

ALEUTS

Tiksi

EVENI

YAKUTS

YAKUTS

EVENI

Magadan

KAMCHADALS

EVENKI

Yakutsk

Okhotsk

NIVKHI

A. Vilyuy S. S. R.

AINU

YAKUTS

Aldan

EVENKI

Komsomolsk

AINU

Buryat
Mongol
A.S.S.R.

EVENKI

NANAI

UDEGE

L. Baikal

Irkutsk

Chita

Ulan Ude

Khabarovsk

Vladivostok

BURYATS

Manchuria

Mongolia

Tokyo

Copyright

3. THE ABORIGINES OF THE SOVIET FAR EAST

III

THE ABORIGINES OF THE SOVIET FAR EAST

There are about 60,000 aborigines in the Soviet Far East (excluding Yakutia and Buryat-Mongolia) belonging to over a dozen different nationalities. The ethnographers divide them into two main groups. The first group, the Paleoasiats, includes the Chukchi, the Koryaks, the Asiatic Eskimos, the Aleuts, Ainu, Nivkhi and Kamchadals. Of the second, the Manchu-Tunguz peoples, the most important are the Tunguz proper, or Evenki, the coastal Tunguz, or Eveni, the Nanai and the Udege. Politically and sociologically all these nationalities must be considered as one single entity. The Soviet régime has treated them quite differently from the Korean, Chinese and Japanese minorities. As the small groups of aborigines are unable to handicap Russian colonization, the Communist Party has patronised them, and Soviet propaganda has always devoted a great deal of publicity to them, even at a time when there was complete silence about the Koreans and Chinese of the Soviet Far East. This does not necessarily mean that Soviet Russia has handled the problems of the Far Eastern aborigines successfully.

TWO VIEWS ON NATIVE POLICY

In the first years following the October Revolution the most authoritative Russian anthropologists felt that the time had come to take special measures to protect the Far Eastern and Far Northern natives from the pernicious influences of European civilization. Demands to that effect were voiced, in the winter of 1921–22, in the organ of the People's Commissariat for Nationalities, *Zhizn Natsionalnostei*. The most remarkable contribution to the problem of the small nationalities came from Professor Vladimir Germanovich Bogoraz-Tan (1865–1936), who had a profound knowledge of the problems of the tribes of North-Eastern Siberia, particularly of the Chukchi. Professor Bogoraz suggested that the Soviet Government should draw the lessons from certain experiments carried out in the native territories of Canada, the United States, Brazil and Argentina. It seemed vital to him that the mode of life and the living conditions of the primitive tribes should be protected against every influence on the part of their more civilized Russian neighbours, or even of other stronger non-Russian peoples. Russians, Bogoraz said, should not be allowed to make any use whatever of the territories inhabited by the 'primitive tribes'. They should not even be permitted to enter them. Exceptions were to be made only for three categories of people, first anthropologists and linguists, secondly certain persons who would render practical services to the territories, such as doctors and technicians, and thirdly the ideologists of the new régime. Professor Bogoraz warned against making any economic experiments with the natives. He said that such experiments would not enhance the welfare of the Far Northern and Far Eastern tribes, but would, in fact, undermine their existence.[1]

To carry out a systematic policy of protection of the natives Professor Bogoraz demanded the foundation of a special committee to be attached to the People's Commissariat of Nationalities. Such a committee was in fact founded with the prominent participation of Professor Bogoraz himself. It was the 'Committee of the North'. It had a huge bureaucratic apparatus consisting of five departments. The first dealt with administrative and legal matters, the second with economic and financial affairs, the third was concerned with scientific research, the fourth with health and the fifth with education. The Committee of the North had a Far Eastern Bureau in Khabarovsk which dealt with the small Far Eastern nationalities.

From the very beginning two tendencies made themselves felt within the Committee. People like Bogoraz-Tan viewed its work primarily from a philanthropic point of view. They thought that the Committee was nothing more than an organization to assist the Far Northern and Far Eastern peoples to recover from the blows which contact with European civilization had inflicted on them. Die-hard Bolsheviks, on the other hand, had a different approach. They considered the Committee to be an instrument of economic exploitation of the Far Northern territories, and for fostering class struggle among the tribes.

Their view did not prevail at once. In the first five years of its existence, between 1924 and 1929, the Committee did not interfere much with the tribal system of the Far North and Far East. The administrative pattern enforced in other parts of the Soviet Union was not extended to the small native peoples. Those living in the Far East were given such forms of local administration as were acceptable and comprehensible to them. Each tribe had a Tribal General Assembly ('Obshchee Rodovoe Sobranie') which elected a Tribal Executive Committee ('Rodovoy Ispolnitelny Komitet'). Several related tribes sent delegates to a Tribal District Congress ('Rayonny Rodovoy Sezd') which elected a Tribal District Executive Committee ('Rayonny Rodovoy Ispolnitelny

Komitet'). The Tribal Committees of the lower order were later described as 'Native Soviets' ('Tuzsovety') of which there were 400 all over the Far East and Far North. The most remarkable fact about this tribal administration was that participation in tribal and native Soviets was not limited by class criteria.

This idyllic state of affairs could not last long. From one plenary meeting of the Committee of the North to the next the intransigence of its more radically minded members increased. In 1929 the Committee firmly decided to apply the principles of class struggle to the Far North, and from 1930 onwards, the tribal administration was abandoned. Regular organs of local government ranging from village Soviets to 'National Areas' ('Okrugs') were created instead. This meant in fact the end of the 'native reserves' which the Russian anthropologists had advocated in the early years of the Soviet régime. Under the new set-up Russian and other European Party and State officials were able to increase their influence in the running of native affairs. The natives were linked politically and administratively as closely as possible with the metropolitan territories of the U.S.S.R. In 1935, the Committee of the North itself was disbanded.

By the time of its abolition the Committee had lost a great deal of its previous importance. Many of its original duties had been taken over either by the Chief Administration of the Northern Sea Route, 'Glavsevmorput', or by local government organs. The Chief Administration of the Northern Sea Route, which had at its disposal a large staff of experts on nationalities problems, was originally launched as a body with extremely wide powers. Among other things, it was supposed to look after the well-being of the Far Northern tribes, direct cultural work among them, organize health services and help to promote their 'sovietization'. In the autumn of 1938 the Soviet Government decided that 'Glavsevmorput' could not carry out these tasks properly. A decree of the Council of People's Commissars stipulated that it was to hand over to the territorial administrations all enterprises and institutions which were not directly connected with the development of the Northern Sea Route.[2]

COMMUNIST ADMINISTRATORS

The abolition of the Committee of the North in 1935, and the curtailing of the powers of the 'Glavsevmorput' in 1938, increased the responsibilities of the administrative authorities and party organizations of Khabarovsk. It cannot be said that the latter have shown great enthusiasm for work in the National Areas and National Districts of the small nationalities. In fact, up to 1939 most of the officials posted to distant parts of the Far Eastern (later Khabarovsk) Territory went there as a punishment. People who were an embarrassment to the authorities, for one reason or another, were frequently sent to the Arctic regions as administrators and Party secretaries. Most cases of abuse of which such ill-suited administrators had been guilty in distant territories were hushed up, but occasionally they became public, as in the case of the Soviet Commander of the Wrangel Island,* which is part of the Chukcha National Area, and situated off its Arctic coast.

The commander, whose name was Semenchuk, had committed the most outrageous arbitrary acts against both Chukchi and Eskimos, the native population of the island. He and his assistant, Startsev, had caused the death of a number of natives, but the Wrangel Island scandal would probably not have come to light had they not also assassinated the local Russian doctor. The two Soviet administrators were brought to Moscow as defendants in a big trial in which Vyshinsky himself acted as prosecutor. A sixty-five page Vyshinsky speech contains an exhaustive description of the Semenchuk régime on Wrangel Island. Semenchuk's authoritarian idea of the role of a Soviet administrator in the land of the Chukchi and Eskimos was summarised in the following pronouncement which he had made. 'I am the GPU here; I am the court, I am the Public Prosecutor. I have the power of life and death.'

Semenchuk and Startsev were sentenced to death and executed in 1936, but it is still a mystery how the Soviet Government could entrust the strategically important Wrangel Island to an outright criminal. Semenchuk had been in prison for the theft of silver cutlery from the Soviet Embassy in Teheran shortly before being dispatched to the Far North.[3]

The case of Semenchuk and Startsev is obviously an extreme one. There is no reason to doubt that some of the administrators are ardent idealists, determined to improve living conditions and promote education among the local peoples. If we can believe the Secretary of the Department of Cadres of the Khabarovsk Territorial Committee of the Communist Party, there has been a better selection of administrators for the distant areas of the Far East since 1939. The secretary in question had promised in that year that Party posts in these territories would be given in future only to particularly trustworthy persons. He had said,

* Russian sovereignty over Wrangel Island was established only with some difficulty Both Canada and the United States had striven to attach the island which has an area of 2,700 square miles to their respective territories. The Canadians established their claim by wintering on the island from 1921. They reasserted it by hoisting the flag there in 1921, and in 1922 the Canadian Prime Minister solemnly proclaimed the annexation of the island in a statement before the Ottawa Parliament. The Soviet régime can rightly claim to have rescued Wrangel Island for Russia. In 1924 the crew of the Soviet gunboat 'Red October' took it over and expelled the only Canadian who lived there, together with a group of 'anti-Soviet' Eskimos, who, they asserted, were engaged in illegal hunting of fur animals. The Soviet authorities then brought their own colonists from the mainland, mostly Chukchi and Eskimos, with a few Russians.

indeed, 'The further away we send a man, the more we must be able to trust him'.[4] It can be taken for granted that a man whom the Communist Party considers particularly trustworthy will be a hard-working official, and that he will not commit any crimes such as those of which Semenchuk and Startsev had been convicted. But a trustworthy communist is not necessarily a man who understands the mentality of the Far Eastern aborigines, and who deals with their problems in the best way.

NATIVES, STATE TRUSTS AND FORCED LABOUR

In addition to the Party and the territorial administration, there is a third influential factor in the Far East which has a great impact on the 'natives', namely the big State capitalist organizations of Kamchatka, Chukotka and the territories around the Okhotsk Sea. Instead of assisting and strengthening native economy the Soviet régime encouraged the growth of State companies such as the 'Kamchatka Limited Company' (later known as 'Glavkamchatrybprom' – Kamchatka Chief Administration for the Fishing Industry), the 'State Reindeer Trust', the 'Dalrybtrest' (Far Eastern Fishing Trust) and 'Soyuzpushnina', the State organization for fur trading. Soviet experts on the Far East themselves have admitted that these enterprises employed people who were guided by a 'narrow-minded business attitude' and who discharged their duties in a 'crudely materialistic way'. All they wanted was to fulfil the target figures of the state plan. They were not interested in assisting the natives either by supplying the most essential food commodities or by encouraging cultural work. The enterprises concerned, in particular the Kamchatka Company and the Reindeer Trust, seized land, and hunting and fishing grounds traditionally belonging to the natives. Even land owned by newly established collective farms of reindeer-breeders was arbitrarily confiscated by State trusts.[5]

Another State enterprise, the previously mentioned 'Dalstroy', which operates around the Okhotsk Sea, has also greatly affected the life of the 'natives' who live in its territory. The first director of Dalstroy, E. Berzin, pointed out in 1936 that the trust had opened schools and hospitals in all centres of the native population. The budget of the native communities ('National Districts') had increased almost ten times during five years.[6] What Berzin did not say was that the native schools and hospitals had been built with the profits which Dalstroy had made by exploiting forced labour. As a matter of fact, some of the schools of which Berzin boasted are 'mixed schools', which are attended both by natives and by children of convicts who were born in captivity and taken away from their mothers.[7] In the area controlled by the Dalstroy we thus meet the most sinister aspect of the 'Soviet nationalities policy', namely, its connection with the forced labour system. A sparsely populated territory on the Kolyma River and around the Okhotsk Sea, which, not so long before, had been the home only of Eveni, Yakuts and other natives, had suddenly become an object of mass colonization by convicts, probably by as many as 400,000. The sudden emergence of huge forced labour camps in tribal territories was bound to have a considerable effect both on the way of life and on the moral outlook of the natives. It is only logical that the N.K.V.D.-M.V.D. should have tried to enlist the support of the natives against camp inmates trying to escape. Former political prisoners have even asserted that the N.K.V.D. pays the natives, either in cash or in the form of vodka, for every escaped person whom they capture.[8] This makes it understandable that the prisoners extend their contempt of the N.K.V.D. to the natives. They charge the authorities with 'coddling and pampering' them in the very areas in which many members of Russia's intelligentsia are gradually being exterminated.[9] It must be said in fairness that the N.K.V.D. is not the first Russian authority to discover that use can be made of Far Eastern natives against convicts from European Russia. The priority for this idea goes to the Czarist governor of Sakhalin Island, General Konotovich. Chekhov, mentioned in his book on Sakhalin that the General had ordered Gilyaks (Nivkhi) to be employed as guards for Russian criminals.

THE REINDEER PROBLEM

Lack of understanding of the 'natives' is manifested not only by the activities of the big State trusts, but also in the day-to-day work of Soviet officials in charge of 'native affairs'. Communist Party officials think in terms of ready-made patterns, and cut-and-dried formulae. They are usually convinced that what is good for Moscow and Vladivostok must be equally good for the most remote parts of the Union. This frame of mind makes it difficult for them to find the right approach to the special conditions of the Far North. Much could be said, for instance, about the peculiar way in which Soviet authorities have handled the basis of Far Northern economy, reindeer-breeding. As late as 1950, the Communist Party of a Siberian province sent large piles of pamphlets on sheep-farming and bee-keeping to the nomads living near the Arctic coast, where there are neither sheep nor bees – only reindeer.[10] This actually happened in North-western Siberia, but it could easily have happened in the Far East. The *Pravda* correspondent in Khabarovsk stated in 1947 that there was not a single specialist in problems of reindeer-breeding in the State and Party offices of that city, although the Khabarovsk Territory includes the largest reindeer population of any administrative unit in the Soviet Union.[11]

Soviet officials failed to understand that the reindeer plays a vital part in the life of the Northern tribesmen, and that it is not a mere subsidiary to their economy as is the cow of the Russian peasants. According to the tribal customs of the Koryaks and Chukchi it is a sin to sell a living reindeer. The Soviet administrators denounced this custom as sabotage, and imposed on the reindeer-breeders not only compulsory sales, but also the confiscation measures which accompany collectivization. The setting up of collective farms and state farms in the native territories of the Arctic regions of the Soviet Far East, led in the 'thirties' to the unleashing of a violent class struggle which, in turn, resulted in a drastic drop in the number of reindeer. Not only did the rich reindeer breeders engage in large scale 'predatory slaughter' of the animals, but they also hampered the collectivization and nationalization measures in other ways. To escape 'de-kulakization', they split their large herds into smaller ones, and distributed them among their shepherds. Moreover pastureland was wilfully destroyed, apparently on a considerable scale.

Loss of reindeer occurred not only in the private but also in the State-controlled sector. The new State farms which were to introduce higher forms of reindeer breeding were, in reality, far more inefficient than the individual reindeer breeding nomad. In the Far East the State reindeer farms lost one-third of their herds within a single year – a catastrophe which could not be attributed entirely to the infiltration of class-alien elements.

Official Soviet statistics about the development of Soviet Russia's reindeer population demonstrate convincingly what damage the collectivization measures caused. In the first years of the communist régime when state interference with the Far Northern economy was slight there was a clear upward trend. The number of reindeer in the entire Soviet Union increased from 1,765,000 in 1923 to 2,193,000 in 1926–27 and to 2,700,000 in 1931. The year 1931 was the turning point. In 1932 the stock fell to 2,333,000, in 1933 to 2,030,000 and in 1934 it was as low as 1,889,000. These figures which apply to Soviet Russia as a whole do not fully reveal the catastrophic consequences of communist reindeer policy in the Far East. In the Koryak National Area, for instance, where full collectivization had been planned for 1933, the number of reindeer decreased from 264,000 in 1926 to 173,000 in 1932 and 127,000 in 1934.[12]

Soviet statistical evidence about Russia's reindeer population after 1934 is contradictory. Figures produced by various official Soviet sources show a large margin of difference. The *Small Soviet Encyclopedia* says that on January 1st, 1938, the number of reindeer was 1,766,000.[13] This would mean that the situation was then even worse than in 1933. On the other hand, a Soviet standard work on Russian reindeer-breeding published in the post-war period claims that the number of reindeer in 1938 was 28 per cent higher than in 1933. But even this book which

71

gives an optimistic picture of the Russian reindeer situation states that a new period of decline set in during the war owing to the increased slaughter for the army and inferior care of the herds resulting from the mobilization of many native herdsmen.[14] After the war the position improved but whether and when the peak figure of 1931 was reached again, is impossible to say. Such increases in the number of reindeer as there were, were brought about, it seems, by a more liberal application of the collective farm statute. Collective farm members were encouraged to own small reindeer herds privately. The maximum size of these privately owned herds is not known but cases have been mentioned of individual collective farmers having as many as 80, 90, 130, and even up to 200 reindeer each.[15]

The reindeer problem has caused difficulties to Soviet administrators not only in the purely economic sphere but also in the field of education. What is needed in the Far North is a school which would help to raise hunting and reindeer breeding to a higher level. The more enlightened Russian pedagogues are the first to admit that such a school does not exist. One of the school inspectors posted to Northern Siberia quoted, not without a certain measure of approval, a reindeer breeder who refused for a long time to entrust his two sons to a Soviet boarding school. The father in question said that he taught his children to hunt game, to catch the polar fox and to ride reindeer. In school, he added, they would not learn all this, and when they had finished they would have no practical knowledge. An article in the *Teachers' Gazette* stated that there was a 'grain of truth' in the complaint of the old reindeer breeder. 'The school is indeed too much cut off from practice and thus not able to prepare children for the life in the Far North.'[16] A similar problem, it is true, also exists in other countries. Richard Finnie, in his book *Canada moves North*, says that Eskimo children, after spending years in boarding schools, return to their families unfitted for the lives they must lead.[17]

THE CULTURAL REVOLUTION

Whatever the quality of school education in the Russian Far North may be, it is a fact that the Soviet authorities have carried out a big cultural revolution in the native territories. The most important part of it has been the liquidation of illiteracy. Until 1931 the Far Northern and Far Eastern peoples could express themselves in writing only in the form of drawings or through the medium of the Russian language. In May, 1931, they received an alphabet of their own, the 'Unified Northern Alphabet' as it was called. It was officially approved by the Ministry of Education of the R.S.F.S.R. The 'Unified Northern Alphabet' was a Latin alphabet and the decision to adopt it was not taken without a long struggle fought out behind the scenes between the supporters of latinization and those who preferred the Russian alphabet or at least a 'mixed alphabet' in which Russian letters would predominate.

In the Soviet Far East the ethnographic section of the Society for Regional Research declared itself with great vigour against all attempts at russification. In a memorandum the Society listed four reasons why only the Latin alphabet could be introduced for the languages of the Chukchi, Koryaks, Nanai, Nivkhi and the other Far Eastern tribes:

1. The successful latinization of the alphabets of the oriental languages.

2. The genuinely international character of the Latin alphabet.

3. The inadequacy of the Russian alphabet which would have to be supplemented by a number of letters.

4. The fact that the Russian alphabet itself would not be long-lived since progressive scholars had already raised the question of its latinization.[18]

These four considerations were shared by the Moscow authorities who had decreed the introduction of the Latin alphabet for the Northern peoples.

The Latin alphabet remained in force for less than six years – until February 11th, 1937, when a new decree abolished and replaced it by a russianized alphabet. The new script was intended for thirteen small nationalities of whom eight lived either wholly or partially in the Far East. The replacement of one alphabet by another rendered necessary the destruction of a large amount of printed material that had been prepared for the Northern peoples. Between 1931 and 1933 alone as many as 200,000 textbooks, 100,000 pamphlets of a political nature and 10,000 books on medical and economic subjects had been issued for them.[19]

Soviet school policy proper did not suffer from such a disturbing lack of continuity as the Soviet literacy campaign. The number of schools increased systematically and steadily and now there are as many as 200 native schools in the Khabarovsk Territory. They are supervised by a Council of National Schools which was created in 1949 and which works under the education department of the Khabarovsk territorial administration. The Council does not only administer schools but also deals with all problems connected with the writing of text-books, and the translation of classical Russian and Soviet literary works into the local languages. The Council relies on the graduates of the teachers' training colleges in Petropavlovsk (for South Kamchatka), Anadyr (for Chukotka), Tigilsk (for North Kamchatka) and Nikolayevsk-on-Amur. The most important and largest of the four is the college in Nikolayevsk. Between its foundation in the early 'thirties' and 1951 it trained 170 Russian and 105 native teachers belonging to ten different Far Eastern nationalities.[20] The most gifted young people from among the Far Eastern aborigines are sent to the Pedagogical Institute of Khabarovsk, where there is a department for the Far Northern nationalities, and a few are even admitted to the Herzen Pedagogical Institute in Leningrad. Courses at the Far Northern Department of that Institute last three years, and the curriculum includes 'Foundations of Marxism-Leninism; the great works of Stalin on questions of linguistics; the history of Russian pre-revolutionary and Soviet literature; folklore, and many other subjects'.[21] In addition every student has lessons in methods of teaching, in the grammar of his own national language, and in the history and ethnography of the peoples of the North.

Native students are also instilled with a feeling of hatred against the non-communist world. The results of this indoctrination can be gauged from the answers which a Yakut student gave, according to *Pravda*, at his final examinations at the Leningrad Pedagogical Institute. 'The Yakut student, E. Sysosyatin, talked at the examination of the situation of the Eskimos, Aleutians and Red Indians in America. He mentioned many facts which unmasked the American imperialists, and their criminal policy directed towards the total extermination of these peoples. To the horrors of misery, starvation, inhumane privations and persecutions to which these nationalities are subject in America, even greater atrocities have been added during the past few years. As has become known, the American imperialists, preparing bacteriological warfare, tried out the effects of the deadly microbes on the Eskimos. As a result of these cannibalistic experiments many Eskimos in America died of bubonic plague.'[22]

Soviet dictatorship indoctrinates all citizens of the U.S.S.R., whether Russians or Uzbeks, Ukrainians or Georgians, Latvians or Chukchi. It gives to all of them a completely distorted picture of the nations outside the communist sphere. This campaign of hatred and distortions, while morally wrong in every single case, is particularly contemptible if directed towards the youth of primitive peoples. By trying to transform young native intellectuals into agitators of the 'cold war', the Soviet régime destroys to a considerable extent the good which it is doing by the spread of culture and knowledge.

COMMUNISTS AND SHAMANS

The young natives trained in Nikolayevsk-on-Amur, Khabarovsk and Leningrad are to help the Russian administrators in the fight against 'local nationalism' in all tribal areas of the Soviet Far East. Naturally, in the territories of the small Far Eastern peoples the Soviet régime does not fight 'local nationalism' in the same way as it does in areas where there are more developed nationalities. There are no parties or political groups which the communists have to suppress; there is no feudal-patriarchal literature which has to be banned, and no cultural societies which have to be closed down because of bourgeois romanticism. Even so the small peoples of the Far East adhere, just as other peoples do, to their national traditions which are closely linked with those primitive religious beliefs usually summed up under the collective name of 'Shamanism'.

Shamanism is fundamentally the belief in good and bad spirits. The exact nature of the belief varies from one tribe to the other. The spirits may be deified animals, they may be ancestors, or they may simply be the forces of nature. Shamanism is not based on an elaborate ecclesiastical organization, but there are, nevertheless, mediators between spirits and ordinary human beings. These mediators are called Shamans. They enjoy a great deal of respect and prestige in the tribal society and this alone would have been sufficient reason to make them 'Enemy Number One' of the Soviet régime in all National Districts and National Areas inhabited by the Far Eastern aborigines.

The régime has charged the Shamans with many crimes, in particular with being dishonest and with consciously deceiving the people. This accusation has been contradicted by many Russian and foreign anthropologists who have had first hand experience of the Far Eastern Shamans. They have made the point that most Shamans sincerely believe in their superior power and are firmly convinced of their ability to cure the sick and to talk to spirits or to deceased relatives. It does not seem that Shamans charged more than moderate fees for their services if they demanded payment at all.[23] According to P. E. Petri, Professor of Ethnology at the Irkutsk University, it was completely erroneous to suggest that the majority of the Shamans were charlatans exploiting the credulity of the natives. For the Shaman, Petri wrote as late as 1928, his vocation constituted a heavy obligation which the spirits had imposed on him. The Shaman knew respite neither by day nor by night. He might at any time be called out and had then to travel dozens of miles in any weather. The Shaman was rarely at home and his household was therefore neglected. As a rule the Shamans were poor and only those living together with their brothers were better off.[24]

According to official Soviet evidence the Shamans engaged in 'mad resistance' to the extension of Soviet power to the north. They disseminated 'provocative rumours' aimed at inciting the tribesmen against the Russians. These charges against the Shamans are reflected in a number of novels which Soviet writers have written on life in the Far East. For example, Syomushkin's novel, *Alitet goes to the Hills*, records the collective resignation of the chairmen of the tribal Soviets in a part of Chukotka, as the result of the evil influences of one important Shaman. These chairmen gathered one day in the tent of the Russian secretary of the Communist Party and surrendered to him their letters of appointment. They tried to get rid of these credentials as quickly as possible, because they were believed to be bearers of the evil spirit. The resigning chairmen suggested that the local Shamans should be appointed in their place, as they would be more successful in dealing with the spirits. The Party secretary refused to comply with this request, and, after a great deal of arguing, most of the chairmen agreed to retain their credentials, and to resume their jobs.[25] In the novel, *Where the Sukpai river flows*, by Kimonko, which deals with the life of the Udege people, the Shaman is both anti-Soviet and anti-Russian. He expresses his political philosophy in the following words:—'It is better to be doomed than to go to the Russians. The Russians will make soldiers out of us and destroy us to a man... The Russians and the Udege are different people. The man of the forest has laws of his own. One must abide by these laws.'[26]

The Shamans preserved their influence throughout the 'twenties' and early 'thirties'. They played an important part in the resistance movement against collectivization. In fact, the terms 'Shaman' and 'kulak' became interchangeable in the official Soviet vocabulary. But this is the usual simplification with which communist anti-religious propaganda operates. An official Soviet analysis referring to the social origin of 300 Shamans showed that between 50 and 60 of them came from poor families (bednota) and only 5 to 10 per cent were 'kulak elements'. More discriminating Soviet writers have stated therefore that Shamans whilst belonging to various social groups constituted 'a reactionary counter-revolutionary force taking sides with native kulaks and semi-feudal elements'.[27]

In addition to collectivization the Shamans obstructed practically every measure taken by the Government in the economic, cultural and sanitary fields. The target figures of the economic plans could not be ful-filled because the Shamans dissuaded the natives from fishing and hunting on certain days or from killing certain animals, for instance walrus. Soviet newspapers and journals were boycotted because the Shamans agitated against their dissemination. Also the new schools in the Far North and the 'kultbazy'* suffered from the sabotage of the Shamans. The latter persecuted and threatened the lives of Soviet teachers, particularly those of Russian nationality.[28] They hindered the re-education of the northern tribes to a more healthy and hygienic life, and intimidated people to such an extent that they did not dare even to go near a Soviet medical station.[29]

Although there is likely to be substance in most of these charges, they

* The 'kultbazy' or 'Cultural Stations' are political, cultural, and scientific research centres which the Soviet régime organized in the Far North. 'Cultural Stations' usually include a boarding school, a kindergarten, crèches, a hospital, a first-aid post, a veterinary station, a metereological station and even a museum. Most 'Cultural Stations' later developed into townships. Out of the fifteen 'Cultural Stations' three were founded in the Far East, one for the Koryaks, one for the Lamuts and the third for Chukchi and Eskimos.

have probably been exaggerated, partly to serve as an excuse for the inefficiency of Soviet administration and partly as a pretext for the anti-Shaman measures taken by the régime. The fight against the Shamans took the same forms as the campaign against other religions of the Soviet Union, ranging from ordinary anti-religious propaganda to administrative terror. The Far Northern cells of the League of Militant Godless were in charge of the former. In view of the complicated character of Shamanism it was no easy affair to combat it and a more thorough picture of its regional diversities had first to be obtained. The League of Militant Godless therefore urged its northern groups to compile a detailed register of the Shamans which was to answer the following questions about each of them: What is the range of activity of the Shaman? Is he a family Shaman or does a larger group of people avail itself of his services? What speciality does he have? Is he a sea-Shaman accompanying fishermen on their expeditions? Is he a tamer of snowstorms? Does he claim to have any influence on the results of hunting? Is he engaged in healing reindeer and people? What sort of cult objects does he possess? Drums? Costumes? Does he hold collective séances? What is his social origin? Detailed information about these and other points was to be sent at least twice a year to the Central Council of Militant Godless, Moscow, Sretenka Street Nr 10.[30]

It does not seem that the League of Militant Godless had many people on the spot with a sufficient knowledge of folklore and anthropology to carry out the 'registration of the Shamans' and it is more than likely that the whole scheme failed. Other anti-Shaman measures were more successful. For instance, pressure was brought to bear on Shamans to give a solemn pledge that they would renounce their activities. Collective statements of several Shamans were even published in the local Press stating that in the past they had been 'wreckers' and 'cheaters.'[31] In other cases where such self-recriminations could not be obtained, Shamans were expelled from their tribal territory or arrested and put on trial. By arresting Shamans the Soviet authorities wanted to show the people that they did not fear their power and that Shamans were not protected by the spirits.

Notwithstanding all these measures of intimidation and persecution the Shamans were still a fairly important factor at the time of the adoption of the Stalin Constitution of 1936. When the constitution was subject to a nationwide discussion the Shamans once more showed their anti-Soviet bias and they did so again during the elections to the Supreme Soviets of the U.S.S.R. and the R.S.F.S.R. in 1937 and 1939 respectively. According to Oleshchuk, one of the leaders of the League of Godless, the Shamans tried 'to falsify the Soviet Constitution, undermine the elections and exploit the electoral campaign for counter-revolutionary aims.'[32]

It would appear from Soviet evidence that Shamanism experienced a certain revival during the war. Shamans, it is alleged, cunningly used the temporary absence of young communist educated people from the tribal areas to regain some of their former influence. The novel of the well-known Soviet writer Azhaev, *Far from Moscow*, which refers to conditions in a Nanai village contains, for instance, the following passage: 'He (the Shaman) had lain low for a time but resumed his evil practices when war broke out. He saw his chance to profit from the war by a crafty and insolent device. Many of the Nanai boys of the village had been called to the colours. They wrote letters home from the front, and the Shaman made his "prophecies" by these letters. His clients were mostly old women anxious about the fate of their sons, and he fleeced and fooled them to the top of his bent.'[33]

Soviet novels about post-war conditions in the Far East try to convey the impression that the Shamans have ceased to be figures that are respected and feared. The Shamans of these novels are desperately isolated and universally despised. In one case the Shaman is even an enemy agent whom the Americans have sent from Alaska to provoke 'acts of diversion' among the natives of the Soviet Far East.

Some of the Soviet charges made against the Shamans coincide more or less with the criticism which a Western colonial administrator would direct against the African witch-doctors and juju-men. Western and Soviet administrators will, however, often differ as to the way in which the Shaman and the juju-man are to be fought. In West Africa, though not in East Africa, the fight against the juju-man is no more than a campaign of enlightenment in favour of a more hygienic way of life. In other words it is an aim in itself. The fight against the Shaman in the Soviet Far East and Far North is only a small part of a great struggle which is aimed at crushing every kind of political and religious opposition.

THE FIGHT AGAINST CHRISTIAN MISSIONS

In the Far East and Far North the régime fights religion on 'two fronts'. If the liquidation of Shamanism is one aim of communist anti-religious policy, the total prevention of Christian missionary activities is another.

Christianity has had a certain influence on the small nationalities of the Far East. Missionaries preaching the faith in a God who loves and helps man, have tried with some success to oust from the hearts of the natives that deep-rooted fear which is accompanied by belief in evil spirits. But the work of the missionaries was far from being finished when the Soviet authorities interrupted it. As it often happens in Africa, the superstitions of paganism survived even where the Church made formal converts. Those Lamuts of Kamchatka, for instance, who accepted the

Christian faith, acquired Christian ikons, but did not want to part with their Shamanist idols. The same can be observed among other Far Eastern and Far Northern aborigines. Many Christian converts wear crosses around their necks, but, at the same time, have idols made of walrus bones and reindeer skin on their belts. Naturally the communists have thrown ridicule on this pagan-Christian dualism, which they have described as 'Shamanism-Orthodoxy', but it is an unavoidable transitory stage in the religious development of any primitive people. Certain sections of the northern tribes of Soviet Russia had been sufficiently Christianized at the time of the establishment of Soviet power to resent the forcible withdrawal of priests, and the removal from forests and ways of crosses which, in the popular belief gave protection against 'devils'. A protest lodged by a group of natives of the Beryozovo district in North-western Siberia was characteristic in this respect. The natives in question wrote a letter complaining that the local communist secretary did not allow them to have a priest. Their actual words were: We can't do without a priest because this is our faith.' ('My ne mozhem bez popa potomu chto vera nasha takaya'.) The letter of protest was printed in 1934 in *Revolyutsiya i Natsionalnosti*, the official organ of the Soviet of Nationalities as a general illustration of the fact that priests still enjoyed confidence in certain parts of the Far North.*

Today most of the Far Eastern tribes are outside the reach of those reduced activities which are still permitted to the Russian Orthodox Church in the U.S.S.R. Whilst churches are tolerated in old towns where their existence is traditional, it has been the consistent policy of the Soviet Government not to allow Christian houses of worship to be erected in the so-called 'socialist cities' which are the products of the Soviet period. In the Far East this applies to Magadan and Komsomolsk, places which among their polyglot population count quite a number of detribalized natives. Members of the two larger nationalities of the Soviet Far East, Yakuts and Buryat-Mongols, are, as far as they are converts to Christianity, in a better position than the members of the smaller tribes. There are churches in the capitals of Yakutia and Buryat-Mongolia and presumably also in other localities of these Republics. These are under the jurisdiction of the Metropolitan of Irkutsk and Chita, whose diocese is larger than the whole of Western Europe.

STALIN – THE SUN

Against Shamanism and Christianity the Soviet régime uses one and the same metaphysical antidote – the Lenin-Stalin cult. In the territories of the Far Eastern tribes this cult has a particularly colourful variant. It takes the form of folk-tales which depict Lenin and Stalin as 'super-

* *Revolyutsiya i Natsionalnosti*, Nr 53, July 1934, pp. 51–57.

shamans' fighting and exterminating the 'evil spirits'. Lenin and Stalin appear in these 'folk-tales' as legendary heroes, as eagles liberating the people from the 'bad black kite' (a Tunguz folk-tale), and, in particular, as something approaching 'sun-gods'.

It is understandable that the idea of the sun must have a powerful appeal for peoples living in Arctic and sub-Arctic regions. Everything associated with the sun is good, wonderful and divine. The Soviet régime has made ample use of this. The Soviet literary journal *Zvezda* rightly said that several volumes could be compiled from all the legends, stories, tales and songs in which Lenin and Stalin are depicted as heroes who gave to the people of the North the inextinguishable sun.[34] Typical of this 'sun literature' produced for the Far Eastern aborigines is the Nanai folk-tale – *Sun of the People*; – 'and there came a time when a hero (who, although living far away from the Nanai people, saw and knew everything) took the sun into his hands, and turned it in such a way that its warmest rays shone where it was dark, and where down-trodden peoples were suffering. And they then knew well-being, warmth and happiness. The name of the hero was Lenin. When a great disaster befell the earth – when Lenin died – bad people were pleased. They thought that the sun would stop shedding its light on the people, but their glee was shorter than the space of a minute, because the people's sun was guarded by another hero. He is the nearest friend and companion of Lenin, and his name is Stalin. Nobody can equal the strength of that hero. His eyes see everything that goes on on earth. His ears hear everything that people say. His brain knows all that people think. His heart contains the happiness and the woe of all peoples. The depth of his thought is as deep as the ocean. His voice is heard by all that inhabit the earth. Such is the greatest of the very greatest in the whole world. And he took the sun out of Lenin's hands, and lifted it very high. And since then happiness shines on earth, because it is impossible for the sun not to shine.'[35]

The same motif as in the Nanai tale *The Sun of the People* is to be found, with slight variations, in the poems and tales produced for the benefit of the other small ethnic groups of the Far East and Far North.

Something could be said even in favour of the Soviet 'sun' propaganda in as far as it banned the fear of 'evil spirits'. Unfortunately, the Soviet régime has replaced the fear of the spirits by the fear of its own power and the institutions and bogies which it has created. One of them is the wicked foreigner, always ready to attack the natives with the most ghastly and devastating weapons.

FAR EASTERN ABORIGINES AND SOVIET FOREIGN POLICY

Destiny has placed the Far Eastern natives into politically and strategically important regions, the mouth of the Amur, the Russian islands of the North-west Pacific, and the territory bordering the Behring Strait. Consequently, the nationalities concerned can only too easily be dragged into the struggle of the big powers for the Pacific. In fact, they have already played their modest part in world politics, and may do so in future. The Nanai, Udege and Nivkhi have participated in Russian-Chinese rivalries. The Udege, Nanai and Ainu have stood between the lines in Russian-Japanese conflicts. The Chukchi, Aleuts and Asiatic Eskimos are involved in the American-Russian antagonism.

The Soviet régime has always been aware of the special position of the small Far Eastern nationalities, and has framed its propaganda accordingly. It has presented itself to the peoples concerned as their saviour rescuing them from 'Chinese merchant capitalism' or from 'Japanese militarism' or from 'American robbery'. The aim of Soviet 'native policy' in the Far East is thus to make the local nationalities anti-Chinese, anti-Japanese or anti-American, as the case may be, and to instil in them a feeling of gratitude towards Russia and the Russians.

Not everything which Russian propagandists tell the natives about other nations is necessarily untrue. It is a fact that Chinese merchants were, for a long time, almost sovereign rulers in the interior of the Russian Pacific province, and exerted a tyrannical overlordship over the aborigines. In some cases the aborigines were reduced to outright serfdom. But even Russian sources have had to admit that the Chinese were interested not merely in profits, but also in spreading their culture. In the absence of any major Russian cultural activities the Chinese ran schools for the aborigines. The latter studied Chinese history, and grew familiar with Chinese institutions. Russia and things Russian were either ignored altogether, or represented in a distorted light.[36] Some of the aborigines completely abandoned their mother tongue, and adopted the Chinese language. The Soviet régime brought about a complete change. It ended the economic exploitation of the natives by Chinese merchants and stopped Chinese cultural propaganda. Cultural domination passed into the hands of the Russians. From a Russian nationalist point of view this was undoubtedly a great success, but whether it is preferable for a Far Eastern people to accept Russian or Chinese civilization is a matter of opinion.

THE NANAI

The most important nationality which the Soviet régime has claimed to have rescued from the Chinese are the Nanai. They are the largest single group of aborigines in the southern part of the Soviet Far East. In the Soviet Union there are between 5,000 and 6,000 Nanai, or Goldy, as they used to be called, while about 1,800 of them live in Manchuria, at the confluence of the Ussuri and Sungari rivers. In the inter-war period this partition of the Nanai between Russia and Manchukuo had a certain political importance. Russia conducted propaganda among the Nanai tribesmen in Manchukuo, and tried to induce them to emigrate and join their brothers on the other side of the border. The Manchukuo Government also did a great deal to obtain the goodwill of the Nanai by associating them with the local administration.

In June 1931, the Soviet régime organized the Nanai National District and the Evenko-Nanai National District. A third National District was founded for the Ulchi or Olchi, a small Far Eastern tribe which is very closely related to the Nanai, and whose number does not exceed 1,000. At the time of their foundation, the three National Districts covered over 60,000 square miles. However, by the end of the First Five-Year Plan, the 'natives' of the three districts found themselves reduced to small minorities. Between 1926 and 1933 alone, the total population in the Nanai and Ulchi Districts was nearly doubled through European colonization, and it increased three times in the Evenko-Nanai National District.

Far from having a sheltered existence in the National Districts, the Nanai hunters and fishermen were thrown into the melting pot of industrialization. In fact, one of the largest industrial centres of the Soviet Far East, the city of Komsomolsk, was built in the midst of former Nanai territory. Komsomolsk has become a magnet attracting the Nanai and regulating their lives. They either work in its industrial undertakings, or have moved to one of the numerous collective farms which supply the 'City of Youth' with vegetables, fruit and dairy products. Many Nanai now have a better command of Russian than of their own language. Their complete absorption by the Russian environment is merely a question of time.

The small Nanai people were greatly exploited for Russia's military effort in the Second World War. As many as 248 Nanai of the Nanai National District and of the Komsomolsk District were awarded military decorations for service on the German front. Some Nanai, including the Nanai poet, Akim Samer, even participated and perished in the Stalingrad battle.

'THE LAST OF THE UDEGE'

The neighbours of the Nanai and their close relatives are the Udege, who live in the Maritime Territory, east of the Amur and Ussuri rivers, in close proximity to the Pacific, particularly in the hinterland of the port Sovetskaya Gavan (previously Imperatorskaya Gavan). Estimates as to the exact number of the Udege differ, they vary between one and two thousand. The official census returns for 1926 recorded 1,347 Udege.

The name 'Udege' became known to the Soviet public through the novel *The Last of the Udege*, by the well-known Soviet writer, Aleksandr Aleksandrovich Fadeev.* The very title of Fadeev's novel has been exploited by Soviet propaganda as a striking example of the solicitude of the Communist Party for the small Far Eastern nationalities, but such an inference is misleading. Fadeev had purposely chosen a title that sounded attractive to the Russian reading public, since it recalled Fenimore Cooper's famous book *The Last of the Mohicans*. Of course, the ideological message of Fadeev is contrary to what Soviet critics have read into the work of the American author. While Fenimore Cooper 'idealized' – in the Soviet view – 'the primitive patriarchal customs of the Red Indians', Fadeev makes the point that there can be no return to the past for the Udege, but only a forward march towards revolution and socialism.[37] *The Last of the Udege* is not primarily concerned with the Udege tribe, although a Udege supporter of the Bolsheviks, named Sarl, is one of Fadeev's principal heroes. Fadeev had planned to write a monumental novel on the Civil War in the Far East, which, when completed, was to comprise as many as six volumes. Only four of them have actually been published. The last came out in 1937. Fadeev seems to have abandoned the idea of completing his work, presumably in view of the re-evaluation which the history of the Civil War in the Far East has undergone since the time of the great purges.

There is another novel which tells us more about the Udege people than the four volumes of Fadeev. It was written by an educated, half-Russianized Udege, Dzhansi Kimonko (1905-1949), who was trained at the Leningrad Institute of the Peoples of the North. After his return to his homeland, he became the chairman of a village council. In his spare time he wrote the history of the Udege people in the form of a novel, *Where the Sukpai River Flows*. The book is remarkable as the first and presumably last step in the development of Udege literature. Its intention is to show the beneficial influence which the Soviet régime exerted on the Udege people, but at the same time it reveals that the Udege have by no means been united in their support of Communist Russia. Kimonko indicated that there had been both a pro-Russian and a pro-Japanese Party among the Udege during the Civil War. One of the Japanese sympathizers was even killed in a violent clash, and so, too, was a wealthy Udege whom Kimonko describes as the 'Udege Czar'.

* Fadeev is the only prominent living Communist who can be considered as a 'Far Easterner'. He was born in the Tver region in European Russia in 1901, but came to the Far East at the age of six. He went to school in Vladivostok, where he joined the Communist Party in 1918. He participated prominently in the Far Eastern Civil War, which is the subject of all his earlier novels.

The Soviet authorities transferred the Udege from the isolated huts which were scattered over a wide area to larger compact settlements. This brought them within the range of medical attention and educational facilities. As a result of this contact with Soviet Russian culture, the young generation of the Udege now speak the Russian language 'almost without any accent'.[38] The next step in the development of the Udege will be that they will forget their own native tongue, and soon 'the last of the Udege' will really have disappeared.

THE NIVKHI

Near the mouth of the Amur is the National District of the Nivkhi. They number just over 4,000, of whom 1,700 live in Northern Sakhalin, and the rest on the Soviet Far Eastern mainland and on three small islands lying off the mouth of the Amur. These islands, Udd, Langr and Kevost, were ignored by the Soviet authorities until 1936, when the famous Russian pilots Chkalov, Baidukov and Belyakov, landed on Udd Island during their trans-polar flight. From that moment the islands became very popular. They were renamed after the three pilots, and it became almost a Russian patriotic duty to develop and colonize the little archipelago. The Soviet Far Eastern fishing industry established a plant there, and Russian workers' settlements were built on both Chkalov and Baidukov Islands, which had previously been inhabited exclusively by Nivkhi.

The Nivkhi of the Asiatic continent are very conscious of the fact that, together with the Nivkhi of Northern Sakhalin, they form one single people. Accordingly, under pressure of persecution by the Soviet authorities in the late 'twenties', the Shamans of the mainland Nivkhi fled to their kinsmen on Sakhalin. But these Shamans only fell out of the frying-pan into the fire, because of the activities of the local anti-religious fanatics. In 1930 the League of Militant Godless in Northern Sakhalin even destroyed the Nivkhi cemetery in an attempt to cure the 'natives' of their religious prejudices. This action caused considerable unrest among the Nivkhi, who lodged a complaint with the authorities. The latter apparently condemned the 'left-wing excesses' of the Sakhalin atheists.[39]

In theory, the Sakhalin Nivkhi live in two National Districts, the 'Western Sakhalin National District', and the 'Eastern Sakhalin National District' which, together cover a large part of Northern Sakhalin. In point of fact, both National Districts have been completely fictitious right from the beginning of their existence. The so-called Western Sakhalin National District, for instance, had, in 1933, only a few hundred natives among its 17,000 inhabitants.

KAMCHADALS

Soviet propaganda has never been very outspoken about the native people of South and Central Kamchatka – the Kamchadals – for a very good reason. Even Soviet historians could hardly claim that friendship between Russians and Kamchadals (or Itelmeny, as they are now called) ever existed in the past. It is a well-established fact that the presence of Russian Cossacks in Kamchatka provoked endless struggles and revolts in the early part of the eighteenth century. While it is true that many Cossacks lost their lives, it is equally undeniable that the first Russian colonizers wiped out the majority of the Kamchatka natives. Only the fact that Kamchatka is rather unsuitable for European colonization saved the Kamchadals from dying out entirely. While their number, which was about 30,000 before the Russian conquest, had dropped to about one-sixth, their relative strength was still fairly important at the end of the nineteenth century. The census of 1897 showed that the Kamchadals then formed over 48 per cent of the population of their homeland. Russian colonization under the Soviet régime changed things rapidly, to the detriment of the Kamchadals. In 1928 they comprised only one-quarter of Kamchatka's population, and in 1939, at the maximum, only 12 per cent.

In absolute figures there were 4,217 Kamchadals in 1926, but only 868 of them were able to speak their national language; the others were, as far as their culture is concerned, completely Russianized. In Petropavlovsk, the capital of Kamchatka, only 69 Kamchadals were counted in the 1926 census.

'ALEUTIAN NATIONAL DISTRICT'

East of Kamchatka are the Commander Islands, consisting of Behring Island, where the famous explorer, Vitus Behring, died in 1741, and Copper Island (Medny). The two islands now form the 'Aleutian National District', which was set up in 1932. There are not more than 400 Aleutians in the Soviet Union. Practically all of them live in the 'District' which is to impress the 5,800 Aleuts of Alaska.

Soviet propagandists have always taken great pride in the cultural successes of the 'Aleutian National District'. Its primary claim to fame is the fact that it was the first administrative unit of the Far East which achieved 100 per cent literacy. However, this triumph was not such a remarkable one as it may seem. Two thirds of the Soviet Aleuts were literate as early as 1926 at a time when the other Far Eastern tribes included only between 1 and 10 per cent of literate people. So the Soviet authorities can hardly take credit for an achievement which in all likelihood was brought about by Orthodox Christian missions. Unlike most other peoples of the Soviet Far East the Aleuts of the Commander Islands had been completely Christianized. In the first five years of the Soviet régime there was one church on Bering Island and another one on Medny. By 1934 the church of Bering Island was closed and that of Medny was reported as 'no longer functioning'. An increasing number of voices could be heard, said an official report, urging that the church building should be used for 'cultural needs'.[40] Such 'spontaneous popular movements' for the closing down of churches have often been reported from many parts of Soviet Russia. On the other hand, it is true that the percentage of communist party members in the Aleutian National District is higher than in any other territorial unit, not only in the Far East but in the whole of the U.S.S.R. 35 per cent of the population is organized either in the Communist Party or in the Communist Youth League, according to the latest figures available.

Before the war the local Soviet authorities of the Commander Islands were composed exclusively of natives. However, no undue significance should be attached to this fact, since the Aleuts as a people are half-Russianized, and Russian is the official language in the District. The Aleutian language, which is used by the Soviet Aleuts in their homes and for private conversation, is actually a mixture of Aleutian and Russian, in which Aleutian endings are added to Russian words.[41] Moreover, the inhabitants of the two Commander Islands speak different Aleutian dialects and can converse with each other only in Russian. Russian is also the language in which a small newspaper is printed on Bering Island for the benefit of the Aleuts and the handful of Russians who are all working on the blue fox State farm 'Komodor'. The name of the paper is *The Aleut Star*. Its sub-title shows that the Commander Islands, despite their tiny population, have a highly organized political life. It reads as follows: 'Organ of the Aleutian District Committee of the All-Union Communist Party, the All-Union Leninist Communist Youth League, the District Executive Committee and the District Trade Union Council.'[42]

In the post-war period considerable attention has been paid to the Commander Islands in connection with the 'cold war'. Their population seems to have increased. An official Soviet report of November 1949 said that the islands had several seven-year schools – only two schools had existed before the war – and that many prefabricated houses had been shipped from the continent.[43]

AINU, RUSSIANS AND JAPANESE

When occupying Southern Sakhalin in 1945, the Soviet authorities took charge not only of a large Japanese population, but also of small groups of aborigines. These included over 300 Tunguz, over 100 Nivkhi* and over 1,500 Ainu. Several hundred Ainu also came under Soviet rule through the annexation of the Kurile Islands. The Soviet Government has tried to strengthen its case for the undivided possession of Sakhalin by asserting that only the Russians were able to establish correct relations with the Ainu, while the Japanese oppressed them. The propagandists of the Soviet régime have even alleged that the Czarist Admiral Nevelskoy, who established Russian rule over Sakhalin, did so with the express purpose 'of defending the Ainu against the acts of violence of foreigners'. The Ainu, the propagandists affirm, gave enthusiastic support to the Russians when they landed in Sakhalin in 1853.[44]

Zadornov, a Soviet writer of historical fiction on the Far East, tries to show that the Ainu are almost fanatically pro-Russian. He asserts in his novel *Distant Country* that the Ainu of Southern Sakhalin looked forward eagerly, throughout the first half of the nineteenth century, to the arrival of the Russian liberators. 'We have been waiting for them for many years, we have been waiting for the time when it will be possible to kill the Japanese', Zadornov's Ainu said.[45]

In reality the Ainu of Southern Sakhalin did not seem to be very keen on killing the Japanese or driving them away. In 1875, when the Russian sovereignty over Southern Sakhalin became final, and when the Japanese formally renounced their rights on the island, 800 Sakhalin Ainu left for Hokkaido. They did not return until 1905, after the re-annexation of Karafuto by Japan. For a long time there was a considerable cleavage between these Ainu re-immigrants and their less advanced former fellow-tribesmen, who had never been away from their home island. This cleavage did not disappear until 1933, when all Ainu were granted Japanese citizenship. Originally the Japanese authorities on Karafuto had put five schools at the disposal of the Ainu minority, but when all members of this minority became full Japanese citizens, these schools were abolished, and the Ainu children transferred to Japanese schools.[46]

Since 1945 the Ainu have frequently been mentioned by Soviet propaganda, and their case has become typical of the hypocrisy of Soviet nationalities policy. While several hundred thousand Japanese were expelled from the new Soviet territories, the Ainu were proclaimed 'equal members of the family of Soviet peoples', and at once granted the right to participate in the elections to the Soviet Parliament.[47] Soviet scholars immediately started to study the interesting Ainu people, and the Soviet Academy of Sciences even set up a special branch in Southern

---

* Under Japanese rule the Tunguz and Nivkhi lived in a native reserve near the town of Shikuka (Poronaysk). Their administrative head was the Karafuto 'reindeer-king', a Yakut, who, with his family, had fled from Soviet territory.

Sakhalin which was entrusted, among other things, with 'raising the cultural and living standard of its native population', the Ainu in particular.[48]

Three years after the establishment of Soviet sovereignty over Karafuto Russian propaganda claimed that 'a revival of the ancient, original culture of the Ainu people' was noticeable, and that an 'Ainu national literary language' was in the process of being created.[49]

THE 'NATIONAL AREAS' OF THE EVENI AND KORYAKS

In 1930 three 'National Areas' were founded in the Far Eastern Territory, one for the Eveni (Lamuts), one for the Koryaks, and one for the Chukchi. The last two are still in existence, but the 'National Area' of the Eveni – Okhotsko-Evensky National Area was the official name – was disbanded after four years. It is doubtful whether the Eveni National Area, which covered 400,000 square miles, ever existed except on paper. The Eveni as a nomad people were not prepared to accept the notion of a territory with stable frontiers and a permanently fixed cultural and political centre. The attempt to erect such a centre, first in Okhotsk, later in Nogayevo, failed.[50] The National Area of the Eveni was formally abolished as a result of the progress which Russian colonization by convicts had made around the Okhotsk Sea in the early 'thirties'. By 1934 the proportion of natives in the population of the National Area had dropped to 40 per cent as against 80 per cent shortly before its foundation.

The Koryak National Area has been able to survive because the Soviet authorities have not yet succeeded in fully exploiting its riches, and have not, up to now, swamped the area with convicts and other settlers. The Koryak National Area covers the northern part of the Kamchatka peninsula, and the adjacent part of the Asiatic mainland. It is 125,000 square miles in area, and had 11,400 inhabitants in 1926. Out of this total, 61 per cent were then Koryaks, 8·9 per cent Chukchi, 7·1 per cent Kamchadals, and 5·5 per cent Eveni. The Russians accounted for 14·3 per cent.

The leading Soviet expert on the arctic and sub-arctic regions of the Soviet Far East, M. A. Sergeev, considers that the Koryak National Area is, politically and economically, one of the most important parts of North East Asia, in view of its close proximity to Japan and the U.S.A. Sergeev, who wrote the only available monograph on the Koryak National Area, pointed out that the Area had a considerable part to play in Russian foreign trade, and that it could develop into a territory earning for the whole Soviet Union an appreciable amount of foreign currency.[51] Among the economic assets of the National Area Sergeev lists its riches in fish, reindeer and fur animals, as well as gold and oil. All these items should be used for export, whereas the chief importance of 'Koryakia' for Soviet Far Eastern economy would lie in its extensive coal deposits. Although Sergeev gave very detailed data about the location of the deposits, it does not seem that exploitation has begun on any noteworthy scale.

The development of the Koryak National Area has lagged behind from the Russian communist point of view, not only in the economic, but also in the political sphere. The small Communist Party organization of the National Area, it is true, has issued statements on behalf of the tribesmen, abounding with such terms as 'dictatorship of the proletariat', or 'creation of a culture, national in form and socialist in content', but it does not seem that this has meant very much to the natives. The few communist agitators – in 1932 the Party organization had 120 members, including 'candidate members' – found it extremely difficult to encourage the class struggle among the Koryaks and other local tribes. The appearance in the National Area of State enterprises which were led and directed by Russians and other strangers, must have consolidated, rather than disintegrated, the primitive tribal unity comprising both the rich and the poor. Sergeev himself said that class consciousness, let alone class struggle, was practically absent in the Koryak National Area at the beginning of the 'thirties'. The 'kulaks', the well-to-do reindeer breeders, operated fairly successfully by stirring up hatred of the Russians, and by using 'tribal traditions, religious prejudices and superstitions' in their campaign against the new Soviet order. Soviet class war propaganda was countered by such simple but realistic phrases as 'rich and poor live together', or, 'the rich are feeding the poor'.

CHUKOTKA – THE RUSSIAN COLONY FACING ALASKA

The National Area of the Chukchi occupies the north-eastern tip of Asia facing Alaska, and is bordered by the Arctic Sea on the north, and the Bering Sea on the east and south. Several islands are part of the Chukcha National Area, including the Soviet island of Big Diomede, which is separated by only four miles from the Little Diomede, which belongs to the United States.*

The Soviet nationalities policy has done its best to take advantage of the indisputable geo-political importance of the Chukcha National Area – in short, Chukotka. This policy had to allow, in the first place, for the fact that the natives of Chukotka, both the Chukchi themselves and the Eskimos, who are related to them, had a long tradition of close economic co-operation with their American neighbours, whereas links between Russians and Chukchi had been tenuous.

* The Diomede Islands are also known as Ratmanov Island and Kruzenshtern Island respectively. Admiral Kruzenshtern commanded the first Russian round-the-world voyage and Ratmanov participated in this expedition.

The danger of an americanization of 'Chukotka' was not caused by a deliberate offensive of 'dollar imperialism' against that territory, but was due to the natural inter-dependence of the more highly developed American Alaska and the underdeveloped Russian territories on the western shore of the Bering Strait. *De jure*, Chukotka has been a Russian possession ever since the middle of the seventeenth century, when Cossacks had first penetrated into the land of the Chukchi. *De facto*, however, the Russians did not exert any sovereign rights over either the territory or the territorial waters around the north-eastern tip of Asia. A few Russians who had settled down in Chukotka in the seventeenth century, became completely intermixed with the native population, and quite indistinguishable from them as far as their exterior appearance was concerned. In 1897 there were 300 Russians in Chukotka, and 500 persons officially described as 'russianized natives', who might easily have been Russians turned native. The bulk of the population – the 11,771 Chukchi – lived in complete segregation from the Russians, and had they not been so primitive, it might have been said that they formed a State of their own. Up to the end of the nineteenth century the Chukchi were completely ignorant of Russia. They were even unaware of the existence of a Russian Czar. Nor did the Chukchi ever pay the Russians any 'yasak', the famous fur tribute by which the Siberian peoples implicitly recognized the overlordship of Russia.[52]

In the middle of the nineteenth century the Americans started the exploitation of Russian coastal waters in the Behring Strait, and in the Okhotsk Sea, with its vast abundance of whales. Since the Russians displayed no interest in whaling, the Americans soon became the un-challenged masters of those Russian waters. 'Predatory American whaling' had nearly exhausted the whale stock of the north-western Pacific before the Russians even thought of organizing whaling expeditions of their own.

After the purchase of Alaska by the United States in 1867, American whalers were almost the only civilized people with whom the inhabitants of the Chukot peninsula came into contact. The Americans sold them all the goods they needed, including rifles and ammunition, and later even little boats in which they went to Alaska, trading and intermarrying with Alaskan natives. Both the Chukchi and the Asiatic Eskimos learned English, and some of them travelled with the assistance of American whalers and traders as far as Seattle and San Francisco. Eskimo children from Chukotka went to Alaska to attend mission schools.

A learned Russian traveller to Chukotka, said, as early as 1888, that nearly all Chukchi of the Chukot peninsula, women and children included, understood some English, and that many Chukchi spoke it as well as a 'genuine American'. Gradually the Americans became so familiar to the Chukchi that they used to call all foreigners appearing on their shores 'Americans'.[53]

It was only in 1889 that the Russian Government transformed the land of the Chukchi into a separate administrative unit – the Anadyr District – and it was not before the 'nineties', when the district was under the command of a young, broad-minded District Commissioner, N. L. Gondatti, that Russian rule over the Chukchi became more effective, and attempts were made to counteract American commercial competition. Gondatti ordered regular fairs to be organized for the benefit of the Chukchi, and every native coming to his headquarters was offered a meal and a small present.

The attempts to consolidate Russian rule in Chukotka were, however, checked by the development of Alaska at the beginning of the twentieth century. To the American public the advance of economic and cultural life in Alaska seemed to proceed at too slow a pace. But what the Americans criticised as 'neglect' the Russians praised as the most astonishing progress. In 1909 the Russian scholar Kokhanovsky described the Alaskan town of Nome as 'an outstanding cultural centre'.[54] Obviously nothing in Chukotka, Kamchatka or around the Okhotsk Sea could bear comparison with Nome during its short-lived boom at the beginning of the century. At that time the danger of the United States expanding economically from Alaska into Chukotka was particularly real. Between 1902 and 1912 there existed an American 'North-Eastern Siberian Company', which eagerly propagated the idea of American investments for the exploitation of Chukotka's national riches – gold, iron-ore and graphite. The company was entitled to exploit 60,000 square miles of Russian land. During the ten years of its existence, it established an American trading monopoly on the Russian side of the Bering Strait. About 200 Americans settled more or less permanently in Chukotka. Their solid, well-furnished houses aroused the envy of the few local Russians, and the admiration of the natives. After the Second World War Soviet propaganda gave a very coloured version of the 'American period' in Chukotka's history. To show the far-flung ambitions of American imperialism, the Soviet Press made great play of a very unrealistic private American project to link Alaska with Chukotka by a submarine tunnel, and to build a railway across Northern Siberia.[55] The scheme had caused a minor sensation at the beginning of the century, but it was never taken very seriously.

THE SOVIETIZATION OF CHUKOTKA

Only the Soviet régime transformed Chukotka into a safe Russian possession and held foreign influence at bay. It could not raise Chukotka to a higher cultural and economic level than that of Alaska, but it could at least destroy the old interdependence of the two territories. Even this could be achieved only gradually and incompletely. Friendly direct contact between Alaska's and Chukotka's natives went on for several years after the establishment of Soviet power in the areas east of the Bering Strait. A fairly large number of Chukchi continued to speak some sort of broken English and there are indications that trips between Chukotka and Alaska went on until as late as 1944. Until that year parties of as many as forty people were observed to arrive from Siberia on the Alaskan coast on hunting, fishing and trading expeditions whilst American Eskimos visited Siberia for similar purposes.[56]

The transformation of Chukotka into an integral part of the Soviet Empire has been described in detail in Syomushkin's novel *Alitet goes to the Hills*. The book, which has already been quoted, was published in 1947. It was awarded a Stalin Prize for prose, for, from the point of view of the régime, it had the great merit of drawing the attention of a large Russian public to the strategic and political importance of the Chukotka outpost in the 'cold war' against America. Later, a film was produced on the basis of Syomushkin's book, but this was not such a great success.

Syomushkin, who had lived eight years in Chukotka, depicted in detail the methods which the Soviet governor employed to achieve the Sovietization of the land of the Chukchi. This man, whom Syomushkin called 'Los', was posted to Chukotka as he might have been to Kursk, Tula, or any other place in Central Russia. He had not the slightest knowledge of the country which he was to administer. He did not know anything about its customs. On the very first day of his arrival in Chukotka, without having gained even a superficial knowledge of local conditions, he stated flatly to his Russian companion: 'We'll make communists and komsomols out of them, mark my words.' And the Soviet administrator did make 'communists' out of the Chukchi, but these 'communists' were unable to understand such words as 'communism', 'Soviet' and 'revolutionary'. His assistant, a young intellectual called Andrey Zhukov, who had studied the customs and languages of the Chukchi, was more sceptical of the transplantation to the Arctic of the Communist Party jargon. When Los asked him to translate the word 'revolutionary' to a Chukcha, Zhukov said: 'I should like to see you translate the word "revolutionary". It is not so easy.' Los was not impressed by this refusal, but assured his subordinate that he would get the word translated, and that the Chukchi would learn the word. After gathering some experience in propaganda work among the local people, Los and his assistant drew up a political vocabulary. Here are some of its principal terms:

Communism	The new law
Lenin	The Russian who invented the new law of life
Communist	A man who wishes to remake life
October Revolution Anniversary Celebration	Feast of the big speech-making. (The Chukchi themselves call it 'The Russian Feast'.)
Communist Party Card	Bearer of the good spirit
Petrol	Good Spirit Benzine

The most difficult thing was to translate the word 'State'. How could one explain to the Chukchi that a thing called 'State' had confiscated the reindeer, and that it had become the most important property owner in Chukotka? A Chukcha woman, Rultina, found an adequate and truthful translation of 'State' by suggesting that the State was just a white man. A young Chukcha communist answered to this that the State was not only the Russian administrator, but 'many, many people'.*

Syomushkin's novel showed that the Soviet régime had to make a particularly great display of its efficiency in Chukotka because the Chukchi had an opportunity to compare the respective merits of Russian and American technical skill, even if only in the form of Russian and American matches. At one point of his book Syomushkin said that a pro-American Chukcha settlement had to be bribed by a motor whale boat before it would agree to join the Soviet hunting and fishing co-operative. Russia's position *vis-à-vis* the United States was also strengthened on a larger scale by the building of new settlements opposite Alaska – the Eskimo village Naukan and the administrative base Uelen, which was mainly populated by Chukchi.

The fight against native kulaks and traders was one of the most important activities of the Soviet authorities in Chukotka. The Russian communist officials tried to take control of fur hunting, fur trading and

* The Soviet régime is not the only one trying to teach the peoples of the North the political A.B.C. in a simplified and even over-simplified language. This is how *The Eskimo Book of Knowledge* of the Hudson Bay Company explained to the Eskimos of Labrador the transformation of Canada into a dominion – 'In his wisdom, the King of Britain said to the people of these new countries beyond the seas, his sons: "You have always loved me and the things which I love. You are now grown to full manhood, you have learned the things which I can teach you, you have your families and your children. It is right that you should direct your ways for the benefit of your children. I will appoint a Governor for your lands, but he shall be guided by your wishes. For are not your wishes my wishes?" '[57]

reindeer breeding. This was a difficult task, since the measures for collectivization were less understood in Chukotka than in most other 'backward' territories of the U.S.S.R. Syomushkin himself had to admit these difficulties when he described the effect of the imprisonment of the 'wicked kulak Alitet' (a Chukcha trader of this name really existed) on the local atmosphere in Chukotka. The local people saw in Alitet's arrest not a measure taken by the champions of the proletariat against the kulaks, but the persecution of a Chukcha by Russians. This is how Syomushkin described the despondency which the 'Alitet case' had created in Chukotka:

'Something amazing had happened on the coast. The Russians had locked Alitet up in a wooden yarang, and he sat there like a seal in a net. The news spread like wildfire, magnified by monstrous rumours. Alitet was in everyone's mouth, in the yarangs of the seal hunters, among the trappers, at meetings on the trail, in the depths of the tundra and wherever men came together in twos or threes.'

'The Shamans said that the Russians were building strong wooden yarangs in order to catch and lock up the Chukchi in them'.

'People dare not live now on the big rivers. The Russians would come down in the summer on their self-going whaleboats, and seize all the reindeer herds in order to do away with them. The reindeer men must not live in big encampments. They must break up into small camps of one or two yarangs, not more. The Russians want to destroy the herds.'[58]

CHUKOTKA DURING THE WAR : ECONOMIC EXPLOITATION AND 'IDEOLOGICAL' CONCESSIONS

The story of Syomushkin's book is carried further in the novel *Swift-moving Reindeer* by Nikolay Shundik. It describes life in Chukotka in the years of the war. The situation is then fundamentally different from that presented in *Alitet goes to the Hills*. The Soviet régime has already won the first round in the fight for Chukotka, the Soviet administration is firmly established, the collective farm system dominates and the young Chukchi are organized in the Komsomol. Many of them, it is true, do not know what the 'Communist Youth League' really stands for* but this does not matter as long as the Chukcha Komsomol members support the régime wholeheartedly and make their contribution to the development of local economy. The emphasis of Shundik's book is on this economic aspect. The Russian officials who figure in his novel are of a quite different type from the Los and Zhukov of Syomushkin. They are no

---

* Shundik's definition of the Komsomol as put into the mouth of a Chukcha girl is very similar to the definitions of political terms in *Alitet goes to the Hills*; 'The Komsomol is a very big family of young lads and girls. These lads and girls are honest and strong. They do one big job that is necessary to all, namely, to build life anew. The Komsomoltsy do not fear anything, neither an enemy, nor heavy work, nor snowstorm, not even death'.[59]

longer interested in indoctrinating the Chukchi and explaining to them the essence of communism and the working of Soviet power, they do not even talk about Lenin and Stalin. Their primary objective is to make the Chukchi work harder and to extract from them greater material contributions, particularly in the form of fur supplies.

The Russian officials and their Chukcha collaborators need all their ingenuity to increase the trapping of fur animals. Although the hunters are working under great strain, day and night, they must raise their targets further – under the pretext that the front expects more. To achieve this every collective farmer must look after a larger number of fox-traps. Women, too, are enrolled into the 'fox-hunting brigades'. One Russian administrator even has the idea of forcing reindeer-breeders to give up their herds and devote themselves entirely to hunting. This scheme is tried out but it does not work. It puts an unfair burden on the remaining shepherds and provokes profound dissatisfaction among the Chukchi who for generations have been used to combining fox trapping with reindeer-breeding. As a result less furs are provided than before. The man responsible for this failure, Karaulin, the head of the economic department of a Communist Party District Committee in Chukotka, is dismissed. He had been highly unpopular with the local population and it is interesting that this final removal occurs over an economic problem and not because of the high-handed way in which he had for several years been treating the Chukchi. One of his 'exploits' was the confiscation of a number of charms and idols belonging to an old Chukcha. Such arbitrary actions against helpless natives must have frequently happened in the past, both in Chukotka and in other native territories of the Far North and Far East. Nobody took exception to them in 1935 or 1938 but in the new situation that existed during the Second World War confiscation of idols became a 'left-wing distortion'.

Far away, in Moscow, Stalin gives the example. He has revised the official policy towards religion and concluded an armistice with the Orthodox Church. The Party secretary in Chukotka thinks that somehow he must adapt this new line to the conditions peculiar to North-Eastern Siberia. So he disowns his too zealous subordinate, Karaulin. The confiscated idols and charms are neatly wrapped up and bundled and restored to the owner who, incidentally, is a first-class and generally respected reindeer-breeder the régime can ill afford to antagonize.

CHUKOTKA AND THE 'COLD WAR'

The situation of Chukotka in 1945, as depicted in Shundik's novel is still not quite satisfactory from the Soviet point of view. The author introduces us to such 'hostile elements' as a reindeer-breeder who still refuses to join the kolkhoz, a kulak who, though formally a kolkhoz member, continues to be harmful and treacherous, and even an alleged American spy who for a certain period successfully poses as an official of a Soviet trading post. What is even more remarkable is the survival in Chukotka of 'devilish superstitions' but about this point at least a more official testimony is available than Shundik's book. 'In the minds of the Chukotka peoples', says *Pravda* of July 2nd, 1947, 'the old times are still surviving.' 'The Party organization', the newspaper adds, 'must carry out a tremendous cultural and educational work among the local population. Books are needed in the languages of the Chukchi and the Eskimos* to expose the prejudices of the past.'

The main handicap to communist activity in Chukotka has always been the fact that the country is ruled from Khabarovsk, which is as far away from Uelen, the settlement of the Chukchi on the Bering Strait, as Murmansk is from Tiflis. The communist leadership of Khabarovsk has found it extremely difficult, for obvious geographical reasons, to become interested in the special economic problems of the Chukchi, and in their cultural and economic needs. When the Party secretary of the distant National Area went to Khabarovsk in 1947, he had more than one reason for complaint. His most urgent grievances were the following: none of the Khabarovsk communist leaders ever visited Chukotka; the Khabarovsk paper *The Pacific Star* (Tikhookeanskaya Zvezda) rarely reported on events in the territory; no literature on Chukotka was published by the Regional Publishing House, Dalgiz; and the Khabarovsk trade organization, Severotorg, did not supply the goods badly needed by the population, such as tea, tobacco and petrol stoves. The publication of the article in *Pravda* coincided, quite accidentally, with the beginning of the 'cold war', and it constituted a turning point in the official Soviet attitude towards the Chukotka problem. Once again events in Alaska had a bearing on the situation in Chukotka. In view of the importance which Alaska acquired in the defence system of the Western hemisphere, the Soviet authorities paid increased

* The 'Russian or Asiatic Eskimos' live in the coastal areas of the Chukot peninsula. The part of the Chukcha National Area which they inhabit, and which also comprises Wrangel Island and the island Big Diomede, forms a special Chukcha-Eskimo National District of 150,000 square miles. It includes about one-sixth of the National Area. The Soviet régime has attached considerable importance to 'its' Eskimos in view of the large number of their kinsmen living in North America. The first expression of a Soviet 'Eskimo policy' was the organization in 1929 of an 'Eskimo Congress of Soviets'. The Soviet Government has also published pamphlets in Eskimo on basic political topics, as well as on reindeer-breeding, and an experiment was made with an Eskimo wall newspaper.

In 1947 the Soviet authorities decided that the Eskimo language hitherto in use in the U.S.S.R. was based on a 'wrong alphabet', and a 'wrong spelling'. The Minister of Education of the R.S.F.S.R., Alexey Kalashnikov, issued a decree by which the existing Eskimo alphabet was changed, and a more phonetic system of spelling adopted. The changes made it necessary to rewrite the existing Soviet literature in the Eskimo language in accordance with the new spelling rules.[60] The new Eskimo alphabet was the third one to be introduced by the Soviet régime within less than twenty years.

attention to Alaska's neighbour, the National Area of the Chukchi. Educational activities, for instance, were greatly extended. At the beginning of 1950 there were as many as 76 schools in the National Area, with more than 3,000 pupils.[61]*

Hand in hand with the development of schools for the children of Chukotka has gone the increase of propaganda activities among the adults. The Party secretary of the National Area stated, in May 1952, that Chukotka had as many as 350 'agitators', who had been recruited from among the Chukchi, Eskimos, and other 'natives'. Some of these locally recruited agitators were trained in the Territorial Party School in Khabarovsk. Others were indoctrinated in Party schools working in the National Area itself. In 1951–52 alone, 900 Party and Komsomol members of Chukotka, including both natives and Russians, studied the 'classics of Marxism-Leninism', and the 'Short History of the All-Union Communist Party'.[62]

All this indoctrination work among the Chukchi is concentrated in the hands of a Russian Party secretary, who shares his political power with the native Chairman of the Executive Committee of the Chukcha National Area. The division is very unequal, for the Party secretary has the powers of the governor of a colony, and the Chairman of the Executive Committee is only a figurehead and a spokesman of native interests. A man called Kukai was chairman just before the war. During the war the job was filled by a graduate of the Leningrad Institute of the Peoples of the North, Otke. He has frequently been mentioned and quoted in the Soviet Press, and there is no other native of the Soviet Far East and Far North who has come into such prominence. Not only does he serve as an example of how the Chukcha people have advanced under the Soviet régime, but he is also used for anti-American propaganda purposes. As a small boy, so his official biography says, Otke was offended by an American merchant, who poured the contents of a whole bag of duck feathers over him. Otke never forgot this episode. Apart from telling the story of the duck feathers, he is credited with making more profound political statements, such as the following: 'From Chukotka to Moscow there are 15,000 kilometres, and to Washington the distance is naturally considerably less. But there are different kinds of distance. There is a very great distance between the thoughts and feelings of people working in Chukotka and the intentions of the people in Washington. In this respect there is no distance whatever between Chukotka and Moscow.'

* The record of the Canadian Government in providing education for the Canadian Indians is at least as good as that of the Soviet government in Chukotka. In 1949, out of the 135,000 Canadian Indians, 23,285 were attending school, that is to say more than one out of six. By comparison the school population in Chukotka is roughly the same, granted that the National Area has about 18,000 inhabitants, which is a very low estimate. The figure includes not only Chukchi and other natives, but also the Russian colonists.

IMMIGRATION OF RUSSIANS AND RESETTLEMENT OF CHUKCHI

It is impossible to say what is the numerical proportion of Russians to natives in Chukotka. It is a fair assumption, however, that the Russian element has greatly consolidated its position after the end of the Second World War, when something approaching a mass immigration seems to have taken place for the first time. Before the war the Soviet Government had mapped out a big colonization plan for Chukotka, the population of which was supposed to increase to 30,000 by 1938, the end of the Second Five-Year Plan. Luckily for the Chukchi, but very much to the detriment of Russia's strategic interests, this plan failed to materialize. Chukotka's population remained stationary, at about 15,000. A substantial increase of the Russian immigrants after the war may be assumed from the fact that, in 1951, as many as 31 per cent of all deputies of local District and Area Soviets of Chukotka were officially classified as not belonging to the northern peoples.[63] In other words, they were Russian and European colonists and officials. If the council seats were distributed in accordance with the proportionate strength of the nationalities inhabiting Chukotka, an inference which cannot be made with absolute certainty, then almost one third of its population must have been European immigrants. This must be compared to the situation around 1930, when only 3·8 per cent of the population of the National Area consisted of non-natives. 76·3 per cent were Chukchi, and almost 20 per cent were Eskimos and other aborigines.[64]

Apart from Russian immigration, the National Area was the scene of yet another important development after the Second World War – the liquidation of nomadism. The complete triumph of the Soviet system in the Far North will be possible only when the entire population becomes sedentary, and within easy reach of the Communist Party and State organs. This is why active measures have been taken to settle the nomads in the various National Areas of the Soviet Arctic. The task has been a difficult one. It has required considerable financial investments, and a great deal of work on the part of the Soviet authorities.[65] In 1947 Chukotka's first nomadic collective farm engaged in reindeer breeding decided (according to an official statement) 'to settle down completely, and for good'.[66] In the middle of 1952 it was stated that a 'mass resettlement' took place, whereby the Chukchi were moved from their yarangs into 'comfortable houses'. This meant a greater concentration of the Chukchi in a number of larger collective farm settlements, probably for many of those concerned a rather painful operation.[67]

Both the immigration of Russians and the resettlement of the Chukchi have set civilization in Chukotka on a higher level. On the other hand, these two measures are bound to pave the way to the extinction of the

Chukchi as a separate national group. Accordingly, the forecast of the great Russian anthropologist Professor Bogoraz-Tan with regard to the Chukchi seems to be coming true: 'If civilization comes too near, the Chukchi will probably follow the way of other primitive peoples, and will die out and disappear.'[68]

BIBLIOGRAPHICAL NOTES TO CHAPTER III

1. *Zhizn Natsionalnostei*, January 10th, 1922.

2. *Pravda*, August 30th, 1938.

3. VYSHINSKY, *Sudebnye Rechi*, Speeches in Court, Moscow 1948, p. 225.

4. *Pravda*, September 12th, 1939.

5. M. A. SERGEEV, *Koryaksky Natsionalny Okrug* – The Koryak National Area, Leningrad 1934, p. 113. A. SKACHKO, *Narody Krainego Severa i Rekonstruktsiya Severnogo Khozyaistva* – The Peoples of the Far North and the Reconstruction of Northern Economy, Leningrad 1934, p. 86.

6. E. BERZIN, Golden Kolyma, *Pravda*, November 11th, 1936.

7. ELINOR LIPPER, *Eleven Years in Soviet Prison Camps*, London 1951, p. 121.

8. Statement by M. L. GOLUBOVICH at the 'Trial of the Soviet Concentration Camp Régime' in Brussels, *La Belgique Libre*, May 23rd, 1951.

9. VLADIMIR PETROV, *It Happens in Russia*, *Seven years forced labour in the Siberian goldfields*, London 1951, p. 260.

10. *Kultura i Zhizn*, April 11th, 1950.

11. *Pravda*, July 2nd, 1947.

12. M. A. SERGEEV, *Narodnoe Khozyaistvo Kamchatskogo Kraya*, The National Economy of the Kamchatka Territory, Moscow-Leningrad 1936, pp. 409–10.

13. *Small Soviet Encyclopedia*, second edition, vol. 7, 1938, p. 703.

14. P. S. ZHIGUNOV and F. A. TERENTEV, *Severnoe Olenevodstvo*, Reindeer-breeding in the North, Moscow 1948, quoted from *Polar Record*, vol. 6, Nr 41, January 1951, p. 109.

15. *Sovetsky Taimyr*, September 19th, 1950, quoted from *Voprosy Istorii*, Nr 2, 1953, pp. 41–2. See also a *Tass* report of August 16th, 1953.

16. *Uchitelskaya Gazeta*, October 13th, 1951.

17. RICHARD FINNIE, *Canada moves North*, The Macmillan Company, New York, 1942, p. 78.

18. *Dalnevostochnoe Obshchestvo Kraevedeniya* (*Etnograficheskaya Sektsiya*), *Yediny Severny Alfavit* – Far Eastern Regional Research Society (Ethnographical Section), The Unified Northern Alphabet, Khabarovsk 1930, p. 6.

19. *Voprosy Istorii*, Nr 2, 1953, p. 45.

20. *Uchitelskaya Gazeta*, June 30th, 1951.

21. *Pravda*, June 2nd, 1952.

22. *Pravda*, June 2nd, 1952.

23. A. V. OBSUREV, *Obshchii Ocherk Anadyrskogo Okruga* – General Outline of the Anadyr District, St. Petersburg 1896, p. 117: I. W. SHKLOVSKY, *In Far North-East Sibéria*, London 1916, p. 248. See also WILLIAM HOWELLS, *The Heathens, Primitive Man and his Religions*, London 1949, p. 126.

24. PROF. B. E. PETRI, *Staraya Vera Buryatskogo Naroda* – The Old Faith of the Buryat People, Irkutsk 1928, pp. 52–3.

25. SYOMUSHKIN, *Alitet Ukhodit v Gory* – Alitet goes to the Hills, Moscow 1948, pp. 259–61.

26. *Zvezda*, Nr 6, June 1950, p. 49.

27. I. KOSOKOV, *K Voprosu o Shamanstve v Severnoy Azii* – On the question of Shamanism in Northern Asia, Moscow 1930, p. 70.

28. OLESHCHUK, *Borba Tserkvi protiv Naroda* – The Fight of the Church against the People, Moscow 1939, p. 104.

29. SYOMUSHKIN, *Children of the Soviet Arctic*, London 1944, p. 221.

30. I. M. SUSLOV, *Shamanstvo i Borba s nim* – Shamanism and the Fight against it, Moscow 1931, pp. 143–5.

31. KOSOKOV, op. cit., p. 71.

32. OLESHCHUK, op. cit., p. 70.

33. AZHAEV, *Far from Moscow*, Soviet Literature, Nr 10, 1949, p. 37.

34. *Zvezda*, April 1950, pp. 263–4.

35. *Skazki Narodov Severa* – Tales of the Peoples of the North, Moscow-Leningrad 1951, pp. 358–9.

36. WLADIMIR ARSENJEW, *Russen und Chinesen in Ostsibirien*, Berlin 1926, p. 79.

37. A. DEMENTEV, E. NAUMOV, L. PLOTKIN, *Russkaya Sovetskaya Literatura* – Russian Soviet Literature, Leningrad-Moscow 1951, p. 372.

38. *Izvestiya*, April 12th, 1952.

39. *Antireligioznik*, November 11th, 1931, p. 26.

40. *Sovetsky Sever*, Nr 4, 1934, p. 45.

41. *Za Industrializatsiyu Sovetskogo Vostoka*, Nr 2, 1933, p. 188.

42. M. A. SERGEEV, *Sovetskie Ostrova Tikhogo Okeana* – The Soviet Islands of the Pacific, Leningrad 1938, pp. 70–8 and 135–8.

43. *Soviet Monitor*, November 11th, 1949.

44. I. VINOKUROV and F. FLORIN, *Podvig Admirala Nevelskogo* – The Feat of Admiral Nevelskoy, Moscow 1951, pp. 127–8.

45. N. ZADORNOV, *Dalyoky Kray*, Distant Country, Leningrad 1950, p. 375.

46. MARTIN SCHWIND, *Die Gestaltung Karafutos im Japanischen Raum*, Gotha 1942, pp. 66–7.

47. *Soviet News*, December 11th, 1945.

48. *Soviet Monitor*, April 8th, 1947.

49. *Geografiya v Shkole* Nr 3, 1947, pp. 16–17.

50. *Sovetsky Sever* Nr 3, 1933, p. 60.

51. M. A. SERGEEV, *Koryaksky Natsionalny Okrug* – The Koryak National Area, Leningrad 1934, p. 129.

52. A. P. SILNITSKY, *Poyezdka v Kamchatku i na Reku Anadyr* – Journey to Kamchatka and the Anadyr River, Khabarovsk 1897, p. 77.

53. *Izvestiya, Imperatorskago Geograficheskago Obshchestva*, St. Petersburg 1888, vol. xxiv, pp. 180–7.

54. *Izvestiya Imperatorskago Russkago Geograficheskago Obshchestva*, St. Petersburg 1909, vol. xiv, p. 516.

55. *Ogonyok*, Nr 2, January 1952, pp. 15–16. MELCHIN, *Amerikanskaya Interventsiya na Sovetskom Dalnom Vostoke* – American Intervention in the Soviet Far East, Moscow 1951, p. 9.

56. *Military Review*, vol. 32, Nr 6, September 1952, p. 11.

57. GEORGE BINNEY, *The Eskimo Book of Knowledge*, Hudson's Bay Company, London 1931, pp. 38–40.

58. SYOMUSHKIN, *Alitet Ukhodit v Gory* – Alitet goes to the Hills, Moscow 1948, pp. 501–2.

59. NIKOLAY SHUNDIK, *Bystronogy Olen* – Swift-moving Reindeer, *Oktyabr*, Nr 10, October 1952, p. 52.

60. *Soviet Monitor*, February 7th, 1947.

61. *Soviet Monitor*, February 27th, 1950.

62. *Pravda*, May 6th, 1952.

63. *Sibirskie Ogni*, Nr 3, May-June 1951, pp. 116–22.

64. M. A. SERGEEV, *Kamchatsky Kray*–The Territory of Kamchatka, Moscow 1934, p. 31.

65. *Uchitelskaya Gazeta*, October 10th, 1951.

66. *Soviet News*, August 26th, 1947.

67. *Pravda*, May 6th, 1952.

68. BOGORAZ-TAN, *Chukchi*, Leningrad, 1934, p. 78.

4

IV

RUSSIANS AND YAKUTS

MULTI-NATIONAL YAKUTIA

Yakutia covers 14 per cent of the entire surface of the U.S.S.R. It is not only the largest of the sixteen autonomous Republics, but also the largest single territorial unit of the whole of the Soviet Union. It is approximately equal in size to the Republic of India.

This vast territory of Yakutia, or the Yakut A.S.S.R., was inhabited by 288,000 people in 1926, and by 400,000 in 1939. No recent data as to the racial composition of Yakutia are available, but in 1926 the Yakuts constituted 82·3 per cent of the entire population, the Evenki and Eveni 4·08 per cent and the Russians 10·43 per cent. The rest were Chukchi, Yukagirs, Chinese and Koreans.

The Evenki and Eveni of Yakutia, though numerically and politically unimportant, live scattered over a large part of the country. In the early years of the Soviet régime, little attention was paid to these minority groups. The turning point came in 1930 and 1931, when 'National Districts' were formed for their benefit. Five 'National Districts' were set up for the Evenki. They covered almost one-third of the whole Republic, and stretched from the western borders of Yakutia to the eastern bank of the Lena river. Nine more 'National Districts' were founded in eastern and northern Yakutia for the Eveni. A fifteenth mixed 'National District' was created in the north-eastern border area of Yakutia for Eveni, Chukchi and Yukagirs. The Yukagirs are a paleoasiatic people who, in the seventeenth century, occupied almost the entire north of Yakutia. The northward-pushing Yakuts decimated them, and compressed them into a narrow area.

In relation to the minor nationalities of Yakutia, the Yakuts have as a rule played the role of a master race. Even under the Soviet régime they have continued to exercise political control over the other nationalities. In 1933, ten of the fifteen 'National Districts' were administered by Yakut district council chairmen. This shows that the Yakuts occupy a special position among the non-Russian peoples of Siberia, and that they have to be considered apart from the small nationalities of the North and the Far East. They differ from them in their numerical strength and in the higher degree of their social and cultural development. From the point of view of the Communist Party they present an incomparably greater problem than do such peoples as the Chukchi, Nanai and Nivkhi. Belonging to the big family of Turkic peoples, the Yakuts had a fairly developed national consciousness before the October Revolution. Unlike many other small nationalities in the Far East, they do not owe the beginnings of a national culture to the Soviet régime.

THE HISTORICAL BACKGROUND: FROM 1630 TO 1924

The Yakuts have been under some form of Russian rule since about 1630. Russian officials collected 'yasak' in Yakutia, but otherwise they left the country alone. Catherine the Second established Russian domination in a more formal way, but Yakuts enjoyed far-reaching autonomy, even under and after Catherine. Their tribal organization, headed by the 'Toyony', the Yakut princelings, remained untouched, although the Russian Government had to confirm them in their dignity. Right to the end of the nineteenth century, Russia practised, in many ways, a policy of non-intervention in Yakutia in both a good and a bad sense. She did not interfere a great deal with local customs, but she also made no efforts to raise the level of civilization. There was no Russian cultural activity worth mentioning in Yakutia. No attempt at russification was made in practice, although theoretically it was the aim of the Czarist régime. Russian colonization was on a very small scale. Many of the Russian colonists who settled in Yakutia spoke Yakut, some to the extent of forgetting their own tongue.

Nevertheless, the fact remained that the Yakuts were a conquered people, and the Russians the conquerors. At the beginning of the twentieth century the Yakuts became aware of this. Their national consciousness awoke. Yakut newspapers and books were published, and in January 1906 a nationalist organization, the 'Yakut Union' (Soyuz Yakutov) came into existence. The 'Yakut Union' demanded that all land in Yakutia alienated by the State, monasteries, and Russian political exiles should be handed back to the Yakut people. It also urged that Yakuts be appointed to local police posts. The Czarist authorities, in an attempt to subdue the nationalist Yakut agitation, arrested the leaders of the 'Yakut Union', an action which only encouraged further Yakut nationalism. The 'Yakut Union' was a genuine home-grown Yakut movement, entirely unconnected with Russian revolutionary forces. The Bolsheviks, in particular, failed to take up any links with the Yakut nationalists, and even denounced their organization as the instrument of a 'clique of kulaks and tribal aristocrats'.[1]

From its own standpoint the Bolshevik Party continued to handle the Yakut problem badly, even after the October Revolution. The first Bolshevik officials who were posted to Yakutia behaved in a tactless and clumsy way, and the Party failed, therefore, to enlist any support from the Yakut people. Stalin's own mouthpiece, *Zhizn Natsionalnostei*, openly admitted this failure. The paper wrote, 'The Soviet Government conducted an incorrect policy with regard to this territory (Yakutia) in 1918. It did not take into account its special climatic and living conditions . . . The Soviet Government did not pay attention to the psychology of the native, particularly to his distrust of the Russian, which was rooted in history. As a result of this mistake, the natives did not understand the nature of Soviet power. They considered it with distrust like everything Russian, and the broad masses kept completely aloof from the efforts to build up the Soviet State'.[2]

The absence of any collaboration between the Bolsheviks and even a section of the Yakut people accounted very largely for the fact that civil war in Yakutia dragged on longer than in many other parts of the Soviet Union. As late as September 1922, almost five years after the October Revolution, the 'Whites' recaptured from the 'Reds' the locality of Verkhoyansk in the Yakut Far North. Even this was not the end of the civil war, for in the winter of 1922–23 General Pepelayev launched a new counter-revolutionary movement in Yakutia. He was finally routed in the summer of 1923, and executed in January 1924.

THE GOLD REPUBLIC

The Yakut Autonomous Soviet Socialist Republic was founded in October 1922. It was roughly identical with the Yakut Province as it existed under the Czars. As a political entity, the Yakut Republic has remained very largely a constitutional fiction, not only because Soviet 'autonomy' in general has very little in common with real autonomy, but also for quite specific local reasons. The vastness of Yakutia and the scarceness of communications make it difficult to rule the country effectively from one centre. It is true that the establishment of numerous airlines has greatly improved the situation, and has made government much easier. Nevertheless, for the bringing up of supplies, civil aviation is of little help, and since there are no railways in the Yakut A.S.S.R., river and road transport have still to do the bulk of the work. Both forms of transport in Yakutia have to overcome great difficulties. River navigation means primarily navigation on the river Lena and its tributaries, and the navigation period on the Lena is shorter than on most other Siberian rivers. It lasts not more than 135 days on the sector Vitim-Yakutsk, and even less on the sector stretching from Yakutsk to the Arctic Ocean. As to roads, a great many are impassable in the summer months, since they are covered with mud. In 1937, out of the 35 districts of Yakutia, only four had communications with the capital, Yakutsk, all the year round, fourteen districts during ten months, eight during eight months, and the remaining nine only during six to seven months. Although the situation is bound to have improved considerably since 1937, the problem of communications is still a very acute one for the Yakut A.S.S.R.

Practice has shown that it cannot be solved centrally from Yakutsk, but only by an economic decentralization of the Republic. This is exactly what has happened. The northern part of Yakutia is no longer dependent on Yakutsk and the southern districts of the country for supplies, but gravitates towards the Arctic sea-port, Tiksi, which owes its existence to the Chief Administration of the Northern Sea Route (Glavsevmorput), and is one of its principal bases. Glavsevmorput has organized supplies to the northern Yakut districts from Murmansk, instead of via Irkutsk and Yakutsk.

In the south-eastern corner of the country, too, an entire district has gone its own way – the gold-mining region on the upper reaches of the Aldan river. Economically, and from the point of view of its communications, the Aldan region is now at least as closely connected with the Khabarovsk Territory as with the Yakut A.S.S.R. The development of the Aldan region into one of the most important gold-producing areas of the country has greatly altered the economic and social structure of the Yakut A.S.S.R., and has also affected its ethnographic physiognomy. Gold deposits on the Aldan river were discovered near a small place which was then still called 'Nezametnoye' – 'the Unobtrusive'. The discovery led to a gold rush. All sorts of adventurers went to the previously almost uninhabited area. In one year, between 1924 and 1925, the population of the area jumped from 1,200 to 13,000. The newcomers included, apart from Russians, people of many other nationalities, particularly Chinese and Koreans. This 'private initiative' soon came to an end. The Government brought order into the Aldan gold-mining business. A powerful State trust, 'Yakutzoloto', was established. It not only organized and greatly increased gold production, but also developed trade, improved housing, and provided cultural facilities in the area. Besides, Yakutzoloto owned the largest lorry park in the whole country.

The name of the gold centre, 'The Unobtrusive', was no longer appropriate for a place which produced such vast wealth. In April 1939 it was therefore changed into 'Aldan'. Although the Russians are a minority in Yakutia, they constitute the majority of the population in the Aldan area. The Russian town of Aldan, the headquarters of Yakutzoloto, is more and more overshadowing the capital Yakutsk, which is 'only' the headquarters of the Government.

Yakutzoloto is not the only big State capitalist enterprise whose wide powers make Yakut autonomy an illusion. There are others in charge of gold, timber, fishing, and the fur trade, and there are, above all, the powerful organizations which look after navigation in the Lena basin. The latter operate in complete independence of the Government in Yakutsk, which does not own a single one of the ships which link one Yakut locality with another.* The navigation is in the hands of three enterprises; one is the 'Lengospar' which belongs to the Ministry for Water Transport in Moscow; the second is 'Lenzolotoflot' which is run by the State trust exploiting the Lena goldfields, and the third is the Chief Administration of the Northern Sea Route.

The development of goldmining and transport under the Soviet régime created a small native proletariat. By 1936 there were 1,845 Yakut miners and industrial workers. They constituted only 4·19 per cent of the entire working class in the country, whilst the Russians supplied the bulk of it (70 per cent), and Koreans and Chinese a very substantial minority (15 per cent).[3]

Russian colonization in Yakutia is expanding, not only in the Aldan area, but also in Central Yakutia, where it is spreading out in the valley of the Vilyuy, a tributary of the Lena river, particularly in connection with the development of coal mines.[4] Northern Yakutia, too, has become more attractive for Russian colonists through the work of Glavsevmorput. It has old Russian settlements such as Ust Yansk, Russkoye Ustye, and Nizhne-Kolymsk, which are situated at the mouth of the rivers Yana, Indigirka and Kolyma respectively. With the development of Arctic and river navigation, these places have become more important. Other ports have been founded as well, and Russians are needed to keep them going.

YAKUT NATIONALISM

Today Yakutia has a new aristocracy, the managers of the gold trusts and transport undertakings, and the Stakhanovites of the gold mines and power stations, and of the new tanning and leather goods factories.

* Although all matters concerning mining, heavy industry and river transport are excluded from the competence of the Yakut Government the latter is, nevertheless, an exorbitantly large bureaucratic body considering the smallness of the population of the country. According to article 42 of the Constitution of Yakutia the Council of Ministers consisted until 1953 of a prime minister, several deputy prime ministers, the chairman of the planning commission, 13 ministers in charge of internal affairs, State security, health protection, municipal economy, timber industry, local industry, food industry, education, social welfare, trade, finance and justice and seven heads of 'administrative boards'. The latter were in charge of highways, cinemas, automobile transport, local fuel industry, industry of building material, cultural and educational institutions and matters concerning the arts. The whole Council of Ministers had at least 25 members, which is more than most governments of Western Europe. The same ministries and 'administrative boards' existed in all Autonomous Soviet Socialist Republics irrespective of the size of their population. In 1953 the number of ministers was slightly reduced.

Most, but not all, of the members of the new upper-class are Russians. To put the new aristocracy firmly into the saddle, the old one, which was Yakut, had to be destroyed, and so had its ideological foundations, Yakut 'bourgeois nationalism'.

Until 1928, the Soviet authorities of Yakutia were rather liberal. They tolerated even a Yakut cultural organization, 'Sakha Omuk' (The Yakut People), which was founded in 1921; and a nationalist literary journal, *Cholbon* (The Morning Star). In its first issue the journal stated that it would deal with Yakut themes to the exclusion of everything else. The editors of *Cholbon*, Leontev and Sofronov, meant what they said. In the middle of the 'twenties' they still had the courage to refuse the publication of a poem carrying the title 'Lenin is alive'. The Soviet authorities had to reconcile themselves to the fact that out of the five or six Yakut writers known in the years 1922 to 1925, only one could be described as 'proletarian'. All the others were 'nationalists'. The most important of the latter was the poet and ethnographer, Kulakovsky.

The essence of Kulakovsky's political philosophy is contained in a poem, 'The Dream of the Shaman'. Speaking through the medium of a Shaman, Kulakovsky warned his people that the 'new-comers', the Bolsheviks, would bring doom to the Yakuts, and would make slaves of them. Only by acquiring modern science and technique could they survive the struggle for their existence. Kulakovsky was an enemy of distinction, who commanded a great deal of respect from his communist opponents. The journal *Revolyutsionny Vostok*, that ardent advocate for the Sovietization of the East, had to admit that Kulakovsky hated the Russians with the sophisticated hatred of an intellectual, and not with that of a petty bourgeois.[5]

Politically more important was the writer Altan Saryn, who preached pan-Turkism among the Yakuts. He advocated the purge of Russian expressions from the Yakut language, and their replacement by terms borrowed from other Turkic languages. No wonder that Saryn soon became the principal antagonist of Bolshevism in Yakutia. His conception of Yakut culture ('Sarynovshchina'), was branded as the ideology of the tribal aristocracy.

In 1928, the Central Committee of the All-Union Communist Party intervened, and imposed on Yakutia the same irreconcilable Bolshevik attitude towards nationalism as was adopted all over the U.S.S.R. The local party leaders of Yakutia, the members of the 'Provincial Committee' ('Obkom') were deposed. In a stiff statement dated August 8th, 1928, the Central Committee enumerated the political mistakes which the Yakut communists had up to then committed, their alleged friendliness towards kulaks and 'toyony', their support for nationalist intellectuals who had been given important posts, and their neglect of the small nationalities of Yakutia.

The new men who took over, following the Central Committee statement, set about their task energetically. They expelled from the territory of the Yakut A.S.S.R. those whom they considered the 'most fanatical representatives' of the Yakut national intelligentsia. They disbanded the 'Sakha Omuk' organization, and reorganized the journal, *Cholbon*. On the economic front, collectivization was carried out in the face of considerable resistance and sabotage.

The final act of this large-scale offensive which the Soviet Government conducted against its enemies in Yakutia took place thousands of miles away from the Lena River along another important waterway of the U.S.S.R., the Baltic-White Sea Canal. Among the workers building that canal there was a considerable number of Yakut deportees. They were kept apart from the Russian convicts employed on the construction site, and, together with a large number of other Asiatics, formed special 'National Minority Brigades'. They were also billeted in special 'National Minority Barracks', the sanitary conditions of which were 'beneath criticism', even according to the Soviet standard book on the canal.[6] This book, to which a large number of eminent Soviet writers contributed, gives a rather contradictory evaluation of the work performed by national minorities, of which only Yakuts, Uzbeks, Tadzhiks and Bashkirs are expressly mentioned. First they are branded with unparalleled idleness, and later they are praised for performing the most herculean tasks. In one case the 'national minority heroes' are said to have worked 38 hours without a stop, and in another case of emergency even as many as 50 hours.

But whether the Yakuts and the other members of the so-called 'Canal Army' were idlers or record-breakers has little importance. What became known of life and work in the National Minority Barracks of the Baltic-White Sea Canal was bound to deter many would-be opponents of the régime in the minority territories themselves, even as far away as Yakutia. Nevertheless, opposition by no means died down entirely, and the big purge of 1937 affected the Yakut A.S.S.R. as much as any other autonomous Republic.

According to the official version, 'Japano-German spies, bukharinist-trotzkyite diversionists and bourgeois nationalists' were its victims. Such elements were discovered in all important State offices, in the Council of People's Commissars, in the State Planning Commission, and in the office of the Yakut plenipotentiary of the Ministry of Supplies, which is responsible for the compulsory deliveries by farmers, cattlebreeders and fishermen.[7]

Even the 1937 purge did not finally dispose of bourgeois nationalism. Nationalist tendencies made themselves felt once again during the Second World War, when Soviet cultural policy for a moment seemed to be inspired by greater magnanimity. Yakut communists used what appeared to be a new situation by reviving the memory of the two outstanding Yakut intellectuals already mentioned, Kulakovsky and Sofronov. Despite their anti-Bolshevik bias, they were, so to speak, smuggled back into the intellectual patrimony of the Yakut people, and rehabilitated.

THE BASHARIN INCIDENT

In 1944 a Yakut historian, Georgy Prokopovich Basharin, published a book in Yakutsk which presented Kulakovsky, Sofronov, and another pioneer of Yakut literature, Neustroev, as progressive people who were spiritually related to such Russian revolutionary democrats as Belinsky and Chernyshevsky. Basharin gave a positive evaluation of the literary work of the three 'enlighteners', as he called them, and considered their nationalist concept as a healthy reaction to the colonial oppression of Czarism. During several years it seemed as if this reinterpretation of Kulakovsky was officially accepted. For a long time no protest against Basharin's thesis came from higher quarters. In 1950 a rehabilitation of Kulakovsky was even incorporated in a book on Russian-Yakut relations, published by the Yakut branch of the Soviet Academy of Sciences.

It was not until December 1951 that Moscow told the Yakut intelligentsia that they must drop the wrong appraisal of their literary heritage, and must revert to an attitude of Bolshevik intransigence. On December 10th, 1951 *Pravda* published an article, 'For a correct elucidation of Yakut literature', which did not mean very much to the readers of the Bolshevik central organ in European Russia, but which was, from the Yakut point of view, a new landmark in Soviet cultural policy. The article was signed by three people who included the well-known Russian poet, Alexey Surkov, and the expert on Turkic literature in the Union of Soviet Writers, Lutsyan K. Klimovich. The three took Basharin heavily to task for his courageous book on the founders of Yakut literature. They charged him with justifying the bourgeois-nationalist views of Kulakovsky, with an uncritical attitude towards his 'fantasies', and with hushing up his reactionary character. The whole thesis put forward by Basharin, so *Pravda* pointed out, was 'clearly erroneous and anti-Marxist'.[8] Not only was the *Pravda* article on Yakut literature one more example of how Moscow interferes with cultural life of the non-Russian nationalities, but it also acquired particular importance in view of the personality involved. By no stretch of imagination could Basharin be described as a 'class enemy'. He was the son of a poor peasant, and spent his entire conscious life in the service of the Soviet régime. First, he was active in the Komsomol, and later in the

Party. Until the publication of the *Pravda* article of December 10th, 1951, his life-story reflected only the positive sides of Soviet nationalities policy in Yakutia. Under the Czarist régime he would have become nothing more than a hunter in the Yakutian taiga, but under the Soviet régime he was able to study at first in one of the new Soviet village schools,* later in the Yakut Pedagogical Institute, and finally in Moscow. In 1943 he became 'Candidate of Historical Science', and in 1950 'Doctor of Historical Science'.[9] There are hundreds of members of small nationalities who went a way similar to that of Basharin. They accumulated knowledge, acquired academic degrees, and became famous, not only in their homeland but also all over the Soviet Union. Then, suddenly, there came a point in their career when they felt the full oppressive weight of the communist totalitarian régime. This is exactly what happened in the case of Basharin. This Yakut communist had digressed from the official ideological line. Although belonging to a new Soviet generation, he had produced a work which was fundamentally nationalistic in Soviet eyes. Such a strange phenomenon had to be denounced in *Pravda*. But whether such a denunciation can stifle the desire for independent thinking and research is a different matter.

'SHORTCOMINGS' AND ACHIEVEMENTS OF YAKUT SOVIET LITERATURE

The *Pravda* article was not written for the sole purpose of settling the 'Basharin incident'. It also drew attention to 'major errors and defects' in Yakutia's contemporary literary output. One of the offences of the Yakut writers consisted in 'an uncritical utilisation of archaic images from ancient folklore to illuminate the Soviet reality of today'. This was a roundabout way of admitting that Yakut folklore was falsified in order to fall in with certain requirements of political propaganda. How this is done in practice was once explained by the Yakut writer, Kulachikov-Ellyay. According to him, some poets simply took an old Yakut national song and made it topical by inserting the word 'kolkhoz' and the 'new names of heroes'.[10] Such manipulations probably account, in part, for the large number of 'folksongs' in honour of Stalin and the Soviet régime in the languages of all Soviet nationalities.

Both the Yakut Communist Party organization and the Union of Soviet Writers of Yakutia repeatedly dealt with the ideological shortcomings of Yakut literature. A conference which the Writers' Union

---

* In 1947 Yakutia had 580 schools in which over 61,000 children were educated. This included 141 seven-year schools, and 28 secondary schools. In the school year 1916-17 there were only 173 schools with 4,460 children (*Uchitelskaya Gazeta*, June 28th, 1947). In 1952 almost two-fifths of the teachers employed in Yakutia's schools were Russians. (*Uchitelskaya Gazeta*, June 28th, 1952).

held in Yakutsk in 1948 denounced the uncritical attitude which some of the Yakut writers were said to have assumed towards the 'survivals of the past', by professing mysticism, inserting 'religious exorcism into their works and indulging in romantic adoration before the River Lena'.

However much the Soviet régime persecuted ideological heresies among Yakut writers and poets, it is a fact that Yakut literature has made great progress, even if it is primarily a Soviet literature in the Yakut language. In the first 25 years of the Yakut A.S.S.R., 3,000 different textbooks and other books were printed in the Yakut language, Yakut state publishing houses turned out many translations from the Russian classics, and a small number of translations from foreign authors. On the other hand, a large proportion of the books printed in Yakutia were worthless from a literary point of view because they consisted of communist propaganda material. The Yakut language is the only one among the languages of the smaller Soviet nationalities into which Stalin's 'Complete Works' are translated. As a rule they are published only in the languages of the Union Republics.

The Soviet literature which is published in Yakut is written in a language which has become to no small degree russianized. This is not entirely the work of the Soviet régime. As many as 2,400 Russian words had penetrated into the Yakut language by the end of the nineteenth century.[11] Under communist rule, it is true, the Russian language gained further ground. Today, every seventh word used in contemporary Yakut literature is a Russian one, quite apart from the influence of Russian on the syntax of Yakut. In Yakut newspapers, Russian words form 30 per cent of the vocabulary used.

RUSSIAN CULTURAL SUPREMACY

The gradual russification of the Yakut language is accompanied by the imposition and propagation of Russian cultural supremacy in the Yakut A.S.S.R. Russian cultural propaganda reached its culmination point in 1950, when the Yakut branch of the All-Union Academy of Sciences published an important work of scholarship, already mentioned. Its full title is *The Progressive influence of the great Russian nation on the development of the Yakut people*. It is interesting that, already, the title of this book expresses a discriminatory patronizing attitude towards the Yakuts. It not only calls the Russians 'great', but refers to them as 'nation' ('natsiya'), whilst the Yakuts are only a 'people' ('narod'). The chapter headings are even more revealing. Here are some of them: 'The great Russian People – the elder brother of the Yakut People'; 'The positive results of Russian colonization in connection with the accession of Yakutia to the Russian State'; 'Russian peasants as pioneers of agriculture among Yakuts'; 'The help of the Russian

111

People in the industrialization of Soviet Yakutia'; 'The leading role of the Russian People in the development of Yakutia's means of communications'; 'The progressive influence of the Russian People on the development of musical culture of the Yakut People.'[12] And so it goes on, until tribute is paid to the Russian contribution in every branch of economy and culture. The characteristic feature of the symposium is that its authors, mostly Yakuts and Russians living in Yakutia, gloss over the negative aspects of Czarist and Russian rule in general. Even the few miserable schools which the Czarist régime had established in Yakutia are hailed as a positive achievement, because the Russian language, and the 'progressive ideas of Russian pedagogical science', penetrated with their help to the Yakuts. The Soviet régime also takes the credit for the work of the orthodox missions in Yakutia, and a few missionaries, who were the first to create an alphabet for the Yakut language, are mentioned in the symposium.

It is tempting to contrast the harmonious picture of Yakut-Russian relations contained in the work of the Yakut Branch of the Soviet Academy with statements which official Soviet organs had previously made on the same subject. This is what the organ of the People's Commissariat of Nationalities wrote in an article published on August 13th, 1921: 'The Yakuts know the Russians as conquerors, as corrupt chinovniks, as merchants and exploiters, as exiled criminals who ridiculed all their best feelings and committed acts of violence, and as neighbouring peasants who oppressed them. Only the political exiles left a good memory.'[13] This statement probably went too far towards the other extreme, although it may be taken for granted that the Yakuts had not been very appreciative of the blessings of Russian rule in the past. Yakut popular sayings, as collected by Soviet folklore experts, even betray a certain hostile scepticism towards the Russians. These include the following: 'Am I a Tunguz nomad or a Russian passer-by that you do not believe me?'; or 'Even on his death-bed will a Russian stretch out his hand for the repayment of a debt.'[14]

Despite everything, a great deal of what Soviet propagandists have said after the Second World War about the civilizing role of the Russians in Yakutia is historically true, but no enlightened colonial power would make such play of the backwardness of a colonial people and force that people to admit it. The symposium on the progressive Russian influence has a certain similarity with literature which the colonial government of the Belgian Congo publishes for the 'natives'. There one can read phrases such as, 'the Belgians, our civilizers, our benefactors'. It is difficult to find any similar exhibitions of enforced, undignified servility towards the European colonizers, either in British or in French West Africa.

1. M. VETOSHKIN, *Iz istorii bolshevistskikh organisatsii i revolyutsionnogo dvizheniya v Sibiri* – From the history of the Bolshevik organizations and the revolutionary movement in Siberia, Moscow 1947, pp. 234-5.
2. *Zhizn Natsionalnostei*, August 13th, 1921.
3. *Revolyutsiya i Natsionalnosti*, April 1936, p. 53.
4. *Izvestiya*, July 16th, 1948.
5. *Revolyutsionny Vostok*, Nr 27, 1934, p. 205-7.
6. *The White Sea Canal*, English edition prepared from the Russian version and edited, with special introduction, by Anabel Williams-Ellis, London 1935, p. 144.
7. KOLESOV and POTAPOV, *Sovetskaya Yakutiya* – Soviet Yakutia, Moscow 1937, p. 13, p. 338.
8. *Pravda*, December 10th, 1951.
9. *Ogonyok*, Nr 13, March 1951.
10. *Literaturnaya Gazeta*, July 7th, 1948.
11. *Sovetskaya Etnografiya*, Moscow-Leningrad 1951, vol. iv, p. 233.
12. *Voprosy Istorii*, 1951, Nr 1, pp. 140-4; *Sovetskaya Etnografiya*, 1951, Nr 4, pp. 230-4.
13. *Zhizn Natsionalnostei*, August 13th, 1921.
14. *Yakutsky Folklor*, Moscow 1936, pp. 276-7.

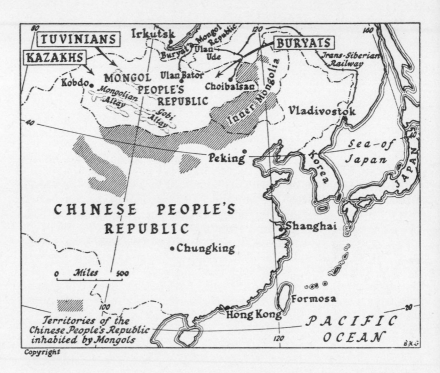

4. THE MONGOL PEOPLE'S REPUBLIC IN RELATION TO CHINA

114

V

THE SOVIET RÉGIME AND THE MONGOLS

In the Russian Far East, the Soviet Government is confronted not only with Chinese, Japanese, Korean and American influences; she has to face yet two other opponents, encountered nowhere else in the U.S.S.R. These are pan-Mongolism and Buddhism.

This pan-Mongol-Buddhist 'danger' must be dealt with in two territories which are closely interconnected, but which enjoy different political status. One is an Autonomous Socialist Soviet Republic within the Soviet Union – Buryat-Mongolia – while the other is formally independent and only *de facto* a Soviet territory – The People's Republic of Mongolia (M.P.R.).

I. THE BURYAT-MONGOL AUTONOMOUS REPUBLIC

The Buryat-Mongols comprise only a quarter of a million people. Nevertheless, they occupy a unique place both in Soviet Far Eastern policy and in Soviet nationalities' policy as a whole. They are the only people of the U.S.S.R. belonging to the Mongol group by both race and language, and they are also the only Buddhist people of the Soviet Empire.*

---

* In the inter-war period there was another Buddhist and Mongol people in the Soviet Union, the Kalmucks, but they have been eliminated from the ethnographical map of the U.S.S.R. Groups of Kalmucks may still live scattered about Russia, but they no longer have any place in the cultural and political planning of the Soviet Government. It stands to reason that the abolition of the Kalmuck A.S.S.R. in 1943 and the deportation of the Kalmuck people must have made a strong impression on the Buryat-Mongols and the Khalka-Mongols of the Mongol People's Republic. There used to be a certain amount of contact between Kalmucks, Buryats and Khalka-Mongols, and during several years the Soviet régime itself promoted their cultural co-operation. In January 1931, representatives of the intelligentsia of the three Mongol nationalities held a meeting in Moscow that was officially described as 'First Cultural Conference of Mongol Peoples'. It dealt with the reform of Mongol spelling on the basis of the Latin alphabet, and with the co-ordination of the scientific terminology of all three languages.[1] Later the Soviet authorities were less eager to develop cultural intercourse between Kalmucks and Buryats or between Kalmucks and the M.P.R. in view of the pan-Mongol danger. Nevertheless, it seems likely that Buryat and Khalka-Mongol intellectuals continued to be interested in the destinies of Kalmuckia.

The Buryats have played a part in Russian policy which is quite out of proportion to their numerical strength. The Czarist Government thought that through their Buddhist connections, they might assist Russia to establish a protectorate over Tibet. Under the Soviet régime their mission in foreign policy consisted in assisting Russia to exercise efficient domination over Outer Mongolia, the Mongol People's Republic (M.P.R.). They did in fact supply a large number of agents for the bolshevization of that country. At a time when Mongolia itself was lacking qualified personnel, the Buryats provided the staff for the leading cultural and economic institutions of the M.P.R., particularly the Montsenkoop, the Mongol State trade monopoly, and the Mongoltrans, the Soviet controlled transport company of the 'People's Republic'. In the Mongol Army the Buryats distinguished themselves as officers and instructors.

The fate of the Buryats provides the most outstanding example of the success of Russian colonization. Although living thousands of miles from the centres of Russian civilization, the Buryats have been split up into groups by wedges of Russian colonists, in the same way as the peoples of the Volga valley were split up. This Russian colonization, which took place in the eighteenth and early nineteenth century, resulted in pressing the Buryats away from the important rivers of their homeland, such as the Lena, Angara, Selenga and Ingoda. It was particularly fateful for the Buryats that the Russians dislodged them in 1799 from both banks of the Ingoda River. This operation not only narrowed down the Buryat 'living space', but also created a small Buryat enclave near Chita, cut off from the bulk of the Buryat people. Russian colonization and Russian policy split the Buryats not only geographically, but also culturally. The Eastern Buryats remained Buddhists and were less exposed to Russian cultural influences, while the Western Buryats became largely christianized and russianized.

In the years following the October Revolution, Western and Eastern Buryats were also politically separated. The former were incorporated into Soviet Russia, the latter into the Far Eastern Republic. The Buryat lake, Lake Baikal, became the frontier between the two. The Far Eastern Republic attached considerable importance to the Buryat question, perhaps less for reasons of principle than out of fear that the Buryats could become a tool of Japanese policy. Five articles of the constitution of that Soviet satellite republic dealt with the special legal position which the Buryats were to occupy. Article 116 said, 'The entire area inhabited by the Buryat-Mongols shall form a special territory under the name of "Autonomous Buryat-Mongol Province".' Article 118 guaranteed to the Buryats the right to establish courts of justice as well as economic, cultural and administrative institutions in their territory.

116

Article 119 provided for the formation of a Buryat-Mongol National Assembly entitled to legislate on local matters.

The communists of Russia proper were less eager than their Far Eastern comrades to grant the Buryats a special status. The communist organization of Irkutsk which was most directly concerned with the problem expressed its outright hostility to Buryat autonomy. The Irkutsk communists argued that the Buryats were not sufficiently civilized to have an autonomous administration of their own. The spokesman of the Buryat communists, Mikhei Nikolayevich Yerbanov, denounced this chauvinistic attitude and complained to the People's Commissar for Nationalities, Stalin. Stalin ruled that an Autonomous Buryat Province was to be organized in Eastern Siberia, in the Irkutsk region, despite the resistance of the local Russian communists. Consequently, during a certain period there were two Buryat autonomous territories, one belonging to the Far Eastern Republic, and the other being part of the Russian Soviet Federation. In 1923 the two territories were amalgamated into one single Autonomous Republic. To draw the frontiers of the Buryat-Mongol A.S.S.R. was no easy task. Whichever way Buryat-Mongolia's frontiers were to be fixed, the Republic was bound to have a Russian majority, in view of the successful Russian colonization which had been carried out in the Buryat country.

SOVIET POWER AND BUDDHISM

The real problems of Soviet policy in Buryatia started only after the framework – the Autonomous Republic – had been created. Should the Soviet régime treat Buddhism in the same way that Christianity had been treated? Could Buddhism and Communism be reconciled with each other? What should the Party do with the Buddhist monasteries? These, and similar questions faced the régime in the early 'twenties'. The Communist Party and the Soviet Government found it difficult to answer them, and vaccilated in their Buryat policy between an attitude of relative liberalism and one of utter intolerance.

In the 'twenties', the Soviet Government was at first inclined to make use of the Buryats as a revolutionary, or at least 'progressive', vanguard of the entire Buddhist world. In the winter of 1926-27 when the situation in China was heading for a crisis, the Soviet Government granted permission for the holding of a 'Congress of Soviet Buddhists' in Moscow, in which most of the participants were Buryats. The Congress produced an 'Appeal to the Buddhists of Mongolia, Tibet and India', calling on them 'to support with all their power the fight for the emancipation of the Chinese people'.[2]

In Buryat-Mongolia itself the local Soviet administration was allowed, for a time, to proceed cautiously in religious questions. The local

People's Commissar of Agriculture, Oshirov, organized the Buddhist priests, the lamas, into co-operatives. His idea that the lamas could be gradually integrated into the new socialist order was widely shared. Buryat cultural workers, in particular, were eager to conserve Buddhist monasteries and religious music. To put the co-operation between communists and Buddhists on solid foundations, a number of Buryat intellectuals conceived the theory of 'Neo-Buddhism', which the Soviet Government at first viewed rather benevolently.

The chief theoreticians of Neo-Buddhism were the head of the Buddhist community in Buryatia, Agvan Dordzhiev, and the Buryat Professor Zhamtsarano. They alleged that Buddhism was actually a 'religion of atheism'. There was no difference between the Buddhist ideas on the emancipation of mankind and those professed by Marx and Lenin. Gautama Buddha was, in fact, a forerunner of Leninist materialism.[3]

From about 1929 onwards, the Neo-Buddhist theories were officially described as 'most harmful', since they served 'to obliterate the class-consciousness of the revolutionary masses'.[4] The régime stopped discriminating between Buddhism and other religious creeds, and launched an anti-religious campaign of great violence throughout Buryat-Mongolia. A small but active group of 'militant godless' communists, by terrorist means, tried to prevent the celebration of Buddhist holidays, interfered with religious processions by deliberate provocations, and by administrative measures, achieved the closing of Buddhist monasteries. All this brought such discredit to the anti-religious cause that the Buryat organization of the League of Militant Godless had to be disbanded in 1930.[5] Anti-religious propaganda was then inactive until about 1937.

In that year a new anti-religious campaign started in connection with misunderstandings which the new Stalin constitution had caused, not only among Buddhist believers, but also among other religious groups of the Soviet Union. Until the coming into force of the new constitution, the lamas had been disfranchised, and the fact that voting rights were restored to them was, therefore, bound to create a certain optimism. The lamas believed, indeed, for a while that there was a fundamental change in Soviet policy towards religion. Their illusions were soon destroyed by the energetic measures which the régime took against them.

Nevertheless, on the eve of the Second World War, Buddhism in the B.M.A.S.S.R. was still a factor with which the Communist Party had to reckon. This is what one of the leaders of the League of Militant Godless wrote at the beginning of 1939: 'In Buryat-Mongolia the lamas have still considerable influence on the masses. It suffices to say that even some pedagogues and medical workers seek the advice of lamas in their capacity of specialists in "Tibetan Medicine".'[6]

PAN-MONGOLISM — REAL AND ALLEGED

Closely connected with the problem of Buddhism is that of Buryat pan-Mongolism. The Buryats had been notorious for their inclination towards pan-Mongol tendencies ever since the Japanese victory in the Russian-Japanese War of 1904-5. In the Civil War many Buryats played a counter-revolutionary role; they sided with the Japanese interventionists who had proclaimed the idea of a 'Greater Mongol Empire'. The 'white guard' puppets of the Japanese, Ataman Semyonov and General Ungern-Sternberg, were able to recruit quite a number of Buryat volunteers for their detachments. A pan-Mongol congress, which was summoned on Japanese initiative in February 1919 in the town of Chita, also enjoyed a considerable measure of Buryat support. The congress demanded that all Russian colonists living east of Lake Baikal should be expelled. It also elected a delegation which was to submit to the Peace Conference in Paris a project for a Greater Mongol State consisting of various Russian and Chinese territories. When the Bolsheviks advanced into the land of the Buryats, and the Greater Mongolia project collapsed, certain sections of the Buryat people propagated the idea of emigration to Manchuria. There the Buryats were to wait until the plan of a Greater Mongolia could be resumed with Japanese help.[7]

Under the Soviet régime pan-Mongol tendencies made themselves felt throughout the 'twenties' and 'thirties'. Communist publications frequently complained about 'bourgeois-nationalist' and 'national-democratic' tendencies among the Buryats, and about the display of pictures of Genghis Khan. The nationalist pan-Mongolist intelligentsia was even able to delay the introduction into Buryatia of the Latin alphabet, which scored its final victory only in 1933, after having been officially introduced in 1931. The Buryat Party secretary, Yerbanov, thought it wise not to provoke the nationalists too much. He sent their representatives occasionally to prison, but did not launch a large-scale anti-nationalist offensive. When in 1933 'local nationalism' was declared in both the Ukraine and Byelorussia to be the 'main danger on the national front', Yerbanov made a statement that this change of policy did not apply to Buryat-Mongolia. There, 'Great Russian chauvinism' would continue to remain the main danger. The Bolshevik Politbureau in Moscow seemed to be satisfied with Yerbanov and his policy. In January 1936 he was invited to the capital as head of a Buryat-Mongol delegation which was received in the Kremlin by Stalin, Molotov, Voroshilov and other Soviet leaders. Molotov delivered a big speech on this occasion; he praised the economic and cultural advance of Buryat-Mongolia, and hailed in particular the emergence of a new Buryat intelligentsia. Yerbanov, too, made a speech in which he promised to establish in Buryat-Mongolia a 'strong rear' for the Red Army. In an emergency, he said, the Buryats would come immediately to the rescue of their great fatherland, the Soviet Union. For his share in transforming the B.M.A.S.S.R. into 'one of the most advanced republics of the U.S.S.R.', Yerbanov was awarded the Order of Lenin.

Between January 1936 and summer 1937 the Politbureau changed its mind completely about the Buryat-Mongol A.S.S.R. 'One of the most advanced Republics' became suddenly one of the darkest spots on the map of the U.S.S.R. The fine Buryat intellectuals were, according to official Soviet statements, but a 'band of gangsters, bourgeois nationalists, Japanese and German spies, diversionists and wreckers'.[8] There was no crime under the sun which the Party secretary, Yerbanov, the president of the B.M.A.S.S.R., Dampilon, and the members of the Council of People's Commissars, were not found to have committed. This is how Yerbanov's successor as Party secretary, Semen Denisovich Ignatev,[*] summarised the activities of his predecessor and his associates: 'The abject dirty dogs of fascism, the ferocious enemies of the Buryat-Mongol people, the bourgeois nationalists, in conjunction with trotzkyite-bukharinist bandits, conducted their dirty, dark and treacherous work for many years. These trebly contemptible Judases poisoned people, infected and destroyed cattle, wrecked industry, incited towards national hatred, and behaved everywhere disgustingly like beasts. They tried to separate Buryat-Mongolia from the U.S.S.R., and to put the country under the protectorate of the black fascist Samurai of Japan.'[9]

We do not know how the N.K.V.D. proved its point about the existence of a pro-Japanese conspiracy in Buryat-Mongolia, but it is possible that it took refuge in deliberate provocations. Such provocations are known to have been tried out with considerable success in other parts of the Soviet Union. One case was mentioned by the former Soviet historian, Avtorkhanov, who is now living in a Western country. In his book, *Genocide in the U.S.S.R.*, Avtorkhanov tells how, in Ingushetia in the Caucasus, a Soviet police official posed as a Japanese agent. He approached all potential enemies of the Soviet régime and recruited them for a fictitious organization. To make the farce complete, he made his victims take the oath on the Koran, and even distributed money and arms among them. As soon as a sufficient number of persons had committed themselves to a pro-Japanese policy, the N.K.V.D. started to arrest 'Japanese spies'.[†] Such tactics may also have been used in Buryat-Mongolia.

* S. D. Ignatev specialized in nationalities problems. Having carried out the purge in Buryat-Mongolia he was sent to Bashkiria and later to Byelorussia and Uzbekistan. In the spring of 1953 he became a secretary of the Central Committee of the Soviet Communist Party, but fell into disfavour a few weeks later.
† A. Avtorkhanov, *Narodoubiistvo v S.S.S.R.*, Genocide in the U.S.S.R., Munich 1952, pp. 31–33.

The 'Japanese spies' and 'Buryat bourgeois nationalists', dominated everywhere, according to official statements – in agriculture, in industry, among the leading personnel of most 'aimaks' (the districts into which the Republic is sub-divided) and in all cultural institutions. The counter-revolutionary nationalists were firmly entrenched in the Buryat State Publishing House, in the local Union of Soviet Writers and in the principal Buryat communist newspaper *Unen*. The Institute of Buryat Culture was 'a jumble of all sorts of human scum', employing four Mongol princes and twenty adventurers, kulaks and white guards.[10]

Were all these charges pure imagination, or did they contain a certain amount of truth? It is difficult to believe that Yerbanov the 'chief-bandit' of Buryat-Mongolia, to speak in the official jargon, was at any time a 'bourgeois nationalist', 'Japanese spy' or 'pan-Mongolist'. Even before the First World War he belonged to a 'Marxist circle' in the Siberian town of Barnaul. From 1917 onwards he was a Communist Party member and took and active part in the fight against the White Admiral Kolchak. After the foundation of the Buryat-Mongol A.S.S.R., in 1923, Yerbanov occupied the highest posts in the Republic, first that of prime minister, and from 1929 that of Party secretary. It is true, however, that Yerbanov advocated moderation in the fight against Buryat nationalism and national culture. He also favoured the 'Buryatization' of the Republic, in as far as this was possible in view of continuous Russian colonization. The Soviet Government on the other hand, haunted by the fear of a Japanese attack on the U.S.S.R., wanted the ruthless suppression of all nationalist elements in Buryatia which might have collaborated with the invader. Buryat nationalism, in the Soviet view, was a natural ally for Japan, just as Ukrainian nationalism was an ally of German imperialism. A half-hearted attitude towards Buryat nationalism, such as that manifested by Yerbanov, was thus a criminal offence and had to be mercilessly exterminated.

The explanation of the fight against the Yerbanov deviation cannot be found in the purely political sphere alone. There is no doubt that the economy of the B.M.A.S.S.R. was in a state of disorganization when the N.K.V.D. launched its big action against the 'enemies of the people' in Buryatia. Buryat-Mongol industry drastically under-fulfilled the Second Five-Year Plan. The most important plants of the Republic under-fulfilled the plan by as much as 40 per cent. The greatest failure was the Locomotive and Waggon Repair Works of Ulan Ude, in the construction of which over 20,000 people had participated. This plant was to be the principal railway repair shop for the whole of the Soviet Far East and for Central Siberia. Russia's transport and supply system in the Japanese border areas depended on its efficiency. The plant was hastily constructed with faulty material, and some of the buildings collapsed soon after their completion. The local Party leadership had to take the blame, although the Railway Repair Works were an 'industrial giant' of all-Union importance and, consequently, a primary responsibility of the central government.

THE DISMEMBERMENT OF BURYATIA

The liquidation of the 'Yerbanov band' proceeded with amazing rapidity. Yerbanov was denounced as a 'Japanese spy' by the Communist Party organization of Ulan Ude on September 26th, 1937, and he was executed barely three weeks later on October 12th. His trial, though short, was one of the biggest which took place in Soviet Russia during the great purge of 1937. It ended with a total of 54 death sentences and executions. This alone shows the degree of nervousness which the Kremlin felt over the situation in the Buryat Republic. Executions, mass dismissals of Party and State officials and their replacement by new people were however, not enough to restore order in the B.M.A.S.S.R. The Soviet Government inflicted on the Republic a sort of collective punishment and deprived it of six of its aimaks (districts). Four of them were located in the westernmost part of the Republic, beyond Lake Baikal, and the two remaining ones formed an enclave in the Chita Province, and were situated 120 miles from the borders of Manchukuo. The 'reform' was justified by the assertion that Yerbanov's misrule had been particularly disastrous in the outlying districts of Buryatia, and required special measures of remedy. The four western aimaks were added to the Irkutsk Province and the two eastern aimaks incorporated into the Chita Province. Within these two provinces the former Buryat territories formed 'National Areas' (okrugi), that lower form of Soviet national autonomy which is otherwise confined to the small tribes of the Far North.

The administrative reform, as such, was not unreasonable from a practical point of view, since the aimaks concerned were organically linked with the two Russian Provinces into which they were formally included by the Decree of September 26th, 1937. The timing of the reform suggested, however, that it was meant to be a reprisal against Buryat nationalism, and, in the case of the eastern aimaks, also a measure of military security. According to the official version, dozens of 'bandits working on the direct instructions of the Japanese secret service were busy sabotaging all efforts of the Soviet Government' in the outlying districts of the B.M.A.S.S.R. These Japanese agents were not powerful administrators who abused their office, but ordinary farmers belonging to kolkhozes with such pretentious names as 'Karl Marx' or 'Comintern'.[11]

The re-drawing of Buryatia's frontier cost the Republic only 12 per cent of its territory, but had considerable economic consequences. The six aimaks affected by the change included one-third of Buryatia's cattle

122

population, whilst one quarter of Buryatia's sowing area was situated within the western aimaks which went to the Irkutsk Province as the 'Ust Ordynsk Buryat-Mongolian National Okrug'. The separated Buryat territories in the east, now the 'Aginsk Buryat-Mongolian National Okrug', contain some of the biggest lead deposits of the U.S.S.R.

Buryat cultural and educational activities, within the strict limits of communist ideology, were safeguarded even in the 'National Areas' with the help of national schools and a Buryat-Mongol department at Irkutsk University.[12]*

In the more important Ust Ordynsk National Area, cultural work in the Buryat language labours under a difficulty for which the Soviet régime bears no responsibility, namely, the far-reaching denationalization of the local Buryats. Of the three Buryat poets and writers of the National Area, two are writing their works in Russian.[13]

The victory of the Soviet central authorities over Yerbanov and his friends made the Russian State safer against a particularly harmful brand of 'local nationalists', the 'pan-Mongolists' of Buryatia. It led to the aggrandizement of Russian Provinces at the expense of an autonomous republic and it probably made Russia's position slightly more secure in the Far East.

THE TRIUMPH OF RUSSIAN INFLUENCE

The victory of Soviet centralism in Buryat-Mongolia was followed by the introduction of the Russian alphabet for the Buryat language on April 7th, 1939, and by the arrival of a new wave of Russian immigrants. The special privileges for new settlers in the Far East, which were included in the decree of November 17th, 1937, expressly applied to the B.M.A.S.S.R.

Russian colonization in Buryatia, it is true, had never ceased under the Soviet régime but, on the basis of the new decree, the influx of Russians became more intense and more systematic. As early as 1926, the Russians formed 52.7 per cent of the population of the B.M.A.S.S.R. against 43.8 per cent Buryat-Mongols. During the first and second Five-Year Plan period, Russians and other Europeans were brought into the Republic because it proved to be difficult to recruit native workers into industry. In 1935 only 16 per cent of Buryatia's industrial workers were Buryats. Even in 1938 the Railway Repair Works of Ulan Ude included hardly 500 Buryats among their 6,000 workers. The

* The Irkutsk University, which is geographically the nearest Russian University to the Soviet Far East, has established a kind of cultural protectorate not only over the Ust Ordynsk National Area, but over the whole of the B.M.A.S.S.R. The Irkutsk University, and not the Ministry of Education in Ulan Ude, decides how the Buryat language is to be taught in the schools of the 'Autonomous Republic', and what reforms are to be introduced into the Buryat language itself. (*Izvestiya*, July 10th, 1952).

growth of Ulan Ude, the Buryat capital, was almost entirely due to the arrival of Russian workers. The town, which had 30,000 inhabitants in 1927, increased its population to 55,000 inhabitants in 1932 and to 129,000 in 1939. It does not seem that the Buryats have formed, at any time, more than 20 per cent of the population of the city.* Also the other towns of the B.M.A.S.S.R., such as Kyakhta and Babushkin (named after the Russian Bolshevik revolutionary, Ivan Vasilevich Babushkin) have a predominantly Russian character. This could hardly be otherwise, for the majority of the Buryats became fully sedentary only during the first two Five-Year Plan periods. In 1928-29 only 9.8 per cent of all Buryats were officially classified as sedentary, 78.6 per cent were described as semi-nomadic, and 11.6 per cent as nomadic.[14]

This semi-nomadic and nomadic past of the Buryat people made it impossible for even the young Buryat Soviet generation to play a major part in the 'new socialist life' of Buryatia. In 1948 the country had over 7,000 specialists with higher and secondary education who worked in industry, transport and agriculture of the B.M.A.S.S.R. Only 1,379 of them were Buryats.[15]

The preponderance of the Russian urban element in Buryatia provoked hostility amongst the Buryats against the towns, which the Soviet régime rightly interpreted as hostility against the Russian proletariat and Bolshevism itself.

CULTURAL AND LINGUISTIC DEVIATIONS

The spokesman of this antipathy to city life was the most gifted Buryat poet, Solbone Tuya, who had enough courage to tell the communist Russian colonizers:

> No, keep your overcrowded cities,
> With their sophisticated air!
> Guileless and free, I need the country,
> The cool wind blowing through my hair.
> Give me the steppe, limitless, windswept,
> Its vastness stretching on each side,
> Where free from orders and surveillance,
> Man's goodness is his only guide.

* The last official statistics giving the ethnic composition of Ulan Ude refer to 1926. In that year 83 per cent of the inhabitants of the town were Russians. A similar Russian predominance existed then and still exists, in the capitals of other Autonomous Soviet Socialist Republics. The capital of Tartaria, Kazan had, in 1926, 70 per cent Russians; Ufa, the Bashkir capital had 76 per cent and Izhevsk, the capital of Udmurtia 91 per cent. In Yakutsk, Yakutia's capital, the situation was more favourable from the point of view of the local people. The Russians accounted for only 56 per cent of all inhabitants and the Yakuts for almost one third. But at the time of the 1926 census Yakutsk had only 10,000 inhabitants. Since then its population has increased sevenfold and the Yakut capital is now ethnically at least as Russian as its Buryat-Mongol counterpart.

The author of these verses, whose real name was Pyotr Nikiforovich Danbinov, was one of the most remarkable personalities whom the Buryat people produced in the twentieth century. During the First World War, the Czarist régime persecuted him for nationalist Buryat activities. The communist government of the Far Eastern Republic recognized Danbinov as Buryat national leader and made him Deputy Chairman, first of the Constituent Assembly, and later of the National Assembly, of the buffer-state. After the amalgamation of the Far Eastern Republic with the Russian Soviet Federation, Danbinov devoted himself entirely to literary and cultural work.[16] *The Encyclopedia of Literature*, published by the Communist Academy, described him as the 'most outstanding Buryat poet'.[17] Until the middle of the 'thirties', Danbinov was frequently criticized as a 'national democrat', but he was respected for his great abilities as a poet and writer. He seems to have been purged at the time when Yerbanov and his supporters were liquidated. His name is omitted from the section of the new edition of the *Soviet Encyclopedia* which deals with the development of Buryat literature. A similar fate befell all other Buryat poets and writers who founded the modern Buryat literature such as Baradiin, Namzhilon and Bazaron. These representatives of 'kulak-noyon* literature', who defended the interests of the Buryat steppe against those of the Russian Bolshevik towns, were all tolerated as long as there were no proletarian Buryat writers but as soon as a proletarian Soviet literature in the Buryat language had grown in communist hot-houses, the nationalist pan-Mongolist writers were doomed to silence.

Pan-Mongolism also strongly affected linguistic problems. Buryat nationalist writers and intellectuals, whilst stressing the cultural differences between themselves and the Russians, endeavoured to draw closer to the Khalka-Mongols of Outer Mongolia. They replenished the Buryat-Mongol language with expressions borrowed from the Khalka-Mongol language and tried to adapt the phonetics, syntax and morphology of Buryat-Mongol to Khalka-Mongol in the expectation that the latter might become the literary la guage common to all Mongol peoples.

Grammars and dictionaries of this artificial Khalka-Buryat synthetic language were published in 1932, but the Communist Party opposed this attempt at linguistic pan-Mongolism. The new language was banned, and the dialect spoken in Southern Buryatia was chosen as the basis of the literary language.[18]

Great pains were taken by the Soviet authorities to eliminate from the officially recognized Buryat language all Mongol expressions for political terms, and to replace them by international and Russian words. It was feared that the sense of the basic notions of communist propaganda

* The 'Noyony' are the members of the tribal aristocracy of the Buryats, Kalmucks and other Mongol peoples.

might be distorted if they were taken from the vocabulary of the 'feudal Mongol language'. There was reason for this anxiety. The Mongol word for 'dictatorship', for instance, meant 'government maintaining itself in power by violence'. This may have been, from the Soviet standpoint, quite permissible if referring to a foreign dictatorship, but it was also applied to the 'dictatorship of the proletariat' existing in Russia, and, in this case, the Mongol term meant an open attack on the Soviet régime.

IDEOLOGICAL STRUGGLES IN THE POST-WAR PERIOD

During and after the Second World War, Buryat-Mongolia, as many other national territories, experienced a certain nationalist revival which found a visible expression in literature. As late as December 1950, the Party secretary of the B.M.A.S.S.R. stated: 'The writers' organization of the Republic committed in the post-war period various serious ideological mistakes. Bourgeois-nationalist elements in their books expressed enthusiasm about the archaic period in which feudal lords and khans ruled. They tried to give a picture full of deceit of the relations between the Mongols and the Russians. The Party helped the writers of the Republic to unmask the exponents of bourgeois-nationalist distortions in literature and to purge them.[19] A year after this statement was made, official quarters still referred to the 'considerable amount of work' which the communist organizations of Buryat-Mongolia carried out to expose 'bourgeois-nationalist and cosmopolitan distortions in the study of Buryat-Mongol history and in literature and art'.[20]

The main target of the campaign against Buryat-Mongol cultural nationalism in the post-war period was, however, not a living poet and writer, but the legendary national hero of the Mongols, 'Geser'. The legend of 'Geser' is several centuries old. In 1715 it was put into print for the first time in the form of an epic. It has always enjoyed great popularity with the Mongols, not only with the Buryats, but also with the people of Mongolia proper. Originally, the Soviet Government and the Communist Party thought it wise to respect 'Geser', and to identify the epic as the expression of an age-long dream of the people about happiness and a better life. Such a positive view was still held in 1948. The publication of the full Russian text of 'Geser' was prepared for the twenty-fifth anniversary of the B.M.A.S.S.R., which was celebrated in June of that year.[21] Also in 1948 the All-Union Academy of Sciences published a book on 'Geser' which was a eulogy of the 'Epic of the Mongol People'. Only in the latter part of 1948 did the Party start challenging 'Geser' as a symbol of feudalism, pan-Mongolism and religious prejudice. The mythical 'Geser', it was suddenly stated, was none other than Genghis Khan and a Genghis Khan cult in disguise could not be tolerated.[22]

The ban against the 'Geser' cult was such an important event in the life of Buryat-Mongolia that it could not be enforced by an order alone. The provincial committee of the Party, in conjunction with the local Union of Soviet Writers, therefore organized a 'discussion'. As usual in the case of such discussions, it was not intended to establish the truth on the problem in question. The 'discussion' was primarily a manœuvre by which pan-Mongol intellectuals were forced into the open. Those who came out in defence of 'Geser' were, of course, labelled as reactionaries and nationalists.

A 'NEW' IDEOLOGY FOR THE BURYATS

However absurd the official attacks on 'Geser' might appear, they are extremely logical from the point of view of the régime. A young Buryat who gets enthusiastic about the exploits of 'Geser' has not the approach befitting a Soviet citizen and patriot. The Soviet régime wants the young generation of the Buryats not to look towards feudal Mongol history, but to focus attention on the positive sides of their association with Russia. It is no longer advisable for a Buryat to lay stress on the wrongs which the Czarist régime did to his people by expelling them from their best lands. The Buryat-Mongol people are now taught to consider even Czarist Russia as a friend. This is the essence of the new historical concept which the Buryats had to endorse in a 'Letter to Stalin'. 'Until the Transbaikal region became united with the Russians', the letter said, 'the Buryat-Mongols were the victims of systematic raids carried out by the savage hordes of the Mongol-Manchurian Khans and feudal lords. These raids were so frequent that complete annihilation threatened the Buryat-Mongol people. The union of Transbaikalia with Russia saved the Buryat-Mongols from this fate.'[23]

In line with this conception, the young generation of the Buryats has been urged to turn away from 'Geser' to Peter the Great. A collector of Buryat folklore conveniently discovered a Buryat ballad paying tribute to the Russian Czar for assistance granted to the Buryat people. The ballad refers to the chiefs of eleven Buryat clans who, in 1703, sent a delegation to Peter asking him to protect them against unjust demands, levies and oppression on the part of Chinese officials. Peter granted their request, and a few years later sent his ambassador, Count Ragozinsky, into the Transbaikal region to fix the Russian-Chinese border in such a way as to include the Buryats, beyond any doubt, in the Russian Empire.

Apart from Peter the Great, there is another 'hero' to whom Soviet Russian propaganda in the Buryat-Mongol A.S.S.R., has attached considerable symbolic importance – Dorzhi Banzarov, 'the first Buryat scholar' (1822-1855). Banzarov demonstrated through his whole life that the place of the Buryat intelligentsia is on the side of the Russians. His biography is striking evidence of the absence of any racial discrimination in the old Russia. The Mongol village boy, Dorzhi, attended a grammar-school together with Russian boys. Later, he studied at Kazan University, and, at the age of 26, was made an official attached to the Governor-General of Eastern Siberia. Shortly before his death, Banzarov became a member of the Irkutsk branch of the Russian Geographical Society, and a splendid career, both as a scholar and civil servant, might have been in store for him had he not died prematurely.[24]

The story of Banzarov is certainly a good and useful one from the point of view of the Soviet régime, but will it be sufficient to bring about the triumph of the new ideology? Will it be able to efface the entire historical traditions of the Buryat-Mongols to a greater degree than abstract Marxist internationalism was able to do?

II. THE MONGOL PEOPLE'S REPUBLIC

The Mongol People's Republic, as big as France, Spain, Portugal, Great Britain and Ireland put together, occupies a unique position in Soviet nationalities policy. The Republic is formally outside the political framework of the Soviet Union, but it cannot be described accurately as a sovereign state. The experiment with the M.P.R. has shown that a state can be, in all essentials, a copy of the Soviet Republics proper, without being formally annexed by the Union and transformed into a fully fledged Soviet Republic.

MONGOLIA'S PLACE IN THE STRATEGY AND THEORY OF WORLD COMMUNISM

Both the Comintern and the Soviet Government thought originally that the example of the Mongol People's Republic might be followed by territories in other parts of the world. Bohumil Smeral, one of the leaders of world communism in the inter-war period, wrote in the official organ of the Communist International in 1930: 'The colonies can learn a great deal from what is taking place in the independent Mongol People's Republic. The M.P.R. is an interesting proof of how a backward people, which until recently lived the life of nomads, is making rapid progress while avoiding the purgatory of capitalism, because it is led by a national revolutionary party which is benefiting from the experiences of the Russian October Revolution.'[25]

Contrary to the expectation of the Comintern the example of the M.P.R. made little impact on colonial territories, but certain features of the Mongolian prototype were, nevertheless, widely imitated. After the Second World War, the model of the M.P.R. influenced the development in the new People's Democracies of Eastern Europe and East Asia. Of course, it could not be a one-hundred-per-cent imitation. Mongolia, a country of cattle-breeders, could not put into effect one of the most fundamental principles of Leninism, the leadership of the proletariat over all other classes of society, peasantry in particular. Soviet politicians in practice, and sociologists in theory, have found ways and means of filling the void in the proletarian hegemony in Mongolia. Since the Mongol proletariat could not lead the transformation of Mongolia into a socialist State, for the simple reason that such a proletariat did not exist, the Russian proletariat had to take over this task. As the Soviet academician, E. M. Zhukov, the Director of the Oriental Institute of the Soviet Academy of Sciences put it, 'the constant disinterested assistance as well as the ideological and political support of the Soviet Union ensured the necessary proletarian leadership for the Mongolian people's régime.'[26] In other words, Mongolia is the classic example of the fact that proletarian leadership in a given 'People's Democracy' need not necessarily exist inside the country, but can be imposed from without. 'The whole teaching of the non-capitalist path of development', says Zhukov, 'lies precisely in the fact that the working class of the land of victorious socialism (i.e., Soviet Russia) takes upon itself the leadership of a backward country with a peasant population.' The history of the Mongolian People's Republic is, therefore, a warning to all peasant countries, particularly those of Asia, against the danger of a Russian 'proletarian imperialism'.

OUTER MONGOLIA AND CZARIST RUSSIA

In the same way as Russian interest in Eastern European countries such as Bulgaria, Rumania and Poland, did not suddenly awake under the Soviet régime, so, too, in Outer Mongolia, Soviet Russian policy has a historical background. This means that the somewhat crude europeanization of this Far Eastern country should not be attributed to communism only, but should rather be interpreted as the work of Russian civilization.

The Russians started economic penetration into Mongolia in 1860 with the foundation of the first Russian business firm in Urga.* By 1910 twenty Russian firms were established in the Mongol capital, but not until Russia obtained political control over Outer Mongolia could she exercise a serious influence on the Mongols. The establishment of political control over Outer Mongolia did not mean a step forward for Russia; it was a consequence of her failure to become a strong Pacific power. Outer Mongolia was a consolation prize which Japan granted

* In 1924 Urga changed its name into 'Ulan-Bator-khoto' or 'Town of the Red Hero'. It is usually called Ulan Bator.

129

Russia for the loss of Port Arthur and Southern Sakhalin by a secret treaty concluded in 1907. The 'concession' could be made the more easily as Japan obtained, on the same occasion, Russia's recognition of the extension of her own zone of influence into Inner Mongolia. A formal treaty between Russia and Outer Mongolia, concluded on November 3rd, 1912, established the Russian protectorate over the country. The treaty reduced Chinese sovereignty over Outer Mongolia to an empty legal fiction, and excluded both Chinese colonization and Chinese influence.

A total transformation of Mongol society was required if Mongolia were to become a factor in world economy, and if the Mongols were to work for the 'White Czar' and for their own advancement. The Mongols, whose ancestors had been the 'vilest butchers of their fellow-men' and the most blood-thirsty warriors of history, had lost their warlike spirit under the influence of Buddhism and succumbed to total lethargy. Caruthers in his book, *Unknown Mongolia*, showed convincingly how the 'indolent life of the lamaseries, the Buddhist monasteries, became the life of the Mongol people as a whole'. Lamaism not only determined the character of the Mongol people but also affected unfavourably Mongol economy. The principle of inactivity inherent in lamaism prevented the development of cattle farming, the economic backbone of Outer Mongolia.[27]

Several years before the Bolshevik revolution with its anti-religious bias, Caruthers forecast that russianization of Outer Mongolia would weaken the power of the Khutukhtu, the religious, and, to a large extent the political, head of the Mongols, and would also lead to an impoverishment of the lamaseries. The establishment of an 'autonomous Mongolia' under Russian protection, added Caruthers in anticipation of further developments, would bring about 'fundamental changes in the life of the people and in the future of the Mongol race'. Mongolia would thus become a 'land of activity and progress' instead of a 'land of stagnation and suppression'.

Any Russian State interested in Outer Mongolia as a huge cattle reserve and as a military base, was bound to awaken Mongol activity. Any Russian State, regardless of its ideological complexion, was bound either to do away with the Khutukhtu, 'the Khan of Outer Mongolia' as he was also called, or to transform him into an instrument of Russian policy. No dual loyalties could be tolerated if Outer Mongolia were to be a *de facto* Russian possession.

The Khutukhtu proved to be an obstacle to Russian policy from the moment that Russia gained political control over Outer Mongolia. He manifested his desire to have Japan rather than Russia as overlord. Towards the end of 1913, he wrote a letter to the Tenno asking him to assist the Mongols in uniting Outer and Inner Mongolia, and to send a

Japanese diplomatic agent Urga. As Russia was then in charge of Outer Mongolia's foreign relations, it developed upon the Russian Ambassador in Tokyo, Malevsky-Malevich, to hand over the Khutukhtu letter to the Japanese Foreign Minister, Baron Makino. Malevsky-Malevich loyally complied with the request, but the Japanese Government asked him to return the letter to the Khutukhtu, as Japan's aspirations did not then embrace Outer Mongolia. The Czarist Government was magnanimous enough not to take the matter too seriously and mildly warned the Mongols to let the incident be a lesson to them.[28]

THE FOUNDATION OF THE M.P.R.

The history of Outer Mongolia under Soviet rule shows that the Soviet Government was more efficient but less liberal than the preceding Czarist régime, in its relations with the Mongols. It is not easy to give a proper outline of this history. The sources are not only very meagre, but also full of contradictions, for the history of the Mongol People's Republic has been officially rewritten in the same way as has the history of the Russian October Revolution and of the Soviet Union. In the case of Outer Mongolia the 'rewriting' has been more successful because the new official history of the Mongol revolutionary movement, and of the M.P.R. itself, cannot easily be contradicted. There is no Mongol Trotzky who has acquainted the outside world with his own version, nor has a foreign observer had an opportunity to follow the crucial periods of Mongol history day by day. However, various material in Russian periodicals of the early 'twenties' makes it possible to reconstruct at least to some extent the origins of the first 'People's Republic'. This material clearly contradicts the claim that the present 'Mongol Revolutionary People's Party' and its creation, the Mongol Republic, owe their existence to two men, Sukhe Bator, the 'Mongol Lenin', and Marshal Choibalsan, the 'Mongol Stalin'.

The Mongol revolutionary movement had at least five founding fathers, and they represented various strata of Mongol society, and various ideological trends. There was the more conservative-minded Lama Chardorzhab, who had important connections with Mongolia's theocratic leadership. There was the liberal centre of the movement, represented by Lama Bodo, an employee of the Russian Consulate in Urga, and by a small official, Danzan, who was an enemy of Mongolia's theocratic rulers. There was the left, formed by Sukhe Bator, a worker in the Russian printing shop of Urga, and a very young man, Khorlogiin Choibalsan (alternative spellings – 'Chobalsan', 'Choibalsang', 'Chaibalsan') who had been educated first in a Lama monastery, and later in a Russian school at Kyakhta, on the border of Mongolia. Whatever may have been the ideological differences between the five, they were united in their desire for a far-reaching Mongol autonomy and, at least temporarily, for close links with the Russian Revolution. One of the first practical steps taken by the 'Young Mongolia' group, as it was then called, was to get in touch with Russian Bolsheviks. In 1920 the five revolutionaries went to Verkhneudinsk and met representatives of the Soviet authorities of Siberia. They also came in touch with a rather strange personality with the name of Rinchino, who described himself first as a 'Narodnik-Maximalist' and later as a 'non-party Bolshevik'. He was a convinced supporter of a communist pan-Mongolia, and played a great part in revolutionizing both the Buryats and the Khalka-Mongols. Rinchino took the Mongol delegation to Moscow, and introduced it to the Kremlin.[29] The Politbureau, including Lenin, Stalin and Bukharin, received the Mongol delegates who had been joined by Agvan Dordzhiev, head of the Buddhist community in Russia, who had once acted as a go-between the Czar Nicholas II and the Dalai Lama.

The Mongol delegates asked for Russian support for the re-establishment of the autonomous Mongol State, which after the fall of the Czarist régime had been reoccupied by the Chinese Army. Soviet Russia granted this help. Thanks to the Red Army, the Government of Mongolia was ultimately restored to the Mongols, but, prior to this, the country was still the scene of a number of dramatic incidents. Whilst the Mongol delegates were on their way back, news reached them that the white guard general, Baron Ungern-Sternberg, had captured Urga. In this situation the Mongol revolutionaries decided to set up a proper organization. In March 1921 they held the constituent congress of the Mongol Revolutionary People's Party in Kyakhta. Only 25 to 30 people attended, but the congress was, nevertheless, a very important event. It decided to set up a Revolutionary Mongol Army, and to form a government, and it also adopted a programme of ten points. This original party programme had nothing in common with the present aims of the Mongol Revolutionary People's Party. It demanded the unification of all Mongol territories, and the formation of a pan-Mongol Republic. The congress did not declare Mongolia's complete independence from China. The delegates, including Sukhe Bator and Choibalsan, considered that the new Mongolia ought to be primarily an ally of the Chinese Revolution and only secondarily of Russian Bolshevism. A fortnight after the congress, the Central Committee of the Mongol Revolutionary People's Party issued a 'Manifesto to the entire Chinese People, to the Chinese Communist Party, and to all revolutionary-democratic groups and real patriots of China' which called for Mongol-Chinese unity of action. Both the pan-Mongol concept of the Mongol People's Party and its positive attitude towards revolutionary China, were endorsed by the Far Eastern Bureau of the Comintern.[30]

Contrary to later accounts, at the First Congress of the Mongol People's Party, Choibalsan played only a secondary role. The key positions in the Party and the State went to Danzan, who became the first party chairman, Chardorzhab, who became first prime minister, and Sukhe Bator, who was appointed commander-in-chief. There was still another person who played an outstanding part in the struggle for power that took place in Mongolia in 1921. His name was Maksarzhab; he co-operated at first with the counter-revolutionary camp, but, at the decisive moment, he deserted Baron Ungern and went over to Sukhe Bator. The Soviet Government recognized the great merits of Maksarzhab by awarding him the 'Order of the Red Banner' in 1922. The story of the involved and cunning manœuvres through which Maksarzhab helped the cause of the Mongol Revolution is told in a Mongol play, 'Khatan Bator Maksarzhab', which was produced in Ulan Bator in 1940.* Maksarzhab was not given full credit for his historic importance, but at least he was not a victim of those many purges which took place in Mongolia after the victory of the revolutionary party. As soon as the revolutionaries had captured the capital, Urga, from the white guards in July 1921, the first internal crisis broke out. Chardorzhap was replaced as prime minister by Lama Bodo. Neither did the latter remain long in power. After having been a year in office, he was not only deposed, but also executed, together with his predecessor and thirteen other prominent politicians. Bodo was accused of being too pro-Chinese, and of having sent a delegation to General Tchan-Tso-Lin to negotiate a Mongol-Chinese reunion.

Even after Bodo there was no real pro-Russian politician in the country to take over, but Mongolia at least obtained its first secular prime minister in the person of Danzan. For two years Danzan was extremely powerful. After the death of Sukhe Bator in February 1923, he also became commander-in-chief of the army. Thus he controlled the Party, The Government, and the Armed Forces. Through his close associate Bavasan, he also supervised the Mongol youth organization, the Revsomol. Danzan wanted genuine independence for Mongolia and

* Maksarzhab ,who had little connection with Russian revolutionary ideas, and who was a real home-grown Mongol revolutionary – his name figures prominently in the history of the revolution which took place in Outer Mongolia in 1911 – has had a stronger appeal to the Mongols than has the rather colourless guerilla leader, Sukhe Bator. Between 1933 and 1938, four plays about Sukhe Bator were performed on the Mongol stage. In all of them Sukhe Bator appeared as a pale figure, whilst all of them described Maksarzhab in much more lively colours. No Mongol playright who remembered the true story of the events of 1921, was able to create that exaggerated picture of Sukhe Bator's historical importance which from a pro-Soviet angle was essential. Two Russian playwrights, A. Borshchagovsky and Ya. Varshavsky, had to be commissioned, therefore, to do this and to produce an 'ideologically sound' play on Sukhe Bator. It was called *Heroes of the Steppe* and was performed in the theatre of Ulan Bator in 1942. (*Uvarova, Sovremenny Mongolsky Teatr*, 1921–1945 – 'The Contemporary Mongol Theatre, 1921–1945', Moscow-Leningrad 1945, pp. 89–91).

not a Russian protectorate. He put out feelers to China, and even to the United States, and he also tried to encourage the development of foreign trade. Formally, Outer Mongolia was then still a constitutional monarchy under the Khutukhtu Bogdo-gegen. When the monarch died in May 1924, Danzan remained, for a few days, prime minister of the Mongol People's Republic. He was overthrown by the Third Party Congress. This strangest of all party congresses transformed itself into a supreme court, sentenced Danzan to death as a plotter against Mongolia's independence, and executed him on the spot, with Bavasan, the chairman of the Revolutionary Youth League.[31]

The Soviet Government had had a hand in the execution of both Bodo and Danzan. The Third Party Congress, which liquidated the so-called 'Danzan conspiracy', carried the hallmark of direct Soviet interference. It decided that the M.P.R. should follow 'the road of a non-capitalist development', a formula which could not possibly have been coined by the Mongol lamas and cattle-breeders, who constituted the bulk of the congress delegates. It was obviously inspired by the Soviet envoy in Urga, and by Russian communist emissaries. Nevertheless, even after Danzan's death, Soviet Russia, then still under the premiership of Alexey Rykov, observed a fairly liberal attitude towards the Mongol Republic. It was still allowed to trade with foreign countries, particularly with China, Germany, the United States and Britain and to allow foreign business men to enter its territory. The country was also free to send students to German and French universities, and to conduct cultural propaganda in the capitalist West. This spell of tolerance came to an end in the winter of 1928-29, when the right-wing political leaders of the M.P.R., were exiled to Leningrad and when the Seventh Party Congress appointed a new left-wing Committee.

This time the deposed dignitaries of the People's Republic could not be charged with plotting against Mongolian independence. They were eliminated from the political scene because they were too independent-minded, adhering to the original pan-Mongolist programme of the Revolutionary People's Party. Shortly before the downfall of the right-wing leaders, a Mongol Government spokesman, the Berlin representative of the Ministry of Education of the M.P.R., Ishi Dordji, had openly admitted that pan-Mongolism was the political ideology of Ulan Bator. He stated that the 'unification of the Mongols around Outer Mongolia' was the aim which the Government and the Revolutionary People's Party of the M.P.R., pursued. 'The cultural activity conducted in Mongolia', he said, 'has its importance and is bearing its fruits far beyond the borders of autonomous Mongolia . . . Independent Mongolia, with her developed national culture and her political and economic programme, is attracting great interest among the intellectuals and youth of the other Mongols living outside Outer Mongolia'.

Ishi Dordji added, that one could meet in Ulan Bator, representatives of all kinds of Mongols ranging from the Kalmucks of the Lower Volga to the Mongols of the Yellow River. Ishi Dordji frankly expressed the view that the cultural and political revival centred in Ulan Bator would ultimately influence both the half-russianized Buryats and the half-sinicized Mongol groups in Inner Mongolia, such as the Tumets.[32]

These amazing utterances of a Mongol Government official were made in the form of an article in the review *Osteuropa*, which was probably written shortly before the purge of the pan-Mongolist elements in the M.P.R. Government, but published only after that event. The article made abundantly clear why Russia, from her own point of view, had to intervene in Ulan Bator and put new people into the Mongol Government. By the end of the 'twenties', the Soviet leaders had lost all previous illusions that pan-Mongolism could ever be used to Russia's advantage. They no longer believed that pan-Mongolism could be made a Soviet tool, or that it could serve the cause of the revolution in East Asia.

LEFT-WING EXTREMISM

When the Seventh Congress struck its blow against Mongol nationalism, the leading Party and Government circles were just about to summon to Ulan Bator a pan-Mongol congress of lamas, for the old leadership was not only nationalistic, but also friendly to Buddhism. It had not only not touched the Buddhist monasteries, owning almost one-fifth of the country's cattle, but it had even granted them loans through the State bank. The Seventh Congress completely reversed the pro-religious policy. The property of the lamaseries was taken over by the State, and a whole chain of legislative and administrative measures forced the individual lamas to return to secular life. A 'Central Anti-religious Commission' was attached to the new government of the M.P.R. to co-ordinate all measures directed against the Buddhist monasteries. It was supported by a mass organization, modelled on the 'League of Militant Godless' in the U.S.S.R.

The new leaders of Mongolia tried to copy not only the anti-religious policy of the All-Union Communist Party, but also its economic policy. It was no longer simply a question of a 'non-capitalist development'. The new slogan was 'socialist transformation of the entire economy of the country'. The transformation was to be carried out during the first Mongol Five-Year Plan, which was supposed to run from 1930 to 1935. Destruction of all private enterprise in cattle-breeding and trade was the main objective of the Mongol plan. With this aim in view, the Eighth Congress of the Mongolian People's Party in 1930, which was entirely dominated by 'left-wing extremists', decided to found collective farms on the Soviet pattern. The decision was implemented so hurriedly that 35 per cent of all cattle-breeder families had joined the new 'Kolkhozy' by 1931. The Russian communist Press, far from disapproving this new course, welcomed it enthusiastically.

This Soviet enthusiasm for the new left-wing trend in Mongolia was of short duration, for it very soon had the most disastrous results. If rapid collectivization was a mistake in the Soviet Union, it was even more out of place in Mongolia. Within two years the number of cattle dropped from 23·4 millions in 1930 to 16 millions in 1932. The crisis of cattle-breeding, and the impoverishment of the population ensuing from it, were made worse by the decline of trade and transport. Private trade had been forcibly liquidated, and the state and co-operative enterprises were not able to cope with their increased responsibilities and to provide goods in adequate quantities. The same was true of transport. The Government had rendered the work of private camel transport undertakings impossible, without developing motor transport on a corresponding scale. Finally, the Mongol State farms, which had been formed on the model of the Russian *Sovkhozy*, could be kept going only at the price of heavy losses to the public finances. Thus, the activities of the left-wing régime brought nothing but misery to the people and bankruptcy to the State.

As popular risings became increasingly frequent in all parts of the country, and as the general situation in East Asia became more and more threatening, Moscow decided to reverse once again its policy in Mongolia. Through the personal intervention of Stalin, the 'left-wing adventurers' were ousted from the Party and the Government. The implementation of the Five-Year Plan was stopped. The collective farms and State farms were liquidated. Private trade was re-introduced. The anti-religious campaign lost in momentum.* On the whole there was a return to sanity. This new policy was not initiated by a congress of the Mongolian Revolutionary People's Party. The Party was in too much chaos to allow for the election of delegates. The new line was decided at an extraordinary meeting of the Central Committee and the Central Control Commission of the Party, and a new congress, the

---

* Legal discrimination against Buddhist ecclesiastical dignitaries continued in the M.P.R. longer than in the Soviet Union. The Mongol Constitution of 1940 expressly deprived higher lamas of their voting rights. No such limitation was inserted into the Stalin Constitution of Soviet Russia which came into effect in 1936. When high ecclesiastical dignitaries in Soviet Russia were used for propaganda purposes, the Mongol Government adapted its policy to the Soviet model. In September 1944, the constitution of Mongolia was revised, and voting rights were granted to such categories of people as had been deprived of them for political reasons, the members of the Buddhist hierarchy included. The head of the Buddhist ecclesiastic organization in the M.P.R. then started to play a part in official propaganda similar to that of the Patriarch of Moscow and all Russia in the Soviet Union. During the 1945 plebiscite campaign, he was reported to have 'prayed for the prosperity of the independent Mongolian People's Republic'. (*Soviet Monitor*, October 22nd, 1945.)

ninth, was not summoned until two years later when order was more or less restored in the country.

MONGOLIA AND JAPAN

In this new period which started in June 1932, all references to a 'socialist transformation' of Mongolia were dropped. 'All-round strengthening of Mongol independence' became the chief slogan. Reasons of foreign policy played a considerable part in this change of tactics. In 1931, Japan had started the conquest of Manchuria, and from year to year, even from month to month, the Japanese armies were becoming more threatening in the Mongol-Manchurian border areas. There were signs of Japan conducting an active Mongol policy. A Mongol Office was attached to the Japanese puppet government of Manchukuo. The Hsingan Province of Manchuria, bordering on both Outer and Inner Mongolia, was transformed into an autonomous Mongol territory where Mongol princes were in charge of the administration under Japanese supervision. In 1937, Japan further extended its co-prosperity sphere by installing in Inner Mongolia a puppet government under Prince Teh.

Moscow reacted to the Japanese challenge by strengthening the ties between the M.P.R. and the Soviet Union. On March 12th, 1936, the Soviet-Mongol Mutual Assistance Treaty was concluded. The most outstanding feature of the treaty was that it no longer mentioned the formal Chinese sovereignty over Outer Mongolia which the previous Russian-Mongol Alliance Treaty had still recognized. Despite the existence of the new treaty, the Soviet Government was still not satisfied with the situation in the M.P.R., and continued to harbour a deep distrust of most Mongol leaders. The Kremlin overrated most probably, the cleverness of the Japanese in handling the Mongol issue, and believed in the possibility of the emergence of a 'Japanese Party' in Outer Mongolia. In 1932, it is true, there had been a pro-Japanese rising in the M.P.R., but since then the situation had changed thoroughly. While in occupation of Manchukuo, the Japanese mismanaged the Mongol problem completely. They showed as little understanding of the mentality and the point of view of the Mongols as the German Nazis had shown to the peoples of the western borderlands of Soviet Russia when occupying those borderlands during the Second World War. In the Mongol territories of Manchukuo there was a 'strong anti-Japanese mood' which led to the execution of Mongol ministers, and other Mongol dignitaries by the Kwantung Army.[33]

THE MURDER OF MARSHAL DEMID AND THE
TRIUMPH OF MARSHAL CHOIBALSAN

Although the Japanese had forfeited such sympathies as they might have had in the M.P.R., the Kremlin continued to fear that some of the leaders of the Mongol Government and the Party, in a moment of crisis, might prefer Asiatics to Russians as their supreme masters. This led to a new decisive change of régime in Ulan Bator, during which Choibalsan, the head of the Russian party, became the ruler of the country. Choibalsan had shown his loyalty to Soviet Russia in many instances, particularly in 1936 when he frustrated Japan's attempts 'to throw the door open into Outer Mongolia'. Making use of a number of incidents on the Manchukuo border, the High Command of the Kwantung 'Army then demanded the admission into the M.P.R. of Japanese military observers and of a Manchukuo consul. Certain of Russian support, Choibalsan braved the Japanese pressure. In his capacity of Foreign Minister, he emphatically rejected the Japanese demands. The War Minister, Marshal Demid, and the Prime Minister, Gendun, until then the strong men of Outer Mongolia, remained on that occasion in the background.

At the time when the purge in Soviet Russia reached its climax, Demid, Gendun, and his successor, Amor, were 'liquidated' and later referred to as 'enemies of the people'. The greatest sensation of all was caused by the disappearance of Marshal Demid who had met with sudden death when travelling to Moscow by the Trans-Siberian express. A statement issued by the official Soviet news agency said that Demid had died from poisoned food on August 22nd, 1937, near the railway station of Taiga, which is a few miles west of Tomsk. Together with Demid died Dzhansankorlo, a divisional commander of the Mongolian Army. Three other members of his entourage, a major and his wife and an official of the Mongol Legation in Moscow, were also poisoned but were rescued 'thanks to efficient medical assistance'. The mortal remains of the Marshal were not taken back to Mongolia which would have been the normal thing. They travelled all the way through Western Siberia and a large part of European Russia until they reached Moscow where they were cremated on the day of arrival. The Soviet authorities marked the occasion by organizing an impressive mourning ceremony in the Russian capital. Mongol and Soviet flags were lowered to half-mast, two cavalry squadrons and one artillery battery of the Red Army stood to attention. Prominent representatives of the Soviet People's Commissariats of Foreign Affairs and National Defence delivered funeral speeches.

All this – the death of Demid, the arrival of the corpse and the funeral speeches–was reported in one single issue of *Pravda* (August 29th, 1937), which also reassured the Mongols that the investigation into all circumstances connected with Demid's death would continue. But nothing further was heard about the whole affair which must have aroused the gravest suspicions throughout Mongolia. The tragic death of Marshal Demid, whose pictures could be seen throughout Outer Mongolia, was in all probability closely connected with the Tukhachevsky affair. All the defence arrangements for Outer Mongolia had been planned in agreement between Marshal Demid and Marshal Tukhachevsky. In view of the dependence of the Mongol Army on the Red Army, Marshal Demid could be nothing else than Tukhachevsky's local representative and had to share his fate.

Demid was hardly a 'Japanese agent', but he was certainly a staunch Mongol nationalist, more attracted by the tradition of Genghis Khan than by Marxism-Leninism. This is borne out by frequently-quoted passages of a speech which the Marshal delivered in 1934 at the Ninth Congress of the Revolutionary People's Party: 'The whole world knows that at the time of Genghis Khan, the Mongol Army distinguished itself by its impetuous attacks on the enemy. Today, when our country finds itself on the way towards national rebirth, we are strengthening in our army again this fine feature of Genghis Khan's forces, so that we can give a worthy answer to the enemy if he tries to attack us.'[34]

After the death of Demid, there were still other Mongols in leading positions to whom Genghis Khan was a greater object of veneration than Stalin. To get rid of these nationalists and romantics, Choibalsan had to purge once more the intellectual elite of the M.P.R. including the 'Academic Committee',* which co-ordinated scientific research work throughout the country. This happened in 1938. Little, if any, documentary evidence about this purge has penetrated into the outside world, but a Russian writer, Mikhail Kolesnikov, dealt with the problem of Mongolia's anti-Soviet intelligentsia in his revealing novel, *The Happy Oasis*. The main theme of the book is a conspiracy of Mongol nationalists who enjoy both Japanese and American support. One of the principal plotters is a learned Mongol, a graduate of Cambridge University, with the name of 'Zhamtso',† whom the Government had appointed to the post of President of the 'Academic Committee'. The opening chapter of the novel includes a conversation between Marshal Choibalsan and a Russian scholar whom Kolesnikov calls 'Andrey Makarovich Turanov', but who in reality is presumably A. Ya. Tugarinov, a Soviet zoologist who worked for many years in Mongolia. Here is a short extract from the dialogue which, with remarkable frank-

* The verbatim translation of the official Mongol title of this body is 'Committee of Books and Letters'.
† His real name was Zhamtsarano, a Buryat by origin and former professor of Irkutsk University.

ness, admits Russian interference in the affairs of the 'Academic Committee':

"Choibalsan asked unexpectedly –
'What do you think of the work of our Academic Committee and in particular of the chairman of the Committee, Zhamtso?'
The question did not find Turanov unprepared. During a week's stay in Mongolia he had succeeded in getting well-acquainted with the work of the Academic Committee. Scientific work was conducted in an unsatisfactory way. The chairman, Zhamtso, suppressed the valuable initiative of young scholars. The funds assigned by the State were not spent in accordance with the provisions of the budget. He was not interested in the requirements of contemporary life.
'It seems to me that the work of the Academic Committee is conducted in a somewhat one-sided way' answered Turanov.
'What do you mean?'
'Well, my main contention is, of course, that the objects of the scientific research work of the Academic Committee and the problems which it solves have little connection with the practical interests of the State.'
'But the Academic Committee has accomplished a great work', interjected the Prime Minister, 'scientific research sections have been formed for various branches of study; philology, history, geology. A network of meteorological stations has come into being. A State library has been established which has now 200,000 volumes. Has all this really no connection with practical interests?'
'Oh yes, it has, but all this is not enough. I am speaking from the point of view of the programme of your party.'
Choibalsan's face assumed a thoughtful expression.
'You are quite right, Andrey Makarovich. It is not enough. Even worse than that. The Academic Committee spends the tremendous funds that are at its disposal in a completely unrational way. Not so long ago, Zhamtso submitted a plan to the Government suggesting the restoration of the ancient Mongol capital of Karakorum, the monastery of Erdeni Tszu and other monuments of the former greatness of Mongolia.'[35]"

The ruins of Karakorum, which was the capital of Genghis Khan, were discovered in 1889 by the Russian archæologist, N. M. Yadrintsev. From the Soviet point of view it would have been better if the ruins of the Mongol cultural and political centre had never been found at all. Their existence has served as an inspiration to Mongol nationalism and to pan-Mongol ideas, and, according to Kolesnikov's novel, they have also diverted the attention of certain Mongol intellectuals from practical economic tasks. Neither Choibalsan nor his Russian advisers could reconcile themselves to such an outlook and Kolesnikov's novel terminates, therefore, quite logically with the reorganization and purge of the 'Academic Committee'.

CHOIBALSAN'S 'FOREIGN POLICY'

Under Choibalsan's rule, the ties between Russia and the M.P.R. were greatly strengthened. The Mongol National Revolutionary Army and the Red Army virtually became one. The Japanese, who between May and August 1939, provoked a number of major border incidents in the area of the Khalkin-Gol River, had to learn by experience that the Soviet-Mongol alliance was something very real. Official Soviet reports on the incidents indiscriminately used such terms as 'Mongol-Soviet forces', 'Soviet-Mongol artillery' and 'Mongol-Soviet air force'. There is, indeed, no doubt that the Japanese attacks were warded off by both Mongol and Soviet troops and that the former lost 1,131 men in the operations. According to an official Soviet version, 25,000 Japanese were killed in the battles on the Khalkin-Gol River.[36]

When hostilities broke out between Germany and the U.S.S.R., the M.P.R. did not join the war officially, nor did it send any troops to the front, but it helped the Soviet Union in every other way. The Mongols had to work hard in order to supply the Red Army with everything that their country had to offer. Here is a short list of what the Mongols sent to the front: 60,000 horses, 47,000 sheepskin coats, 51,000 fur jackets, 60,000 pairs of felt boots, 'and many other valuable things'.[37]

In addition, the Mongols sent 28,000 so-called 'individual presents' to Soviet soldiers and officers. Throughout the war the M.P.R. also had the patronage of a tank brigade, 'Revolutionary Mongolia', and of an air squadron, 'The Mongol Arat'.* It is not quite clear what the word 'patronage' entailed in these two cases, but it is a safe assumption that it was a rather costly affair, and that both the brigade and the squadron were financed and supplied out of Mongol State funds.

It does not seem that these material sacrifices were gladly accepted by the Mongols, particularly not in the early part of the war when the Soviet armies suffered defeat. The initial victories of Germany are likely to have provoked some doubts in Mongolia about the wisdom of Choibalsan's policy of Mongol-Soviet co-operation. Opposition re-emerged within the Party. In the years 1942 and 1943 it was again purged from 'alien and unsuitable elements'.[38] Later in the war when the military situation was reversed Choibalsan recovered his prestige and 10,000 new members joined the Party ranks. The popularity

---

* The original meaning of the term 'arat' (new Mongol spelling 'ard') is nomadic toiling cattle-breeder. It is now applied to the entire working population of Mongolia and in its widest sense it simply means the whole Mongol people.

of the régime was further enhanced by the so-called Soviet-Japanese War of August 1945 in which the Mongol army, then 80,000 men strong, played an active part. The M.P.R. proclaimed a 'Holy War' against Japan, and the Mongolian army suffered 675 casualties in the campaign. However small this contribution might have been, Mongolia got ample credit for it. Stalin's Order of the Day of August 23rd, 1945, announcing the capitulation of the Kwantung army mentioned the 'Mongolian army under Marshal Choibalsan' twice, and stated expressly that the 24 artillery salvoes from 324 guns which were fired in Moscow in honour of the victory saluted both the Soviet and the Mongol troops.

The next event in Mongolia's history was a farce, namely, a plebiscite about the independence of the M.P.R. The plebiscite was carried out on October 21st, 1945, in compliance with an agreement which the Soviet Government had concluded with the Chiang Kai-shek régime on August 14th, of the same year. The plebiscite was arranged for purely formal reasons; it was to end, from the point of view of international law, Mongolia's theoretical inclusion in the Chinese Republic. On the basis of Mongol constitutional law, Mongolia had been independent ever since the adoption of the constitution of June 30th, 1940, which had proclaimed Mongolia an 'independent state'. There was nobody in Mongolia who would have dared to oppose the so-called independence of the M.P.R. at the plebiscite, and not a single person voted against it, not even one of the numerous Chinese working in Ulan Bator.

The Mongol-Soviet relations of the post-war period were regulated by two treaties which were concluded in February, 1946. They were not very explicit in their wording, but they provided, in fact, for a total co-operation between the two countries in the military, economic and cultural spheres. One of the treaties referred to detailed agreements which were to be entered into by the various economic and cultural organizations directly. These special agreements have never been published, but it may be taken for granted that all important Soviet State institutions have by now established direct contact with the corresponding institutions of the M.P.R.

THE NEW CONSTITUTION

As far as the internal development of the M.P.R. is concerned the Choibalsan régime narrowed down the differences in the political structure between Mongolia and the Soviet Unicn. Choibalsan and his associates gave the M.P.R. a new constitution which is largely identical with the constitutions of the thirty-two Soviet Republics and Autonomous Soviet Republics of the U.S.S.R.

The constitutional reform was carried out in two stages. Most of the provisions of the constitution now in force were adopted as early as 1940 by the Tenth Party Congress, but in February 1949 this original text was redrafted and altered in a number of essential points. Under the 1940 constitution there existed two national assemblies, the 'Little Khural', which performed the ordinary legislative work, and the 'Grand National Khural' which was summoned only for the discussion of fundamental problems of policy. The 1949 version of the constitution abolished this dualism. It vested all legislative power in the Grand National Khural, which now fully corresponds to the Supreme Councils (Soviets) of the Republics forming the Soviet Union. Moreover, the 1940 constitution provided for indirect elections to the central legislature, and to the provincial (aimak) and district (somon) councils. The revised text of the constitution introduced direct elections on all levels, including the election of judges of the lower courts, exactly as in the Soviet constitution of 1936.

A minor change concerned Outer Mongolia's national flag. Article 93 of the 1940 constitution said that the flag of the Mongol People's Republic should consist of a red cloth. Article 106 of the amended constitution stipulated that the Mongol national colours should be red-blue-red. Here, at least, Mongolia seems at first sight to depart from the Soviet model, for, until 1949, all Soviet Republics had the plain red flag as their 'national' symbol. But the Kremlin has decided that there is no need for a uniformity of symbols as long as there is uniformity of policy. Since 1949 one Soviet Republic after another has been allowed to change the red banner for a red-blue one or a red-green one, with the red colour always comprising two-thirds of the whole flag. Thus, what appeared at first as a special concession to Mongolia has also been granted to the official member States of the Soviet Union.

Apart from small variations of terminology there is only one fundamental difference between the Mongol and the Soviet constitutions. The constitutions of the Soviet Republics proper are constitutions of countries where, in the official view, socialism is a reality, while the Mongol constitution is one of a country which is moving on a non-capitalist road, but where socialism is still an aim for the future. Soviet sociologists and experts on the Far East have been unable to agree so far as to whether Mongolia has really marched on the way to socialism since the adoption of the 1940 constitution. One school of thought considers that the anti-feudal programme of the Mongol Revolution was exhausted by 1940, and that since then Mongol socialism has been developing. The protagonists of this concept have shown, with the help of statistics, that the socialist sector already plays an important part in many branches of Mongol economy.

The other, and more authoritative, group of sociologists and experts believes that the 'struggle against remnants of feudalism in the economy and the minds of the people' is still not terminated. This view is held, by among others, academician E. M. Zhukov, who, in November 1951, stressed at a conference in the Oriental Institute of the All-Union Academy of Sciences that the existing level of industrial development was not capable of ensuring the transition of the bulk of Mongol livestock breeders to a collective economy.[39]

The following comparison between ten characteristic articles which are contained in both the Mongol and Buryat-Mongol constitutions, shows to what extent Choibalsan copied the Soviet original.

CONSTITUTION OF THE MONGOL PEOPLE'S REPUBLIC.	CONSTITUTION OF THE BURYAT-MONGOL A.S.S.R.
Article 3.	*Article 3*
All power in the Mongol People's Republic belongs to the working people of town and khudon as represented by the *Khurals** of Working People's Deputies.	All power in the Buryat-Mongol A.S.S.R. belongs to the working people of town, ulus and village as represented by the *Soviets** of Working People's Deputies.
Article 5.	*Article 6.*
All the land and its natural resources, forests, waters and all the wealth contained therein, factories, mills, mines, gold production, rail, automobile, water and air transport, means of communication, banks, *Hay-Cutting Stations** and State farms are State property, that is, belong to the people as a whole. Private ownership of the above is forbidden.	The land, its natural resources, waters, forests, mills factories, rail, water and air transport, banks, means of communication, large State organized agricultural enterprises (State farms, *Machine Tractor Stations** and the like) as well as municipal enterprises and *the bulk of the dwelling houses in the cities and industrial localities,** are State property, that is, belong to the people as a whole.
Article 34	*Article 39.*
The Council of Ministers of the M.P.R. is for its activity responsible and accountable to the *Grand National Khural** and in the intervals between sessions to the *Presidium of the Grand National Khural.**	The Council of Ministers of the Buryat-Mongol A.S.S.R. is responsible and accountable to the *Supreme Soviet** of the B.M.A.S.S.R. and in the intervals between sessions to the *Presidium of the Supreme Soviet of the B.M.A.S.S.R.**
Article 67.	*Article 80.*
Judges are independent and subject only to the law.	Judges are independent and subject only to the law.

144

Article 71.

Local Public Prosecutors exercise their functions independently of any local organs whatsoever, being subordinate solely to the Public Prosecutor of the Republic.

Article 85.

The organs of the Public Prosecutor's Office exercise their functions independently of any local organs whatsoever, being subordinate solely to the Prosecutor-General of the U.S.S.R. and the Public Prosecutor of the R.S.F.S.R.

Article 86.

Candidates for elections are nominated by electoral constituencies. The right to nominate candidates is secured to public organizations and societies of the working people: the organizations of the *Revolutionary People's Party** co-operatives, trade unions, youth organizations, Arat unions and cultural societies.

Article 109.

Candidates for elections are nominated by electoral constituencies. The right to nominate candidates is secured to public organizations and societies of the working people: the organizations of the *Communist Party,** trade unions, co-operative societies, youth organizations, and cultural societies.

Article 95.

In conformity with the interests of the working people, and in order to develop the organizational initiative and political activity of the toiling masses, the citizens of the M.P.R. are ensured the right to unite in public organizations: trade unions, co-operative organizations, youth organizations, sport and defence organizations, cultural, technical and scientific societies; and the most active and politically-conscious citizens in the ranks of the workers, toiling arats and intellectuals, are united in the *Mongol Revolutionary People's Party,** which is the vanguard of the working people in their struggle to strengthen and develop the country *along non-capitalistic lines,** into a party which is the leading core of all organizations of the working people, both public and State.

Article 93.

In conformity with the interests of the working people, and in order to develop the organizational initiative and political activity of the toiling masses, the citizens of the B.M.A.S.S.R. are ensured the right to unite in public organizations, trade unions, co-operative organizations, youth organizations, sport and defence organizations, cultural, technical and scientific societies; and the most active and politically-conscious citizens in the ranks of the working class and other sections of the working people unite in the *Communist Party of the Soviet Union,** which is the vanguard of the working people in their struggle to strengthen and develop *the socialist system,** and is the leading core of all organizations of the working people, both public and State.

* The italics are the author's.

145

Article 101.	Article 96.
The M.P.R. affords the right of asylum to foreign citizens persecuted for defending the interests of the working people, or for their struggle for national liberation.	The B.M.A.S.S.R. affords the right of asylum to foreign citizens persecuted for defending the interests of the working people, or for scientific activities or for struggling for national liberation.

Article 103.	Article 99.
Compulsory military service is law. Military service in the Mongol People's Revolutionary Army is an honourable duty for the citizens of the M.P.R.	Compulsory military service is law. Military service in the Armed Forces of the U.S.S.R. is an honourable duty for the citizens of the B.M.A.S.S.R.

Article 104.	Article 100.
The defence of the motherland is the sacred duty of every citizen of the M.P.R. Treason against the motherland – violation of the oath, desertion to the enemy, impairing the military power of the state and espionage – is punishable as the most heinous of crimes.	To defend the motherland is the sacred duty of every citizen of the B.M.A.S.S.R. Treason against the motherland – violation of the oath, desertion to the enemy, impairing the military power of the state and espionage – is punishable as the most heinous of crimes.[40]

The statute of the Revolutionary People's Party which its Tenth Congress adopted in 1940, copied that of the Soviet Communist Party as closely as the Mongol constitution imitated the Soviet constitution. The Tenth Mongol Congress walked in the footsteps of the Eighteenth Congress of the Soviet communists of March 1939. Like its great example, it was a landmark in the Party's history and was followed by an organizational strengthening of the Party ranks. Between the Tenth and the Eleventh Congress in 1947, the Party increased its membership from 14,000 to 28,000.* The Soviet Communist Party also doubled its membership during this period.

CHOIBALSAN'S ECONOMIC POLICY

The most important task of the Eleventh Party Congress was the introduction of the new Mongol Five-Year Plan. The plan came into force

* During the period between the wars, the membership figure of the Mongol Revolutionary People's Party had developed like a fever curve. From 3,000 members in 1923, it went up to 15,000 in 1928, and reached its peak in the first half of 1932, when there were as many as 44,000 members. Of this record number, only 8,000 were left after a thorough purge following the change of policy carried out in June 1932.

on January 1st, 1948, twenty years after the introduction of long term economic planning in the Soviet Union. The Five-Year Plan running from 1948 to 1952 was officially described as the 'first', although in fact, the first Mongol Five-Year Plan had been introduced and abandoned as a failure in the early 'thirties'.

The purpose of the plan was to increase the general well-being of the country and to put the Mongol People's Republic firmly 'on the way towards socialism'. In the field of cattle-breeding, this was to be done by strengthening collectivized cattle-farms, the so-called 'Arat Unions'. Their number has increased every year. There were 34 of such Arat Unions in 1938, 121 in 1949, and 139 in 1951. It is obvious that the Mongol Government is anxious not to enforce collectivization too hastily, in view of the negative experiment of the early 'thirties'.

Together with the 'Arat Unions', so-called Hay-Cutting Stations have been set up all over the country. Their number grew from 10 in 1937 to 55 in 1951. The Hay-Cutting Stations have very much in common with the Machine Tractor Stations (M.T.S.) in the Soviet Union. In the same way as Soviet collective farms depend on the M.T.S. for the supply of agricultural machinery, the Arat Unions rely on the Hay-Cutting Stations for the supply of feeding-stuff for their cattle. In addition to 'Arat Unions' and Hay-Cutting Stations, the Mongol Government tried to promote State farms. The latter have been the pioneers of agriculture in Mongolia, though on a small scale; but in future they are supposed to devote themselves primarily to quality stockbreeding.

The industrial targets of the Five-Year Plan were modest, but not unimportant. Apart from raising Mongolia's coal production to over half a million tons, it provided for the extension of the food and light industries of the country. The most important industrial plants of Mongolia are the 'Choibalsan Kombinat', in Ulan Bator, which supplies shoes, underwear and clothing of European style to the urban population, and the highly mechanized meat factory which is called after Stalin. Output increase of these two plants was an important item of the Five-Year Plan. The Mongol workers staffing these and other enterprises, far from constituting the political basis of the régime, which they ought to be doing according to Leninist theory, are a backward element that causes considerable uneasiness to the Revolutionary People's Party. Many of the so-called industrial workers of Mongolia have only just abandoned their nomadic way of life. In 1947, of all industrial workers, 35 per cent had less than one year of factory work to their credit. In these circumstances one can well imagine that labour discipline is still very low.

THE DEATH OF CHOIBALSAN

The M.P.R. is copying the Soviet Union not only in fundamental institutions, such as the constitution and the Five-Year Plan, but also in matters of detail. Choibalsan, for instance, imitated Stalin in every respect. When, in 1939, the Soviet Government introduced Stalin Prizes for literature, art and inventions, the Mongol Government very soon afterwards created 'Choibalsan Prizes'. The Mongol constitution is officially referred to as the 'Choibalsan Constitution', despite being, as we have seen, only a free translation of the 'Stalin Constitution' of the U.S.S.R. At elections to the Mongol Parliament, Choibalsan appeared as the candidate of the 'Choibalsan constituency of Ulan Bator', in the same way as Stalin usually stood as candidate for the Stalin constituency of Moscow.

There is no evidence that Choibalsan himself started this cult out of personal ambition. It is more likely that the initiative for it lay with the Mongol Revolutionary People's Party, or even with the Soviet Government. Both may have wanted to consolidate the pro-Russian trends in Mongolia by creating a mystique around a 'Fuehrer'. But the moment came when Moscow and the Russian Party in Ulan Bator probably regretted the almost complete identification that had existed since 1938 between Choibalsan and the Mongolian régime. This was when Marshal Choibalsan died in Moscow on January 26th, 1952. His death seems to have thrown the country into considerable confusion. It certainly took four months before a successor was appointed, in the person of the Secretary-General of the Party and first deputy premier, Tsedenbal. Before the problem of Choibalsan's succession was settled, the Mongolian Revolutionary People's Party organized a big propaganda campaign popularising the Soviet Union with the help of lectures, exhibitions, cinema shows, and the opening of Russian language courses. Also, the Grand National Khural, was summoned to send a letter of allegiance to Stalin. The entire campaign was to convey to the people that Choibalsan, although an object of great veneration during his lifetime, was only a gifted pupil of the Soviet generalissimo. This was also more or less the tenor of the speech which Tsedenbal delivered at Choibalsan's funeral, a speech which was very largely inspired by the one which Stalin had made in 1924 at Lenin's funeral.

The real historical importance of Choibalsan for Mongolia is difficult to assess, but it is fairly certain that, rightly or wrongly, some of the most remarkable reforms which took place in his country will be for ever associated with his name.

THE CULTURAL REVOLUTION

Between 1940 and 1950 it was not only the economic and political structure of the M.P.R. that underwent many changes; the health services and the cultural life of the country were also 'revolutionized'. During this period the number of hospitals in the country increased from 17 to 50, that of medical and first aid posts from 157 to 421, that of chemist's shops from 6 to 63. In 1940 there was only one maternity home in the country, whereas in 1950 there were over 100 of them.[41]

As far as education was concerned, Mongolia boasted 412 schools in 1949 with 60,000 pupils and 3,000 teachers (against 417 teachers in 1940). The country had in 1949, furthermore, 14 technical schools and 345 libraries and reading rooms. Since 1942 the M.P.R. has possessed a State university; it has a musical and dramatic theatre, and a new theatre was opened in 1950.[42]

The number of newspapers increased from ten in 1940 to twenty-seven in 1950, and that of journals from eight to sixteen.*

The increase in the number of schools and newspapers was the natural consequence of the growth of literacy in the M.P.R. At the time of the Mongol National Revolution, only 6,000 people in the country were able to read and write. This was less than 1 per cent of the total population. In 1947, 42 per cent of the adult inhabitants of the country were literate and in 1951, 87 per cent.

A decisive turning point in the literacy campaign was the introduction of the Russian alphabet decreed by the Central Committee of the Mongol Revolutionary People's Party and the Mongol Government on March 25th, 1941. Until then the Mongol language had been written in the vertical ancient Mongol script, or, since 1931, also in Latin characters. The decree of March 1941 was inspired by a similar decree which had been issued in Buryat-Mongolia two years earlier, as well as by identical measures taken in other Asiatic Republics of the Soviet Union.† As the M.P.R. is formally outside the Soviet Union, its Government had to be more explicit in justifying the new cultural revolution than the Soviet

* The Mongol press is organized completely on the Soviet pattern, and even the titles of the Moscow newspapers are imitated. The three principal newspapers published in Ulan Bator are the organ of the Mongol Revolutionary People's Party, *Unen* (meaning 'Truth' just as *Pravda* means 'Truth'), *Zaluchudun Unen* or 'Truth of the Revsomol', which corresponds to the *Komsomolskaya Pravda* in Moscow, and the organ of the Mongol army, *Ulan Odo*, the exact translation of the title of the newspaper of the Red Army, *Krasnaya Zvezda* ('Red Star'). As in Moscow, the Party in Ulan Bator publishes a periodical, *Propagandist*, and the leading Mongol literary journal is named in the same way as is the Moscow illustrated *Ognoyok* ('Little Fire').

† In Uzbekistan, the Cyrillic alphabet came into force in May, 1940, and in Tadzhikistan in June of the same year. In Kirghizistan and Kazakhstan, it was introduced in the schools in September, 1941.

149

Republics of Central Asia needed to be. The Mongol decree stated first of all that the Latin alphabet lacked certain signs essential for the transcription of the Mongol language, and was thus unsuitable. There were, of course, other considerations which were more important in prompting the 'reform', particularly the necessity of a further Mongol-Russian *rapprochement*. The decree made this point very clearly. It said that most of the skilled personnel employed in various branches of Mongol economy had received their training in Russia. It mentioned that the revolutionary literature, essential to the Mongol people, was written in the Russian language, and it emphasized very frankly that the further cultural development of Mongolia was possible only through the absorption of Russian culture.[43]

This was an open admission that the growth of literacy was to be used for the superimposition of a Soviet Russian culture, and not for the development of an authentic and original Mongol cultural life. No immediate action followed the publication of the decree on the Cyrillization of the Mongol script. The new Mongol orthography was not ready until 1946.[44]

MONGOL LITERATURE

After the introduction of the new alphabet, State control over Mongol literature was tightened, but a severe censorship had already been in existence for a long period. In the early years of the M.P.R. there had been quite a few Mongol writers who had tried to take an independent line, and who had defended the cause of a Mongol literature standing outside party politics. These writers were very soon denounced as representing the interests of feudal circles, the trading bourgeoisie, and foreign intelligence services. They were also charged with stirring up disagreements between the nationalities living in the M.P.R., and with attempting to sever the ties between the latter and the Soviet Union.[45] This group of anti-Soviet writers (Buyan-Nekhe, Shi-Ayushi, Idam-Surun and Radia-Bazar) was ultimately liquidated after a prolonged and sharp ideological struggle between the protagonists of so-called 'oriental symbolism', and the representatives of 'revolutionary realism', the counterpart of socialist realism in the Soviet Union. It was easier to destroy the 'reactionary' trends in Mongol prose and poetry than to build up a new 'realistic' Mongol literature. This can be gathered from the statements by Soviet Russian critics who are as outspoken in denouncing the alleged mistakes of Mongol writers as they are in exposing the 'shortcomings' of Buryat and Yakut literary works. Soviet criticism of Mongol literature is primarily concentrated on the neglect by Mongol authors of contemporary themes. The Soviet journal *Zvezda* complained, for instance, that certain Mongol poets depicted life as if the revolution of 1921 had never taken place, and as if the people had not changed since then.[46] Another Soviet literary journal, *Oktyabr*, expressed regret at the absence of Mongol works about the 'new (Mongol) man, and Mongolia's fight for peace'.[47]

Greater uneasiness has, however, been shown in Moscow about certain nationalist tendencies in Mongol literature. The latter have been fairly strong in the post-war years, and the Mongol Government has had to take several measures to suppress them. To achieve a greater measure of streamlining, the Government organized a 'Union of Mongol Writers' on the pattern of the 'Union of Soviet Writers'. Its first congress in spring, 1948, adopted a statute which made it the duty of every writer to 'participate in the ideological transformation and education of the toiling masses in the spirit of the great ideas of the Mongol Revolutionary People's Party, and in the spirit of socialism'. Mongol writers continued to commit ideological offences even after the foundation of the new body. The Central Committee of the Party therefore considered it necessary to issue its decree of December 31st, 1949, which initiated a large-scale campaign against heretics. The decree admitted that 'nationalist ideas hostile to Marxism-Leninism, and the programme of the Party' were still reflected in literature and art as well as in the teaching in schools and educational institutes. The decree stated in particular that there was too much bias in favour of Mongol feudalism to which the school curricula for history and literature devoted an almost exclusive attention. The decree constituted a further attempt to 'debunk' various outstanding figures of Mongol history, and dealt once again with the problem of Genghis Khan, which had already played a considerable part in the purge of 1937–38. Some writers had glorified the military marches of the great Mongol khan, and the decree had to remind them sharply that these marches had led to nothing but robbery, and that Genghis Khan himself was an 'oppressor and strangler of the Mongol people'.[48] This argument must have been unconvincing to Mongol intellectuals who could see the cult of Ivan the Terrible, surely an oppressor and strangler of the Russian people, encouraged in Soviet Russia.

Another Mongol national hero, Tsoktu Taidzhi, was dethroned by the same decree. This political leader and poet of the seventeenth century, who is much venerated in Mongolia, led the Mongols in a war against Manchuria. For a long time the Mongol Government not only tolerated the cult of Tsoktu Taidzhi, but even actively contributed to it by arranging the production of a film dealing with his life and deeds. The film had its première in the autumn of 1945, and was at first considered to be one of the most outstanding artistic achievements of Mongolia. The December decree of 1949, however, condemned the film because it implied that there were good, as well as bad, feudal lords.

As historical themes are becoming increasingly taboo, and as nonpolitical literary works are undesirable, Mongol poets and writers have to devote themselves to those topics in which the Mongol Revolutionary People's Party and its Soviet protectors are interested, for instance, the 'great friendship between the Soviet and Mongol peoples'. Works falling under this heading include novels and poems extolling the Soviet-Mongol comradeship in arms in the fight against Japan, particularly in the battle on the Khalkin-Gol river; and expressions of admiration for Russia's fight against Hitler. Another theme of Mongol literature is the glorification of the 'great leaders', Lenin, Stalin, Sukhe Bator and Choibalsan. During Stalin's lifetime the cult of his person was as effusive in Mongolia as in the Soviet Union. One poet, Lubsan Kurch, described Stalin as 'the wisest man', another, Puntsuk, called him 'the symbol of happiness of the people', and Damdin-Surin, the most official of all the official Mongol poets, referred to him as 'our father'.[49]

Finally, literature is taking shape in the M.P.R., which is more or less identical with the 'Five-Year Plan literature' of the Soviet Union. It pays tribute to outstanding cattle-breeders, and to the shock-workers of Mongolia's new industrial enterprises.

More important than the still rather small original Mongol literature are the translations from other languages. The selection of books for translation into Mongol is a highly responsible task. How should it be solved, and how has it been solved? The great Russian writer, Maxim Gorky, thought a great deal about this problem and the result of his reflections were contained in a letter which he wrote to Mongol writers in 1925. This is what Gorky told them:

'The propagation of the principle of activity would be for your people the most useful thing of all. Active relationship to life is at the bottom of all the marvellous things which Europe possesses and which are worthy of being adopted by all races. Buddha taught that desire is the source of suffering. Europe is ahead of other peoples of the world in the field of science, arts and technical progress just because she was never afraid of suffering and always desired to improve on what she already had. Europe was able to stir in the masses of her people, the longing for justice and freedom, and for that alone we must forgive her a great number of sins and crimes. I think, in acquainting the Mongolian people with the European spirit and the aspirations of European masses in our times, you should translate those European books expressing more clearly than others the principle of action.'

Gorky wanted revolutionary European spirit, but none the less European spirit, propagated in Mongolia. What the Soviet régime brought to the Mongols was less europeanization than spiritual sovietization and russification. Between 1925 and 1948, 227 literary works were translated into Mongol, including 104 works by Soviet authors, 80 by pre-revolutionary Russian writers and poets, and 43 by authors of all other nations, including, apparently, a number of communists and near-communists.[50]

The works of Soviet authors translated into Mongol included amongst others the following: Vsevolod Ivanov, *Armoured Train* 14–69 (a play about the Civil War in the Far East); Nikolay Ostrovsky, *How Steel was Tempered* (a novel about Soviet youth during the first few years of communist rule); Aleksandr Fadeev, *Young Guard* (the story of a Komsomol underground organization in the rear of the Nazi army), Aleksandr Korneichuk, *Platon Krechet* (a play about the new Soviet intelligentsia); Konstantin Simonov, *Russian People* (a play about the Russian resistance against the Nazi invaders); Dmitry Furmanov, *Chapaev* (a novel about the famous hero of the Russian Civil War).

The other works which had the privilege of translation into Mongol dealt with similar themes and were of similar ideological content, but some are of less literary value than the ones mentioned. The translated works also include the Communist Manifesto of Marx and Engels, Stalin's *Problems of Leninism*, and the *Short History of the Communist Party of the Soviet Union*.

THE MONGOL THEATRE

Russian influence has also dominated the Mongol theatre, at least since the beginning of that more active Soviet interference in the affairs of the M.P.R., which started in 1928. Until then, Chinese plays in Mongol translation were still performed. After the Seventh Party Congress of 1928, the Mongol Government disbanded the 'reactionary right wing' drama circle of Ulan Bator, and founded a new one which described itself pompously as 'Central Drama Circle bearing the name of the Central Committee of the Revolutionary People's Party and of the Revolutionary Youth League'. At the same time it was decreed that all plays had to pass through Government censorship, and that in future no play could be performed which was devoid of 'revolutionary ideas'. The Mongol Theatre thus became, first and foremost, a propaganda instrument, putting across the party line of the moment.[51]

The situation changed to some extent in the late 'thirties', when a number of plays, which were based on Mongol folklore were performed and enjoyed great popularity. A case in point was the play *The Three Sharaigol Khans*, which showed the fight of the Mongol national hero, Geser, against the forces of darkness personified by the three khans. The play, which was first performed on the occasion of the twentieth anniversary of Mongolia's independence in 1941, dominated the Mongol stage for three years but was then suddenly rewritten. The main theme the fight of light against darkness, was eliminated and the action of the play was almost entirely confined to battle scenes.[52] The play in its second version was produced by a Russian Jewish producer, Rabinovich, in co-operation with the Mongol Oyun. The music was composed by a Russian, another Russian was in charge of décor, the choreographer, too, was Russian. No wonder that there was little genuine Mongol atmosphere in the would-be folklore play. Even the official organ of the Mongol Revolutionary People's Party, *Unen*, stated that the specific features of Mongol national customs had been neglected in the play, and that the producers in the Mongol Theatre should study them more carefully.[53]

MINORITIES IN THE M.P.R.

The M.P.R. is ethnographically as little homogenous as any Asiatic Soviet Republic. Although the Khalka Mongols form the large majority, there are quite a number of minority groups in the country. About the relative strength of the dominating nationality and the minorities, Soviet specialists on Mongolia have produced slightly conflicting statements. There is not even full agreement between the authors of two monographs which were published in the same year, in 1948. Murzaev, whose work was published by the Institute of Geography of the All-Union Academy of Sciences, stated that the Khalka Mongols formed 70 per cent of the 850,000 inhabitants of the M.P.R. The other author, Tsapkin, believes that they account for 80 per cent. Murzaev gives the strength of Outer Mongolia's minorities as follows: Dyurbets and other Western Mongols – 7 per cent; Dariganga (Eastern Mongols) – 2 per cent; Kazakhs – 3 per cent; Tuvinians – 3 per cent; Buryats – 3 per cent. Tsapkin lists the same minorities, and gives them slightly different percentages: Kazakhs – 3·5 per cent; Dyurbets – 3·1 per cent; Buryats – 3·1 per cent; Dariganga – 2·2 per cent; Tuvinians – 2·1 per cent; and 'Others' – 6 per cent.[54]

Neither of the two Soviet authors gives the relative strength of the two minorities which are politically the most important ones, the Chinese and the Russians. On the eve of the foundation of the M.P.R., the Chinese constituted a fairly strong element, even from the merely numerical point of view. A Bolshevik expert on Mongolia, Ivan Maisky, who later became a distinguished diplomat, estimated in 1919-20 that out of a total population of 647,000 there were then as many as 100,000 Chinese. The Chinese formed the majority of the urban population of Outer Mongolia which Maisky estimated at 140,000.[55] A few years later, in 1930, the Chinese numbered 50,000 according to authoritative Soviet sources, and accounted for roughly 6 per cent of the total population of the M.P.R[56].

It seems that the Chinese are still forming a not unimportant community in the M.P.R. and that a substantial section of the young working class is recruited from them. The Chinese working class element in at least numerous enough to warrant the formation of a Chinese section within the Mongol trade union organization, and the publication of a Chinese newspaper, the title of which has been translated as *Workers' Path*. Chinese are also engaged in petty trading and horticulture.[57]

As to the Russian ethnical group in the M.P.R., this consists not only of people who work as experts and advisers in the capital and other urban centres, but also of agriculturalists in the northern districts of the Republic. In 1921, there were 5,000 Russians in Mongolia and in 1930 about 30,000. Today the Russian element is still in all likelihood, smaller than the Chinese. The aggregate strength of the 'peoples of the Soviet Union' in Outer Mongolia is, however, very nearly 10 per cent of its total population. The most important of them are the Kazakhs who have a special national Kazakh aimak or, as it is officially called, the Bayan-Ulegei Aimak where the Kazakh language is used in administration and education. The Bayan-Ulegei Aimak is situated in the westernmost part of the M.P.R., and is 18,000 square miles in size. Tuvinians and Buryats live in the northern aimaks of the M.P.R. in the neighbourhood of the Tuvinian Autonomous Province and the Buryat-Mongol A.S.S.R. respectively. In addition, there is a small Uzbek minority in the town of Kobdo, which is situated in the western part of the Republic.

In the past, the Soviet Union intervened on several occasions in favour of the minorities. In 1931, in particular, the Government circles were accused of 'Khalka chauvinism', not so much in their relations towards the 'peoples of the Soviet Union', but because of their attitude towards such Mongol groups as the Dyurbets.[58]

In future, the Chinese People's Republic may also take an interest in the minorities of the M.P.R. Just as the Buryats or Tuvinians in the northern aimaks are naturally gravitating towards their kinsmen in the Soviet Union, there are groups in the south, such as the Dariganga, who maintained in the past the closest contact with Inner Mongolia and even China proper.[59] These contacts had to be broken off in the period between the wars but the emergence of a communist China has created a strong case for their resumption.

RUSSIA, CHINA AND MONGOLIA

The change of régime in China, the replacement of a decaying State by a vigorous and potentially expansionist system of government, has put the problem of Mongolia into a new light. Soviet Russia has certainly won the first rounds in the battle for Mongolia. The Soviet régime has come very near to making the aim of the Mongol nationalists – the unification of all Mongol territories in one independent national state – a utopian impossibility. Both by their political and economic integration into the U.S.S.R., and by their spiritual russification, the Mongols of Outer Mongolia have been cut off from the Mongols of Inner Mongolia and Jehol. Even from the point of view of communications, Outer Mongolia is now connected with Russian Siberia, instead of being linked with the Mongols of the Chinese Republic. The first Mongol-Soviet railway line was constructed in 1938, and the second, the Stalin Railway Line which runs from Ulan Bator to the Soviet border, was opened in 1949. Thus, everything has been done to make a change in the orientation of Outer Mongolia as difficult as possible. Nevertheless, the Russian protectorate is not the only future which can be visualized for the M.P.R. for the presence of a communist China on the borders of Outer Mongolia means a challenge to that protectorate. The political monopoly which Soviet Russia has tried to create for herself in Mongolia during many years was threatened for the first time in 1950 when a Chinese Embassy was opened in Ulan Bator. This event was followed up by the visit of a Mongol Government delegation to Peking in 1952, the conclusion in that year of a Sino-Mongol Agreement on economic and cultural co-operation and trips to Mongolia of various groups of Chinese communists, particularly representatives of arts and literature. All this could not fail to make a considerable impression on the Mongols who, for such a long time, had been completely cut off from any contact with the non-Russian world. If China goes a step further and manifests a more active interest in Outer Mongolia, she is sure to meet with a certain response. Indeed, as has been mentioned, the original programme of the Mongol People's Party provided for union with a revolutionary China, and according even to official Soviet sources there was a major pro-Chinese uprising in the M.P.R., as late as 1930.[60]

The Chinese communists have even obtained the promise that the Mongol question will not be solved without their participation. At the congress of the revolutionary organizations of the Far East, which took place in Moscow in 1922, Zinoviev said, on behalf of the Comintern and the Russian Bolshevik Party: 'I consider that the final settlement of the Mongol problem will only be possible at the moment when the Chinese themselves have liberated themselves from the yoke of their oppressors, when they have driven out of their country the imperialist soldiers of foreign nations, when revolution has been victorious. Only then, will the Chinese people be in a position to say that its fate is in its own hands. Only then will it be possible to put the Mongol question on a new basis whereby it is a matter of course that its final settlement will depend on the liberation movement in Mongolia itself.'[61]

The fact that Zinoviev was later expelled from the Bolshevik Party and executed has, of course, no bearing on the matter. What he said about the right of a revolutionary China to participate in the solution of the Mongol problem was a true expression of Russian Bolshevik policy at that time, and it could still be considered as a binding promise. In point of fact, the Soviet Government did not abide by the pledge which Zinoviev had given. It settled the Mongol question, from its own point of view finally, at a time when the Chinese had not yet liberated themselves from 'foreign oppressors', to use the Soviet jargon. It might even be said that the U.S.S.R. has shown a peculiar haste in concluding the agreement of 1945 with the weak bourgeois Chinese State of the Kuomintang, in order to put an accomplished fact before a new revolutionary and more vigorous China.

However weighty the economic and political reasons which might be advanced in favour of a continuation of the Russian protectorate over Outer Mongolia, there are other, perhaps even more convincing, arguments which the new China could put forward against it, arguments of a racial and geographical nature. One day the Chinese may ask whether it is logical that the Asiatic Mongols should be ruled from European Moscow, rather than from the much nearer Asiatic Peking.

BIBLIOGRAPHICAL NOTES TO CHAPTER V

1. *Revolyutsionny Vostok*, 1931, Nr 11–12, p. 238.

2. *International Press Correspondence*, February 25th, 1927.

3. *Revolyutsionny Vostok*, 1932, Nr 13–14, p. 250.

4. *Antireligioznik*, 1930, Nr 7, p. 22.

5. *Antireligioznik*, 1930, Nr 8–9, pp. 55–56.

6. OLESHCHUK, *Borba Tserkvi protiv Naroda* – The Fight of the Church against the People, Moscow 1939, p. 104.

7. These plans of the 'Buryat counter-revolution' are aptly and dramatically described in a novel by the Buryat writer, ZHAMSO TUMUNOV, *Step prosnulas* – The Awakening of the Steppe, Moscow 1950, pp. 367–70.

8. M. I. POMUS, *Buryat-Mongolskaya A.S.S.R.* – The Buryat-Mongol A.S.S.R., Moscow 1937, p. vii.

9. *XV let B.M.A.S.S.R.*, Ulan Ude, Burgiz 1938, p. 19.

10. *Pravda*, September 7th, 1937.

11. *Pravda*, September 26th, 1937.

12. *Pravda*, April 17th, 1950.

13. *Poeziya Sovetskoy Buryat-Mongolii*, Moscow 1950, pp. 460–62.

14. *Large Soviet Encyclopedia*, second edition, Moscow 1951, vol. 6, p. 350.

15. *Izvestiya*, June 6th, 1948.

16. *Sibirskaya Sovetskaya Entsiklopediya*, Moscow 1932, vol. 3, pp. 223–24.

17. *Literaturnaya Entsiklopediya*, vol. 1, p. 225, Moscow 1929.

18. *Za Industrialisatsiyu Sovetskogo Vostoka*, Moscow 1933, Nr 3, pp. 210–19.

19. *Pravda*, December 22nd, 1950.

20. *Pravda*, January 17th, 1952.

21. *Izvestiya*, December 17th, 1947.

22. *Literaturnaya Gazeta*, March 26th, 1949.

23. *Pravda*, July 4th, 1948.

24. *Istorichesky Zhurnal*, 1944, Nr 10–11, pp. 84–86.

25. *International Press Correspondence*, November 6th, 1930, p. 1037.

26. *Izvestiya Akademii Nauk SSSR* – Proceedings of the Academy of Sciences of the U.S.S.R., History and Philosophy Series, Nr 1, January-February 1952, pp. 80–87.

27. DOUGLAS CARUTHERS, *Unknown Mongolia*, London 1913, vol. 1, pp. 306–16.

28. *Krasny Arkhiv*, 1939, vol. 37, pp. 58–60.

29. *Severnaya Aziya*, 1928, Nr 2, pp. 80–84.

30. *Revolyutsionny Vostok*, 1927, Nr 2, p. 73.

31. *Severnaya Aziya*, 1928, Nr 2, p. 90.

32. ISHI DORDJI, *Kulturelle Aufbauarbeit in der Mongolei, Osteuropa*, March 1929, vol. iv, Nr 6.

33. DIETRICH SCHAEFER, *Kommunistische Propaganda in der Mongolei, Zeitschrift fuer Geopolitik*, January 1939, Nr 1, p. 166.

34. *Bolshevik*, May 1st, 1936, Nr 7, p. 74.

35. MIKHAIL KOLESNIKOV, *Shchastlivy Oazis* – The Happy Oasis, *Dalny Vostok* 1952, Nr 1, pp. 7–8.

36. *Soviet Monitor*, October 10th, 1946, quoting an official note of the Mongol Government to the U.S.S.R., U.S.A., France, U.K. and China. The note enumerated Mongol losses in the fight against Japan, and demanded the inclusion of a Mongol representative in the Far Eastern Commission.

37. *Izvestiya*, February 28th, 1946.

38. MASLENNIKOV, *Mongolskaya Narodnaya Respublika, na puti k sotsializmu* – The Mongol People's Republic on the Way to Socialism, Moscow 1951, p. 61.

39. *Izvestiya Akademii Nauk SSSR* – Proceedings of the Academy of Sciences of the U.S.S.R., History and Philosophy Series, Nr 1, January-February 1952, pp. 80–87.

40. The constitutions of the M.P.R. and the B.M.A.S.S.R. were published in Russia by the State Publishing House for Juridical Literature in Moscow. (*Konstitutsiya Mongolskoy Narodnoy Respubliky* – The Constitution of the Mongol People's Republic, Moscow 1952. For the Buryat-Mongol constitution see *Konstitutsiya RSFSR, Konstitutsii Avtonomnykh Sovetskikh Sotsialisticheskikh Respublik* – The Constitution of the R.S.F.S.R. and the Constitutions of the Autonomous Soviet Socialist Republics, Moscow 1952, pp. 115–37.)

41. MASLENNIKOV, op. cit., p. 143.

42. *Problemy Ekonomiki*, May 1951, Nr 5, pp. 89–92.

43. MASLENNIKOV, op. cit., p. 146.

44. V. Kh. TODAYEVA, *Grammatika Sovremennogo Mongolskogo Yazyka* – Grammar of the Contemporary Mongol Language, Moscow 1951, p. 11.

45. B. KAMESHKOV, *Literatura Narodnoy Mongolii* – The Literature of People's Mongolia, Zvezda 1951, Nr 9, p. 149.

46. KAMESHKOV, op. cit., p. 153.

47. *Oktyabr*, Nr 6, June 1952, p. 166.

48. *Oktyabr*, Nr 6, June 1952, p. 168.

49. *Literaturnaya Gazeta*, July 13th, 1946.

50. KAMESHKOV, op. cit., p. 152.

51. UVAROVA, op. cit., pp. 45–46.

52. UVAROVA, op. cit., p. 104.

53. UNEN, May 9th, 1944, quoted by UVAROVA, op. cit., pp. 177–78.

54. E. M. MURZAEV, *Mongolskaya Narodnaya Respublika*, Moscow 1948, pp. 23–25; N. V. TSAPKIN, *Mongolskaya Narodnaya Respublika*, Moscow 1948, pp. 23–24.

55. I. MAISKY, *Mongoliya, Novy Vostok*, Moscow 1922, Nr 1, pp. 163–64.

56. *Sibirskaya Sovetskaya Entsiklopediya*, Moscow 1932, vol. 3, p. 513.

57. *Soviet Monitor*, October 25th, 1945.

58. *Revolyutsionny Vostok*, 1931, Nr 11–12, p. 35.

59. GERARD M. FRITERS, *Outer Mongolia and its International Position*, London 1951, p. 43.

60. *Revolyutsionny Vostok*, 1931, Nr 11–12, p. 35.

61. *Novy Vostok*, November 1924, Nr 8–9, pp. 218–19.

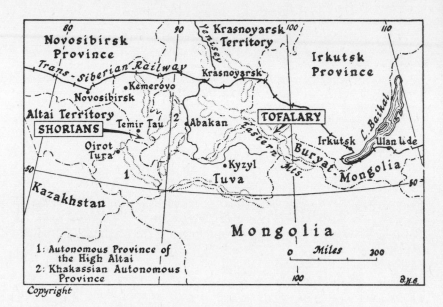

5. THE TUVINIANS AND THEIR COUSINS

VI

THE TUVINIANS AND THEIR COUSINS

I. THE REPUBLIC OF TUVA

Tannu Tuva, or more simply, Tuva, would be a state of medium size if situated in Europe, but in the vast space of Asia it is a mere speck. Tuva, known under its Mongol name of Uriankhai until 1922, deserves more attention than its 100,000 inhabitants* may seem to justify, not only because of its economic potentialities, but also as a classic example of Russian and Soviet methods of expansion.

Being an almost complete *terra incognita*, Tannu Tuva offers an interesting field for studies in history, geography and popular customs. From a political point of view, Tuva deserves interest for the fact that Russia annexed the territory twice within thirty years, without the outside world paying the slightest attention. In both cases Russia made use of a European war to settle the Tuva problem to her own advantage, the first time in 1914 by proclaiming her protectorate over Tuva, the second time in 1944 by discreetly transforming the People's Republic of Tuva into an administrative unit of the U.S.S.R.

Tuva, whose size various geographers have estimated at between 50,000 and over 75,000 square miles, is by no means an artificial creation. On the contrary, Tuva is a natural fortress, a kind of Asiatic Switzerland, bordered by two powerful mountain chains – the Sayan in the north, and the Tannu Ola in the south – separating the country, which forms the headwater region of the Yenisey, from both Siberia and Mongolia.

THE FIRST RUSSIAN ANNEXATION

Uriankhai became a political issue when Russians and Chinese signed the Treaty of Peking in 1860. By this treaty, Russia acquired commercial rights for Russian merchants, which excluded, however, the building of permanent Russian settlements. The first penetration of Russian merchants into Uriankhai, carried out on the basis of the Peking Treaty, led to such incidents as the burning down of Russian stores by the Chinese.

* According to Russian sources the population of Tuva was 64,000 in 1913, 70,000 in 1926, 86,000 in 1939 and 95,000 in 1941.

A mixed Russian-Chinese commission investigated the situation on the spot in 1869, and, as a result, the Chinese had to pay an indemnity, while the Russians reiterated the pledge that Siberian colonists would not settle in Uriankhai. Russian traders, when in Uriankhai on business, were forced to live in tents and boats to demonstrate the temporary character of their presence in Chinese territory. These limitations were brushed aside by a new treaty concluded in 1881. China then allowed the Russians to establish permanent settlements not exceeding 200 people in one place. The Russians were even permitted to build churches and cemeteries, and to sell arms and spirits, which until then had been excluded from trading.

Subsequent developments confirmed the original Chinese fears that the progress of Russian colonization would ultimately endanger Chinese sovereignty over Uriankhai. Indeed, Russian colonists pouring into the area in the 'nineties' of the nineteenth century, and in the first years of the twentieth century, were preparing the ground for the Russian civilian authorities. These colonists consisted of greedy traders trying to rob the natives, and of hard-working Russian peasants, including the god-fearing 'Old Believers', members of a religious sect which promoted the success of Russian colonization in many parts of the Czarist Empire. The Russian colonists immediately acquired fishing and grazing rights which neither the Chinese nor the Tuvinian natives, who had completely ignored fisheries until the arrival of the Russians, could effectively challenge. Caruthers indicated that a *de facto* Russian protectorate existed over the whole country before the annexation was made formal. Russian authorities living in the Siberian frontier village of Ussinskoye carried out official duties among the colonists of Uriankhai before the First World War, exactly as if the area belonged to the Russian Empire.[1]

The Government of Imperial Russia, much more hesitant in questions concerning Russia's territorial aggrandisement than Stalin's Russia, was full of doubts as to Uriankhai. As late as 1911, the Russian Council of Ministers rejected the annexation of the territory, and only in 1913, after the establishment of the Russian protectorate over Outer Mongolia was Russia's political penetration into Uriankhai officially decided.

The first formal incorporation of Uriankhai into Russia in 1914 resulted in increased Russian colonization. 3,500 new colonists arrived in Tuva between 1914 and 1917, and the beginning of a new Russian era in the history of the little country was marked by the foundation of a township, Byelotsarsk – the 'Town of the White Czar'.

The Stalinist conception of Russian history refuses to consider Czarist Russia's annexation of Uriankhai as a logical outcome of economic infiltration and colonization. The official Soviet thesis is that the Tuvinian people have linked their fate to that of the Russian people, and that progressive Tuvinians 'always relied upon the help of the

Russian nation in the struggle for a better future'. This is how the Secretary of the Communist Party of Tuva, Salchak K. Toka, described in 1946 the first annexation by Russia: '. . . the most far-sighted political leaders of the Uriankhai area, reflecting the mood of the arats, approached Russia with the request that she would take Tuva under her protection. In 1914 Tuva was taken under the protection of Russia. This was the most favourable solution of the problem'.[2]

The true history was somewhat different from Toka's statement. The Tuvinians feared all strangers and disliked the Russian newcomers as much as they disliked their former Chinese masters. They spoke of the Chinese only as 'yellow devils', and their attitude to the European colonists can be characterized by the Tuvinian saying, 'The Russian is not a man'.[3] In the early period of colonization, the Tuvinians carried out numerous raids on Russian factories, for which they were heavily punished by the Chinese officials. Later the Russian authorities themselves dealt with such cases of banditry, and took the culprits to the prison at Minusinsk, the nearest Russian town. There may have been a few Tuvinians who actually favoured Russian annexation, but the young Soviet State did not recognize them as spokesmen of the true aspirations of the Tuvinian people. In the view of the Soviet People's Commissar for Foreign Affairs, Chicherin, the idea of Tuva's annexation by Russia was fostered only by 'cunning Czarist officials'. Accordingly, in a statement of September 23rd, 1921, Chicherin declared the annexation of Tuva illegal, and proclaimed that the Workers' and Peasants' Government of Russia had no designs of any kind on the territory,

TUVINIAN PAN-MONGOLISM

Chicherin's statement was a solemn denunciation of all Russian territorial claims on Tuva, but it was not the birth certificate of the Tuvinian People's Republic (T.P.R.). Although in later years Tuva dated its independence back to 1921, Russia failed to acknowledge its independence until the autumn of 1925. The Soviet Government hesitated to commit itself with regard to Tuva out of consideration for the Mongols, who had hoped that the Tuvinians would eventually join the Mongol People's Republic. As Mongolia was in a permanent state of internal chaos, the Soviet Government ultimately thought it safer that Tuva should link its fate with the U.S.S.R., rather than with the M.P.R., the more so since the number of Russians in the country was considerably larger than the Mongol minority. From 1925 onwards, the Soviet envoy in Tuva discouraged pro-Mongol tendencies, but these continued to exist in both the Government and the Tuvinian Revolutionary People's Party. In fact, there was every conceivable reason for the Tuvinian élite to look to Mongolia for cultural and political guidance. A Tuvinian national culture and literary language did not exist. Mongol, on the other hand, was the language of the few educated people of the country, and of the holy Buddhist books. Mongol was also the official language of the Tuvinian Government and of the Revolutionary People's Party. The minutes of its first congresses were taken down in Mongol, and the only newspaper of the country, *Unen*, was written in that language.

The first political leader of 'independent Tuva', the Prime Minister Donduk, was an ardent pan-Mongolist. He felt that the so-called political independence of the country would benefit only the Russians, and that geographical and political commonsense demanded the amalgamation of Tuva with the Mongolian People's Republic. 'The Tuvinian people', said Donduk, 'is small, poor and backward in the cultural respect. That is why it must be united with Mongolia.'[4] The ambitious plan of a Mongol-Tuvinian union could not be carried out but Donduk, in 1926, at least signed a Treaty of Friendship with the M.P.R.

Donduk and his principal associates were not only pan-Mongolists but also devout Buddhists, and they insisted on a religious education for the Tuvinian youth. In 1928, they even passed a law limiting anti-religious propaganda and proclaiming Buddhism as the State religion of Tuva. This was more than the Soviet Government could tolerate. The ideological cleavage between the Tuvinian leaders and the Kremlin became such that a conflict between the two was bound to break out. The Soviet envoy in Tuva, Starkov, was instructed to bring about the downfall of the Tuvinian régime. This was no easy task, for the Buddhist and pro-Mongol leadership enjoyed the confidence of the population, and could be removed from office only by a *coup d'état*. Moscow engineered the latter by making use of the differences between the old and the young generations in Tuva. The pro-Russian and pro-Bolshevik elements in the country first succeeded in getting control over the Tuvinian Revolutionary Youth League, the 'Revsomol', and with its help the right-wing chiefs were then ousted from the party itself in the summer of 1929. Otto Mänchen-Helfen, a German social-democrat, who as far as is known, was the only foreigner ever to have visited the T.P.R., asserted that the purge of 1929 was mainly carried out by five Tuvinian students. The Soviet Government had dispatched them to Tuva to assist the Russian envoy in restoring order. These five, who were graduates of the 'Communist University of the Toilers of the East' in Moscow, toured the Republic as commissars extraordinary, and expelled two-thirds of the party membership.[5]

THE CREATION OF A 'TUVINIAN CULTURE'

It was not enough to change the leading personnel of the T.P.R. The pro-Mongol tendencies in Tuva could be eliminated only by the creation of a Tuvinian national culture. The birthday of this Tuvinian culture was June 28th, 1930, when the Government published a decree on the introduction of the Tuvinian Latin alphabet, which had been compiled by a commission of Russian scholars. The introduction of the alphabet was the beginning of a cultural revolution. It meant not only the end of the Tibetan-Mongol script in Tuva, but also the end of the Mongol language. The State Publishing House of Tuva ceased publishing Mongol literature, and turned out Tuvinian pamphlets instead. The Mongol newspaper, *Unen*, was bi-lingual Mongol-Tuvinian for nine months, and then switched over to Tuvinian altogether. The campaign for the new alphabet was carried out with great enthusiasm. In the capital of Tuva, Kyzyl (formerly Byelotsarsk), alone, twelve literacy courses were opened, and all Government Offices were transformed into class-rooms after working hours. The Tuvinian alphabet, the 'State script' as it was officially called, was not well received by everybody. The conservative, theocratical opposition tried to sabotage it by spreading all kinds of rumours. It was even asserted that the literacy classes were haunted by bad spirits, and, moreover, that the new alphabet was bad for pregnant women. The opposition was, not however, entirely unconstructive, for the opponents of the new alphabet tried to organize rival literacy classes, in which the Mongol script was taught. There was one other group in Tuva, which was not against the Tuvinian alphabet on principle, but which resented the fact that it was imposed by the Russians. In fact, a learned lama, Lobsan Dshigmid, had compiled a Tuvinian Latin alphabet in 1928, and a number of Tuvinians had started learning it. The Russian advisers of the Tuvinian Government rejected it, however, for philological reasons. This caused a great deal of bad blood among a section of the Tuvinian intellectuals, who asserted that the Russians had spoiled the spelling of their language.[6]

The Tuvinian literary language, which was made official on the insistence of the Soviet Government and its local plenipotentaries, was not identical with the Tuvinian language as spoken by the people. It contained a fairly large number of Russian words which became even more numerous later on, particularly after the replacement of the Latin by the Russian alphabet. The Russian words taken into the Tuvinian language included such political terms as: 'Soviet'; 'Bolshevik'; 'Party'; 'kolkhoz'; as well as the equivalents for 'bread'; 'garden'; 'school', and many others. The director of the Tuvinian Scientific Research Institute for Language, Literature and Art, pointed out that Tuvinian had borrowed not only from the Russian vocabulary, but also from Russian grammar.[7]

The man who, apart from Russian scholars, was primarily responsible for the emergence of the so-called Tuvinian national language, was the Party Secretary, Toka. No person in Tuva had done so much for the consolidation of Russian influence. Toka was trained in Moscow, married a Russian girl, and in 1929 played a prominent part in the liquidation of the Buddhist and Mongol trends in the country. He was Minister of Education during the crucial months in which the language reform was carried out. Finally, it was only natural that Toka became the founder of a Tuvinian literature. One of his first works was a play with the not very exciting title, *Three Years as a Cell Secretary*. It depicted the class struggle in Tuva, and 'the beastly hatred of the enemies of Tuva's revolutionary society'.[8]* Most of the 'Tuvinian' literature consisted not of any original contributions but of translations of Gorky, Pushkin, Tolstoy, Mayakovsky, Lenin and Stalin.

It was not only Russian cultural influence that increased in Tuva. The Russian colonists acquired an ever increasing influence over the destinies of the small country. As early as 1927 they numbered 12,000 or almost one sixth of the entire population of the T.P.R. Until the end of the 'twenties' the Russians of Tuva had not been allowed to interfere with internal Tuvinian politics. They had had the status of privileged foreigners enjoying exterritorial rights and formed an organization which called itself 'Self-governing Colony of Russian Toilers' ('*Russkaya Samoupravlayushcheisya Trudovaya Koloniya*' – R.S.T.K.). A treaty concluded between this Soviet Russian colony and the Tuvinian Government protected the economic interests of the local Russians. Following the *coup d'état* of 1929, the situation changed. The Russians were given full citizens' rights. They became entitled to representation not only in the Grand Khural, the Tuvinian National Assembly, but also in the Little Khural, the principal legislating body. This does not mean that all Russians in Tuva sympathized with the Soviet and left-wing Tuvinian régimes. The land confiscation measures introduced in 1930 even led to an uprising of a section of the Russian peasant colonists. It broke out almost simultaneously with a revolt of the Tuvinian cattle-breeders. Both risings were suppressed but they forced the Tuvinian Government and its Soviet advisers to take up a more moderate attitude with regard to the ownership of land and cattle. A number of Russian peasants living in Tuva were able to keep individual farms until the end of the Second World War.

THE SECOND ANNEXATION

On August 17th, 1944, the 'Little Khural', which comprised only thirty people who were more or less identical with the members of the

* Toka was the first Tuvinian to be awarded a Stalin Prize for literature. The Prize was awarded in 1951 for the autobiographical novel *Slovo Arata* – 'The Word of the Arat'. A further great honour was bestowed on him at the Nineteenth Congress of the Communist Party of the Soviet Union. He was made an alternate member of the Central Committee, from which representatives of the smaller nationalities are usually excluded.

Central Committee of the Tuvinian Revolutionary People's Party, took the 'historic decision' to ask for Tuva's admission into the U.S.S.R. Two months later, the Presidium of the Supreme Soviet of the U.S.S.R. granted this request. The T.P.R. became the Tuvinian Autonomous Province of the R.S.F.S.R.

The incorporation of Tuva into the U.S.S.R. put an end to such formal attributes of sovereignty as the country had possessed, its special criminal code, its constitution of 61 articles, its postage stamps, national flag and coat of arms. The Tuvinian Government which had as many as seven ministers, including one for foreign affairs and one for war, was disbanded and so was the 'People's Revolutionary Army'. The Mongol Legation in Kyzyl was closed down. The Russian rouble replaced the Tuvinian currency, the 'Aksha'. There was no need to abolish the Tuvinian Latin alphabet for it had already been abandoned for the Russian script in July 1941.

As a logical consequence of the annexation, the Revolutionary People's Party was transformed into a provincial organization of the Soviet Communist Party. This was more than a formality. The Revolutionary People's Party, however much an instrument of Soviet policy, had been exclusively Tuvinian in its composition, and the Russian communists in Tuva had had a separate organization of their own. After the annexation the two organizations were merged into a single body which had over 4,500 members, a higher proportion of the population than in the rest of the U.S.S.R. Many of the Russian members of the amalgamated party were given important posts as party officials and administrators.

A list of leading personalities, published in 1949 on the occasion of the fifth anniversary of the Tuvinian Autonomous Province, showed that the following Party and State dignitaries were Russians or Ukrainians: the heads of the local branches of the Ministry of the Interior (M.V.D.), and of the Ministry of State Security (M.G.B.), the head of the Propaganda and Agitation Department of the Communist Party, the second secretary of the Tuvinian Party organization, the head of the education department of the Province, the public prosecutor and the two officials in supreme charge of agriculture. On the other hand, all the figureheads were Tuvinians, such as the chairman of the Executive Committee of the Provincial Council, the first secretary of the Communist Youth League, the first Party secretary and the president of the Provincial Court of Justice.[10]

The reasons prompting the second Russian annexation of Tuva may be summarized as follows:

First, Tuva was very rich in cattle. This made it desirable for the Soviet authorities to bring the country within the reach of Soviet planned economy. The cattle of Tuva were of particular importance

167

for Russia in time of war, in the Russo-Japanese War of 1905, in the Civil War, and in the 'Great Patriotic War' of 1941–45. In the last-mentioned war alone, Tuva supplied 40,000 of her best horses, and 600,000 head of cattle.

Secondly, Tuva forms a national fortress guarding the approaches to the Kuzbass (Kuznetsk Basin), one of the main coal and steel producing centres of the Soviet Union. It was preferable to have this fortress inside the Soviet Union than to grant it even a sham sovereignty.

Thirdly, and perhaps the most important point, Tuva has large deposits of metals and minerals, including gold (exploited by the trust, 'Tuvzoloto'), platinum, and even uranium. It may or may not be a coincidence that Tuva, with its uranium deposits, was annexed to the Soviet Union at a time when atomic research in the western hemisphere was heading towards its climax.

Fourthly, the Tuvinians are closely related to some small Turkic peoples living in Soviet Russia proper, to the west and north of the former Tuvinian-Soviet border. The peoples in question are the Oirots, Shorians and Khakassians.* Certain groups of the Oirots even refer to themselves as 'Tuba' or 'Tuva'. From the point of view of Oirot nationalists in particular, there was no reason why these peoples should belong to the Russian Empire instead of uniting with the Tuvinians into an independent State. As long as there was an independent Tuva, there was always the possibility that Oirots and Khakassians might gravitate towards that country. Also, for this reason, it was safer to have Tuva inside the U.S.S.R. Although the Oirots and Khakassians themselves were discouraged from stressing their racial connections with the Tuvinians, the Tuvinian communists made great play of these links, when propagating the union with Russia.

The territories occupied by the Shorians, Oirots and Khakassians experienced a remarkable economic and cultural development under the Soviet régime. Nevertheless, their fate could hardly have been an incentive for the Tuvinians to join the U.S.S.R., for the recent history of the three nationalities offers a particularly striking example of the

---

*Another small Turkic people to whom the Tuvinians are closely related are the Karagasy, now called Tofalary or simply Tofy. They live on the north-eastern border of Tuva, near the frontiers of the Buryat-Mongol A.S.S.R. Although the Tofy are not more than 438 in number, according to the last available statistics, their history under the Soviet regime is interesting. In 1930, collectivization and denomadization measures were imposed on what was then the 'Tof National District.' All native households had to join one of three newly founded collective farms. Their managers were Russians who had unlimited powers and no knowledge of native economy. The local party and administrative organs, in a clumsy attempt to make collectivization more attractive, introduced strange 'premiums' for collective farms in the form of alcoholic spirits with the result that quite a number of natives died from alcohol poisoning. When this happened the higher administrative authorities at last intervened. They dismissed the incompetent party leaders of the Tof district and put them on trial. An official representative and later a whole working party were despatched to the Tof people. These emissaries, it is officially claimed, restored economic prosperity. (*Sovetsky Sever*, No. 2, 1934, pp. 95–6.)

doom which small Asiatic peoples have to expect under the Soviet régime, as a result of ruthless industrialization and European colonization.

II. THE SHORIAN NATIONAL DISTRICT

All three Turkic nationalities who live in the south of Central Siberia, near the Tuvinian border, enjoyed national autonomy during the inter-war period. Today this autonomy has become meaningless, both for Oirots and Khakassians, who are completely swamped by Russian immigrants, while the autonomy of the Shorians has come to an end even nominally.

The Shorian National District was founded in 1929. It then comprised an area as big as Belgium, and the Shorians, numbering 16,000 people, seem to have been in the majority in the territory which bore their name. In 1931, the Shorians formed only 38.8 per cent of the population in the District; in 1938, only 13 per cent, and since then they have shrunk to an even more insignificant percentage. It was only logical for the Soviet Government to disband the Shorian National District altogether, and to make it, in 1939, a part of the Kemerovo Province, which provides the administrative framework for the 'Kuzbass'. The Shorians were outnumbered in their homeland chiefly by Russian and Ukrainian miners, whose arrival in Shoria was an economic necessity. Shoria, or High Shoria, as it is also called, supplies the iron-ore for the blast-furnaces of the 'Kuznetsk-Metallurgical Combine'. By the end of 1950, Shoria produced 2,000,000 tons of iron-ore a year, and it may be taken for granted that Shorian iron-ore has now supplanted the iron-ore which the Kuzbass previously received from the Urals. An attempt was made to associate the Shorians with this magnificent development of the mining industry of their homeland. Quite a number of them did become miners, and they exercise this new trade either in Shoria itself, or in other parts of the Kuzbass.

It seems, at least according to official Soviet sources, that the indus-trial development of Shoria was facilitated by a number of Shorian hunters, who informed the Soviet authorities of the location of iron-ore deposits. Indeed, one of the richest ore mines of the area has been named after a Shorian who first discovered it.[12] The real story behind the discovery of the Shorian iron-ore mines is more involved. It has never been told in a straightforward way, but the well-known Soviet writer, Fyodor Panfyorov, has written a play which indicates that the Shorians were for a long time not very co-operative in their attitude towards the communist régime. Panfyorov's play, *When we are beautiful*, does not mention the Shorians by name; he refers only to an anonymous 'small nationality'. However, there can be no doubt as to the identity of the latter, for the action of the play takes place in Temir Tau, a mining town in Shoria. One of the main themes of the play is the search for iron-ore, the 'red stone', as the Shorian hunters call it. The ore is badly needed by the local metallurgical plant. Geological expeditions are sent into the mountains, but they fail in their task. No sufficient iron-ore deposits can be found in the more easily accessible areas. The reason for this failure is the obstruction by the local population, described by the Party Secretary of Temir Tau as 'not a nation, only a handful of people'. He adds: 'We are convinced that they know where the ore is situated, but they don't tell us; they don't show these places to us. Somehow they are on their guard. . . They have no confidence in us. They fear us.'[13]

To state so bluntly that a small people has no confidence in the Soviet régime was an amazing and daring admission for a Soviet writer. No wonder that Panfyorov had great hesitation in publishing his heretical play. He started writing it in 1939, but its final version did not appear in print until thirteen years later. To make the play acceptable to the communist censors, Panfyorov had to invent a 'happy ending'. The spokesman of the mountain people suddenly drops his cautious attitude towards the local Soviet authorities, and, in the last scene of the play, tells the Party Secretary where the 'iron heart' of the mountains is to be found. This sudden *volte-face* sounded unconvincing. It did not save the author from bitter attacks by official Soviet quarters who reproached him with having distorted the 'friendship of the peoples' of the U.S.S.R. The Russian heroes of Panfyorov's play did, in fact, express some doubts about the meaning of this Soviet *cliché*, 'friendship of the peoples', in a case where it applies to the relations between the huge Russian nation and a small mountain tribe. As must be agreed, 'friendship' is hardly the right word to describe a process by which a small nation is absorbed by a large one, as in the case of the Shorians.

Today the Shorian nationality exists no longer, either politically or culturally. In addition to the suppression of Shorian territorial autonomy, attempts at building up something like a Shorian literary language have been virtually abandoned. All Shorians have become bi-lingual, and talk Russian everywhere except in their narrow family circle. But before the Shorians arrived at the present stage of lost national identity, they had to pass through all the various experiments which the communist régime has imposed on the culture of all Soviet nationalities. At first, they were encouraged to work out an alphabet for their language, taking the Russian alphabet as a basis. The first Shorian book in Russian characters was printed in 1927. Then, in 1930, the Soviet Government ordered the latinization of the Shorian script. A few years later, the Russian alphabet was again introduced. A number of works by Pushkin and Gorky have been translated into Shorian, as have some pamphlets on political and agricultural problems. This does not mean that a Shorian literary language is actually in existence. A Russian ethnographer, Potapov, said that the translators of Russian works into Shorian had to borrow all abstract terms from the Russian language. The literature thus created could not, therefore, be considered either Shorian or Russian.[14]

III. THE AUTONOMOUS PROVINCE OF THE HIGH ALTAI

Oirotia, the second Turkic territory on Tuva's borders, is even richer in minerals than Shoria. It contains manganese ore, iron-ore, silver, lead and wolfram. The exploitation of all these riches, as well as the development of the local timber resources, demanded a great deal of manpower, and resulted in the usual influx of Russian elements. During the first Five-Year Plan period, the percentage of Oirots in the Autonomous Province dropped from 41·8 to 36·4. During the second Five-Year Plan period and after, many thousands of Russians entered the country and changed the ethnographical balance still further to the detriment of the local people.

As the Oirots are more numerous than the Shorians – they numbered 47,700 in 1939 – they are still granted the privilege of living in an 'Autonomous Province', where special provisions are made for the use of the Oirot language. But this Autonomous Province is no longer associated with the name of the Oirots. Early in 1948, the Soviet Government passed a decree that the 'Oirot Autonomous Province' was to be known in future as 'Autonomous Province of the High Altai', in deference to the wishes of the local Russian workers. On the same occasion, the capital of the Province, 'Oirot-Tura', previously 'Uala', had to give up its Oirot name. This was changed into 'Gornoaltaisk', or 'Town in the High Altai'. Even the name of the people was altered, although not by decree, but only in point of fact. Suddenly all Soviet reference books and text books dropped the word 'Oirots', and spoke of 'Altaitsy' instead. This was the very name which the Czarist authorities had given to the Altai people, and it had an imperialistic and chauvinistic flavour. All these changes of terminology were not only connected with the immigration of Russians into Oirotia, but were also aimed at inflicting a blow on a people which, despite its small numbers, had caused considerable difficulties to the Soviet régime. The ideological independence which the Oirots have shown *vis à vis* the communist State was fed by the memories of a heroic past. At one time, the Oirots were the terror of Central Asia. In the first half of the eighteenth century, they left their Western Chinese homeland, Dzungaria, invaded the Kazakh nomad states and other areas, captured Tashkent, and went almost as far as the Urals. In 1758, China practically wiped out the Oirots and abolished their State. Only a few thousand Oirots survived in the Altai mountains. Those who lived in the High Altai were subjects of both Russia and China until 1866, when Russian sovereignty over that area was finally established.

'BURKHANISM' – THE OIROT RELIGION

The more powerless and impoverished the Oirot people became under Czarist rule, the more did they cling to their ancient legends and traditions. So strong was the spiritual resistance against the colonizers that it led ultimately to the foundation of a new religion which was called 'Burkhanism' or 'White Faith'. This Oirot religion is very similar in character to the new religions which emerge from time to time in various parts of tropical Africa, such as the Kibangism and Kitawala, messianic creeds whose prophets forecast the end of European rule.

In the centre of the Oirot religion stood the legendary figure of Oirot Khan, a descendant of Genghis Khan, whom the Oirots considered their last great ruler. Oirot Khan was the Messiah who was supposed to free the Oirots from their plight under alien rule, and to lead them to a better life. Oirot Khan appeared on a white horse to the Oirot shepherd Chot Chelpanov in 1904, and gave him a very detailed message to the Oirot people, containing an entire code of behaviour, which was anti-Christian and anti-foreign. Oirot Khan demanded that his people must not maintain ties of friendship with Russians, that they must not eat from the same pot with Christians, and that they must call the Russians not 'Orus', but 'thin-legged people'. The alleged appearance of Oirot Khan, who predicted that Russian rule would soon end, caused a great deal of unrest among the Oirots. The Czarist authorities intervened, despatched punitive expeditions against them, and arrested the main protagonists of 'Burkhanism', including the initiator of the trouble, Chot Chelpanov.

On the whole, the Czarist authorities handled the problem of 'Burkhanism' in a liberal way. The trial of Chelpanov was conducted with great fairness. A progressive ethnographer, D. A. Klements, whipped up a great deal of public sympathy for the 'Burkhanists', and even induced several outstanding lawyers of St. Petersburg to take over the defence of the accused. This defence was conducted so convincingly and so skilfully that the proceedings ended with a verdict of not guilty for all defendants. In giving it, the court overlooked the political implications of 'Burkhanism', and considered the case entirely from a religious angle. This attitude, which is in striking contrast to the conduct of Soviet courts in similar cases, was the more remarkable since the Oirot Khan cult had acquired a very pronounced pro-Japanese bias in connection with the defeat of the Czarist régime in the Russo-Japanese War. Popular imagination identified Oirot Khan with 'Yepon Khan', the Japanese Emperor.

'Burkhanism' has confronted the Bolshevik specialists on nationalities policy with a difficult problem. Originally they hesitated to condemn the Oirot religion as 'reactionary'. 'Burkhanism' was, after all, a national liberation movement directed against 'colonial robbery, Christendom, and the Altai Church Mission'. As it was persecuted by the Czarist authorities, it was, *ipso facto*, entitled to a certain consideration on the part of the Soviet régime.[15]

Soviet indulgence towards 'Burkhanism' came to an end in 1933, when it was denounced as a creation of Chinese merchant capitalism, and of Mongol-Lamaist theocracy.[16] But at least 'Burkhanism' was challenged from a purely class and ideological point of view. After the Second World War, Soviet criticism of 'Burkhanism' assumed a more outspoken national Russian character. The 'Burkhanists' were then charged with attempting to sever cultural and economic ties with the Russians, and to exchange them for a Japanese protectorate.[17]

THE DREAM OF 'GREATER OIROTIA'

Oirot nationalism took forms other than the messianic 'Burkhanism'. After the Russian February Revolution of 1917, it appeared on the scene in a more modern attire, as one of the many movements for national autonomy and self-determination that sprang up all over the Russian Empire. The aims of this secular Oirot nationalism were formulated by the Oirot nationalist, B. I. Anuchin, at the 'Constituent Congress of the High Altai', which took place in February 1918 in the village of Uala. Anuchin demanded the creation of an Oirot Republic, including, apart from the Oirots proper, the Khakassians and Tuvinians. According to him, these peoples were one by origin, language and customs. If united, said Anuchin, they would form a 'great Asiatic republic', several times larger than Germany and France put together. The hundred or so delegates who attended the Constituent Congress of the High Altai were greatly impressed by the ambitious nationalistic programme which was submitted to them. They fully endorsed the plan for an Oirot republic, and decided that it should be formally proclaimed by a 'Kurultay',* which was to meet in a place on the Mongol-Russian border in June 1918. Until the summoning of the 'Kurultay', negotiations were to be conducted with Russia, China and Mongolia. Each of these countries was supposed to give up certain territories to the

* An ancient Turkic term for National Assembly.

Oirot republic. China was to part with Dzungaria, the northern part of the Sinkiang province, Mongolia was expected to abandon the 'Mongol Altai', with all the territories inhabited by the Tuvinians, and Russia was to lose a considerable portion of her Altai region. Pending the implementation of the Greater Oirotia scheme, the High Altai was to be administered by the 'Karakorum Altai Administration' (Karakorumskaya Altaiskaya Uprava). This name is characteristic of the frame of mind of the Oirot nationalists. It reflects their romanticism that they should have identified their movement with Karakorum, the capital of Genghis Khan's Empire.

Considered retrospectively, the plan of Greater Oirotia might appear a romantic Utopia, but in 1918, when Russia seemed to disintegrate into a multitude of autonomous and independent states, the situation was different. The unification of the Oirot peoples appeared then as a possibility and, from the point of view of the Oirot nationalists, as a last chance to prevent the final triumph of russification in the High Altai. The Oirot nationalists had to realize, only too soon, that the gigantic struggle of Red versus White left no room for an independent Oirot policy. Therefore, they linked their fortunes with those of Admiral Kolchak, and put a whole 'Native Division' at his disposal. In December 1919, the coalition between 'Kolchakovtsy' and 'Karakorumtsy' was defeated. Soviet power was established in the High Altai, and in February 1920 the first Communist Party and Komsomol organizations were set up in Uala.

In the following months, some of the most prominent people among the Oirots went over into the Soviet camp. The Soviet Government, consequently, proclaimed an amnesty in favour of the 'citizen-natives' of the High Altai, who had originally sided with the counter-revolution, but who had since then repented of their attitude.[18]

SOVIET POWER AND OIROT NATIONALISM

This change of heart by some leading Oirot nationalists was determined by their expectation that the Greater Oirotia State would be ultimately established with Soviet help. Indeed, during a short period, it seemed that the Soviet Government had decided to create a large Turkic autonomous territory in the south of Siberia. In December 1921, the official organ of the People's Commissariat for Nationalities stated outright that the question of the 'Autonomous Oirot-Khakassian Province' was to receive a positive solution.[19] According to the Oirot nationalist leader, Sary-Sen Kanzychakov, the Province was to be 75,300 square miles in size, with 208,000 inhabitants, including 135,000 belonging to various Turkic nationalities. Between December 1921 and May 1922, the Soviet Government changed its mind about 'Greater Oirotia'. On

June 1st, 1922, the All-Russian Central Executive Committee issued a decree about the foundation of an 'Oirot ('Oirat' in the original spelling) Autonomous Province', which covered less than half the territory which was originally earmarked for the Oirot-Khakassian Province. Nevertheless, the Soviet Government made two important concessions to the Oirot nationalists. The first was that some of the more prominent nationalist representatives should be associated with the administration of the new autonomous unit. These included the above-mentioned Sary-Sen Kanzychakov, who became vice-president of the provincial administration. The other concession was the granting of official recognition to the terms, 'Oirots' and 'Oirotia'.

As everywhere else in the Soviet Union, the co-operation between communists and nationalists in Oirotia was only temporary. The Oirot nationalists seemed to have made various attempts to satisfy their aspirations towards national unity with other Turkic peoples, both inside and outside the Soviet Union. The concept of Greater Oirotia was still alive in the middle of the 'thirties'. Official Soviet sources asserted then that Oirot nationalists had exploited the situation of Oirotia as a border territory for their aims. This meant that they had been in contact with 'counter-revolutionary elements' of the Chinese Province of Sinkiang. At the same time, it was alleged that a 'counter-revolutionary nationalist group' had penetrated deep into the provincial administrative machinery, and also into the village councils. In connection with the liquidation of the 'counter-revolutionary conspiracy', the entire leadership of the Communist Party of Oirotia was dismissed for 'lack of vigilance', and for not fighting 'local nationalism'.[20] It is a fair assumption that Oirot nationalism with all its peculiarities, like the cult of Oirot Khan, survived not only the purges, but even the Second World War. Otherwise, the Soviet Government would hardly have taken the trouble to ban the 'provocative' term 'Oirot' in 1948.

THE 'HOUSE OF THE ALTAIWOMAN'

Soviet nationalities policy in Oirotia, whilst preventing the national liberation of the Oirots in the political sense, has done a great deal to raise their cultural level. On the whole, the development in the Oirot Autonomous Province has proceeded on the same pattern as in other autonomous territories of the U.S.S.R., but there is one institution which seems to be peculiar to Oirotia. This is the 'House of the Altaiwoman'.

These 'Houses' were founded only after the Second World War, presumably in 1950. There are six of them in various parts of the 'Autonomous Province'. In these 'Houses', wives and daughters of the native collective farmers of the High Altai are taught how to exchange

175

native for Russian habits. A fairly good picture of the atmosphere at these Houses, and of the curriculum of the courses, is available from descriptions by Russian reporters who have visited them. In the 'House of the Altaiwoman' in Shebalino, the native women learn cooking in the Russian way, knitting and sewing. Child welfare, vegetable-growing, and poultry-breeding are also part of the course. Some women also learn to read and write. In addition, the 'House of the Altaiwoman' is the scene of intense political indoctrination. There are lectures on the 'fight of women for peace', and on the hydro-electric giants on the Volga, Don and Dnieper. There are also anti-religious lectures in which the native women are told 'the truth about the Shamans'.[21]

The training in the Shebalino 'House' lasts two months. In the Elikmonar House it takes only six weeks. The pupils for the latter are picked from among the most efficient women workers of the local collective farms. Since this is done on a compulsory basis, the villagers regard the 'Houses' with some scepticism. A Soviet reporter, who described the departure of a milkmaid to the 'House' in Elikmonar, could not help noticing the mixed feelings with which the Oirots looked at the innovation. He said it was not certain whether the other women envied the girl who went away, or whether they felt that the girl in question should envy those who stayed at home.[22] This is not to be wondered at. Every progressive measure in any colony encounters the resistance of the more backward groups of native society. British policy, for instance, faces the same difficulties in Africa with some of its mass education schemes. There is, however, one great difference. The British ultimately carry out these schemes with the help of the local nationalists; whereas the Soviet Government implements them by annihilating the latter.

IV. THE KHAKASSIAN AUTONOMOUS PROVINCE

The Khakassians have so far been more lucky than the Shorians or Oirots. Their Autonomous Province has not been abolished, nor has its name been changed to please the local Russian colonists. Nevertheless, the position of the 52,000 Khakassians, who live in a territory as big as Belgium and Holland combined, is precarious.

A Soviet propaganda article on the Khakassians said that they were doomed to extinction under the Czarist régime, but were saved by the Soviet Government.[23] In fact, Soviet critics were right in denouncing Czarist colonization for having relegated the Khakass people, or 'Minusinsk Tatars' as they used to be called, to areas where the soil and climatic conditions were unfavourable. Russian colonization in Khakassia under the Czarist régime reached its peak between 1840 and

1850, when the population of the country increased by 25 or 30 per cent. Under the Soviet regime, Russian colonization assumed a much more powerful impetus. Within seven years – from 1926 to 1932 – the population of Khakassia increased by almost 100 per cent from 88,800 to 173,300. In 1944 the population was given as 270,000 and considering the small number of Khakassians, this meant that their share in the total population of the Province had dropped to below twenty per cent. The newcomers flocked primarily into the capital, Abakan, and into three workers' settlements – Chernogorsk, Kommunar and Saral. By the outbreak of the Second World War, these four places had more inhabitants than the country's entire population in 1926. This growth was in the first place due to the large coal deposits in Khakassia, believed to amount to between 17 and 20 billion tons. The country also produces gold and various rare metals.

The growing Russian influence in Khakassia met with protests even on the part of the native communists. In their meetings they used the slogan, 'Khakassia could do without Russians', which, however, was soon denounced as a manifestation of bourgeois nationalism. Some leading Khakassians went beyond mere verbal protests in their attempt to check the increase of the Russian elements. In the same way as the Oirot nationalists, they thought that the various Turkic peoples of Siberia would be in a better position to resist Russian pressure by joining hands and forming a single autonomous unit within the Russian Soviet Federation. Without consulting Moscow, some Khakassian Soviet officials started to negotiate with their opposite numbers in Oirotia and Kazakhstan for a unification of the Turkic peoples. Kazakhstan, as the largest country involved in these secret talks, was probably expected to assume a kind of protectorate over Khakassians and Oirots. The Moscow Communist Party leaders were informed in time of the counter-revolutionary pan-Turkic project. The nationalist promoters of the plan, who included representatives of the new Khakass Soviet intelligentsia, members of the Khakass Students' Club in Moscow, and graduates of the Khakass Teachers' training college, were purged in the middle of the 'thirties'.[24]

In the post-war period, there has been no evidence of any open trouble on the 'national front' in Khakassia but difficulties have arisen from the inferior constitutional status of the Khakass Autonomous Province. Like all other Autonomous Provinces of the R.S.F.S.R., with the sole exception of Tuva, Khakassia is not directly under the Council of Ministers of the Russian Federation, but under a territorial ('kray') administration. The territory to which it belongs has its centre in Krasnoyarsk. This administrative set-up has enabled the Krasnoyarsk territorial Executive Committee and the territorial Party Committee to practise a policy of petty interference in the local affairs of Khakassia.

Dissatisfaction at the arbitrary attitude of the territorial authorities came into the open at a provincial party conference held in Abakan in September 1952. There it was stated bluntly that the Kranoyarsk party and administration chiefs had the habit of drawing up economic and cultural plans for Khakassia without consulting the local organs about them.[25] In other words, Khakass autonomy exists only on paper.

BIBLIOGRAPHICAL NOTES TO CHAPTER VI

1. DOUGLAS CARUTHERS, *Unknown Mongolia*, London 1913, vol. i, p. 166.
2. S. TOKA, *Prazdnik Tuvinskogo Naroda* – The Festival of the Tuvinian People, *Pravda*, August 17th, 1946.
3. *Severnaya Aziya*, 1926, Nr 4, p. 20.
4. S. A. SHOIKHELOV, *Tuvinskaya Narodnaya Respublika* – The Tuvinian People's Republic, Moscow 1930, p. 87.
5. OTTO MÄNCHEN-HELFEN, *Reise ins Asiatische Tuva*, Berlin 1931, pp. 162–3.
6. *Revolyutsionny Vostok*, 1935, Nr 30, pp. 169–70.
7. *Literaturnaya Gazeta*, April 28th, 1951.
8. *Novy Mir*, April 1941, Nr 4, p. 17.
9. *Small Soviet Encyclopedia*, first edition, vol. 8, Moscow 1930, p. 869.
10. *Pravda*, October 11th, 1949.
11. *Large Soviet Encyclopedia*, second edition, Moscow 1950, vol. 2.
12. *Sovetskaya Etnografiya*, 1950, Nr 3, p. 129.
13. *Oktyabr*, June 1952, Nr 6, pp. 107–8.
14. *Sovetskaya Etnografiya*, 1950, Nr 3, p. 133.
15. *Revolyutsionny Vostok*, Nr 7, 1929, p. 223. Various books on Oirotia published in the early thirties included a positive appraisal of 'Burkhanism', among them being MANET's *Oirotia*, Moscow 1930; and POTAPOV's *Ocherk Istorii Oirotii* – Outline of the History of Oirotia, Novosibirsk, 1931.
16. *Revolyutsiya i Natsionalnosti*, June 1933, Nr 3, pp. 121–4.
17. POTAPOV, *Ocherki po istorii Altaitsev* – Essays on the History of the Altaitsy, Novosibirsk 1948, pp. 41–42.
18. *Zhizn Natsionalnostei*, February 25th, 1922, Nr 1.
19. *Zhizn Natsionalnostei*, December 14th, 1921, Nr 29.
20. *Revolyutsiya i Natsionalnosti*, October 1936, Nr 80, pp. 15–17.
21. *Ogonyok*, March 1952, Nr 11, pp. 4–5.
22. GENNADY GOR, *Po Gornomu Altayu* – Through the High Altai, *Zvezda*, April 1951, Nr 4, pp. 117–18.
23. *Soviet War News*, June 28th, 1944.
24. *Revolyutsionny Vostok*, 1935, Nr 32, p. 191.
25. *Pravda*, September 9th, 1952.

VII

THE SOVIET FAR EAST IN PERSPECTIVE

1.

Communism as a materialistic teaching cannot aim at the preservation of national groups and minorities. Their right to an existence as separate political and cultural individualities depends on their contribution to the communist cause. If they fulfil a useful and 'progressive' task, from a communist point of view, they are able to enjoy the very considerable material blessings which communism has in store for backward areas. On the other hand, if they are an obstacle to communism they may be exterminated.

The extermination of ethnic groups can take many forms both in communist and non-communist societies. Open violent genocide has been practised only in a few exceptional cases, for instance, by Imperial Germany which wiped out entire tribes in South-West Africa, by Hitlerite Germany which destroyed the bulk of the Jewish population of Eastern and Central Europe or by Soviet Russia which suppressed such nationalities as the Chechens, Ingushi, Crimean Tartars, Balkars and others. But genocide does not always culminate in one single dramatic event, it may be spread out over many years. A large number of political, economic and cultural measures may be put into effect to bring about the ultimate extermination or at least disintegration of an ethnic group. Let us recapitulate shortly the principal measures leading to national oppression which we have seen at work in various parts of the Soviet Far East and Eastern Siberia:

1. Industrialisation and de-tribalisation which is linked with migration of natives to big urban centres.
2. Destruction of the native economy through state interference such as the fostering of class struggle and the confiscation of cattle.
3. Mass colonization of 'national territories' by Europeans.
4. 'Liquidation' of the native upper class and of the intellectual *élite*.
5. Persecution of religious beliefs peculiar to minority nationalities.
6. Prohibition of cultural and political integration of kindred tribes and nationalities.
7. Imposition of an alien ideology, of a foreign language and culture.

8. Suppression of historical and cultural traditions which are essential to the survival of the national consciousness of a given ethnic group.

It may be argued that none of these eight measures is the exclusive weapon of communist nationalities policy. Their application may be traced not only in Russia but also in areas which are notorious as 'dark spots' of Western colonial policy. Ruthless industrialization and de-tribalization, for instance, may be seen in operation in a city like Johannesburg or in the mining areas of the Belgian Congo. The liquidation of the intellectual *élite* does seem to be the result of the policy pursued in Madagascar. Mass colonization by Europeans has jeopardised the interests of the native peoples of Kenya and the Rhodesias. Attempts at establishing unity have been frustrated in the case of the Ewe people in West Africa and in the case of the Somali in East Africa. But in comparing conditions in Siberia to those in the more problematic parts of the African continent one important reservation must be made. The numerical strength of the African people is such that ultimately they will triumph over the limitations which result from European colonial rule. Ultimately Africa will belong to the Africans. In Siberia things are different. There the peoples can have no hope of an end of European rule. They are too small in numbers to withstand the communist offensive which combines the implementation of economic development schemes with social experiments and attacks on tribal institutions and customs.

Another important factor which makes national oppression in the Soviet Union even more intolerable than in most other colonial Empires is the lack of freedom of expression in Russia's metropolitan territories. Protests about injustices committed in colonial territories often reach the public in Britain and France, they are discussed in the press and in Parliament. The interest which British public opinion takes in colonial affairs in particular, is a very important factor in the discovery and remedy of local inequities, and the local political leaders in the colonies know that there are always British members of parliament, British newspapers and British missionary societies ready to take up a 'cause'. In Soviet Russia it is unthinkable that a Moscow newspaper should defend the cause of a local nationality against the Central Government or against the Central Committee of the Communist Party. It is equally unthinkable that a Yakut or Buryat delegation should give a Press conference in Moscow to a sympathetic Russian audience challenging certain measures or plans pursued by the Kremlin in Eastern Siberia or that a member of the Soviet Parliament should expose the execution of nationalist leaders, say, in the Tuvinian Autonomous Province.

The reason for the absence of such Russian criticism of Soviet colonial policy is not that all Russians are in agreement with the policy pursued in the Soviet East but that they themselves are an oppressed people. To remember this fact is of cardinal importance for the appraisal of Soviet reality although it might easily be overlooked in view of the forcible imposition of Russian culture and the encouragement of Russian colonization by the communist régime. Naturally, the Russians are not oppressed in the same way as the other peoples of the Soviet Union. In view of their large numbers and their geographical distribution all over the U.S.S.R. they are bound to occupy a place in communist strategy that is different from that of the minority nationalities. The régime uses the Russian language and it uses a diluted and falsified form of Russian culture for the strengthening of communist centralism. Russian culture as a free Russian intelligentsia would understand this term and the 'Russian culture' propagated by the Soviet régime are by no means identical. In the first place, a number of Russian philosophers, particularly Russian religious thinkers, have remained on the Soviet 'index' and without them Russian culture will remain incomplete. As long as Russian culture is without its Christian elements it will be as crippled as British civilization would be without the Bible. In addition, the Soviet régime has given Russian culture and Russian history an aggressive and one-sided interpretation which the best elements of the Russian intelligentsia would never accept if they had a real opportunity to express their views.

2.

The Soviet nationalities policy as pursued in the Russian Far East helps to solve the question of whether the Soviet Union is predominantly a European or an Asian power. This question is of more than academic interest since on its answer depends the future shape of relations between Russia and the nations of Asia. The methods by which Russian culture and language are encouraged in Soviet North-East Asia, Russian nationalist leanings are fostered among colonists, Buryats and Yakuts are treated and Mongolia is ruled through 'remote control' show that the Soviet Union is behaving as a European colonial power in the worst old-fashioned sense of that term.

When determining whether Russia is 'Europe' or 'Asia' other factors too must be taken into account. If we look at the problem geographically and historically, then it must be recognized that Russia is a combination of Europe and Asia. But the vastness of the Soviet Far East and Soviet Asia in general can only too easily lead to an over-rating of the Asian aspect of the U.S.S.R. while in fact the political and ideological centre of gravity of the Soviet State is clearly in Europe and more so now, since the Second World War, than ever before. The European character of Soviet Russia has been strengthened by the territorial annexations which she carried out in the years 1939–45. The Western territories which the Kremlin added to the Soviet Empire have as many inhabitants as all five Central Asian Soviet Republics. A small slice of the new 'Soviet Far West', the Baltic States alone have a larger population than the entire gigantic Soviet Far East which covers one-seventh of the surface of the Soviet Union. Nor are they superior in numbers only, they are also more advanced culturally. The Russian territories east of Lake Baikal have not a single cultural centre which could rival a Vilnius, a Riga or a Tartu (Dorpat).

The emergence of half a dozen satellite countries in Central and Eastern Europe has further consolidated the specific weight of Europe within the Soviet Empire. The satellite countries, it is true, have caused considerable worries and difficulties to the Kremlin but from a long-term Russian communist point of view the advantages outweigh the disadvantages. Seen from the angle of the internal security of the Soviet State the satellites are considerable assets. The existence of 'loyal' governments in Poland and Eastern Germany means safety for Russian colonization in the Baltic States and the Kaliningrad (Koenigsberg) Province. The communist régimes of Poland, Czechoslovakia, Hungary and Rumania isolate Ukrainian nationalism and reduce the danger which it constitutes to Soviet centralism. A Bulgarian 'People's Republic' at the gates of Istanbul is an additional safeguard against that city becoming a rallying point of pan-Turkism, an idea which still has its attractions for the Turkic peoples of the U.S.S.R.

The communist sphere, it is true, has expanded further in East Asia than in Eastern Europe but there it has a quite different meaning. The establishment of the so-called European 'People's Republics' or 'People's Democracies' is an obvious gain both from an international communist and from a Russian viewpoint. These countries are not only Russia's political satellites, they are also part of the Russian cultural sphere. For instance, the Russian language is being persistently and to some extent even forcibly imposed on them as the 'language of socialism', With regard to the Chinese People's Republic things are different. Its existence is certainly a gain for world communism, but whether it is in the long run a gain for Russia is doubtful.

It is difficult to imagine a situation in which Russia could 'swallow up' a communist China culturally and politically. On the other hand, the victory of Chinese communism may have, from the Soviet Russian standpoint, adverse effects on the destinies of the European population of the Soviet Far East, on the Mongols of the M.P.R. and even on the Buryats and other nationalities of Siberia. Could not a new vigorous China try to draw these nationalities into its orbit in the same way as a strong Japan did in the past?

If communist China decides to take up the problem of Asiatic immigration into the Soviet Far East and the problem of the unification of all Mongol territories this will have not only considerable political but also great ideological significance. In taking up these issues China will force the Soviet Union to decide whether it wants to adopt towards the Far East a Russian nationalist or an internationalist communist approach.

But whichever way Soviet Russia decides will ultimately make little difference. If she continues to uphold the nationalist Russian 'mystique' and the policy of the White Soviet Far East with all that this implies she must necessarily encounter the open hostility of China and possibly of a new strong Japan, even if we assume for the sake of argument that it might be a 'Japanese People's Republic'. The position of the Russian Far East will then become untenable. If, on the other hand, the Soviet régime decides to drop its European bias, then it must throw its frontiers wide open to Eastern immigrants, both Chinese farmers and Japanese fishermen. In such a case there would no longer be any sense in an artificially fostered European immigration into the Pacific coastal areas. Nor would there be any sense in Russia keeping such outposts as Sakhalin and the Kurile Islands. In other words, if Soviet Russia remains nationalistically Russian, then she is bound to be involved in a conflict with the Far Eastern nations as a result of which she might lose her Far Eastern possessions. If she adopts an internationalist communist attitude she must honour this change of heart by a voluntary retreat. Naturally, in a world situation where Russia and China are bound together by the common fear and hatred of the West, questions like those of Chinese immigration into the Soviet Far East and the future of Mongolia are of secondary importance but these problems do exist and will require a solution one day.

The peoples of the Soviet Far East would gain little if Russian communist rule were replaced by Chinese communist rule. There could only be a change for the better if a régime were established which would guarantee the freedom of the person and the freedom of conscience. One of the most important consequences of the restoration of freedom would be the liquidation of the forced labour system which is a more important institution in the Russian Far East than in most other parts of the U.S.S.R. The disbandment of the forced labour camps would lead at least temporarily to a weakening of Russian colonization and to the virtual depopulation of certain less accessible parts of the Russian Far East. It would also result in the abandonment of various development schemes which are economically wasteful and can be kept going only with the work of convicts.

3.

As soon as the Russian people are freed from the fetters of communist materialism and police rule the Russian attitude towards the small peoples of Siberia and the Far East will have a chance to be inspired by a new and genuinely democratic ethical nationalities policy. The aim of such a policy can only be the preservation of the life of ethnic groups, even of the smallest, instead of their submission to the requirements of a political apparatus and a rigid economic plan. 'Preservation of life' does not mean non-interference, does not mean leaving undeveloped areas to themselves but means guaranteeing them material well-being without destroying their souls. To combine the two is a problem which confronts every society including the Russia of the future.*

For the non-Russian nationalities of the present Soviet Far East and Siberia the restoration of freedom in Russia will be the beginning of a new spiritual revolution. Various philosophies and creeds will enter into competition to heal the moral wounds and confusion which the brusque transition from Shamanism to Communism must have inflicted. Christian missions will be one of the factors in this new situation arising in Siberia. The missionaries in the lands of the Far Eastern and Far Northern tribes will require a profound psychological understanding of the local nationalities, an infinite amount of tact, and a thorough knowledge of history, languages and tribal customs. This tremendous task can probably not be shouldered by the Russian Church alone, it may have to be shared by the entire Christian world.

However, it is not likely that Christianity will have a spiritual monopoly in the Russia of the future. There will be other alternatives to communist materialism in various parts of the Russian Empire – Islam, Buddhism and other beliefs, as well as various brands of nationalism without pronounced religious attachments. All these forces are at present kept in check by the communist police state but on the purely spiritual plane they have not been vanquished yet. Even after many years

* Nobody has defended the 'preservation of life' of the small ethnic groups in more brilliant terms than the Indian philosopher Radhakrishnan when he wrote:
'The trail of man is dotted with the graves of countless communities which reached an untimely end. But is there any justification for this violation of human life? Have we any idea of what the world loses when one racial culture is extinguished? It is true that the Red Indians have not made, to all appearance, any contribution to the world progress, but have we any clear understanding of their undeveloped possibilities which, in God's time, might have come to fruition? Do we know so much of ourselves and the world and God's purpose as to believe that our civilization, our institutions and our customs are so immeasurably superior to those of others, not only what others actually possess but what exists in them potentially? We cannot measure beforehand the possibilities of a race. Civilizations are not made in a day and had the fates been kindlier and we less arrogant in our ignorance the world, I dare say, would have been richer for the contributions of the Red Indians.' (S. Radhakrishnan, *The Hindu View of Life*, London 1927, pp. 94–5).

of purges and persecution religious and nationalist trends are alive in the Soviet Empire. This survival of religion and of nationalism is not only characteristic of conditions in the U.S.S.R. itself, but also gives a clue to the future development of the Asiatic territories outside the Soviet Union. If complete ideological uniformity could not be imposed on even such small peoples as Buryat-Mongols and Yakuts how can we expect communism to succeed in the larger Asian countries with their great and ancient civilizations? To become a victorious ideology in addition to a victorious political system communism would have to change its character and increase its spiritual striking power. It would have to rise to the same heights as the religious teachings of the Asian continent. Up to a certain point the Kremlin itself has been aware of this problem. It has deliberately encouraged certain aspects of communism which would lend themselves to expansion into component parts of a new pseudo-religious mysticism – for instance the cult of Stalin and the cult of Moscow which comes very near the myth that surrounds the 'sacred city' of any religion. Both these cults are propagated on a worldwide scale but nowhere did they find such exaggerated expression as in the Eastern Republics of the Soviet Union. However persistently propagated, they could not make communism a serious competitor of the recognized creeds and philosophic teachings of the East, least of all the Stalin cult which may turn out to be short-lived. It has already given way to the colourless cult of the Party which is far less attractive to the Eastern mind. Other attempts have been made too, to put communism on a higher level by restating as communist principles what are Christian principles or general moral principles common to all religious creeds. This is the purpose of the teaching on so-called 'communist morality' in Soviet schools as well as of the new statute which the Communist Party of the Soviet Union adopted in October 1952 and which put stronger emphasis on honesty and truthfulness to secure a smoother running of the Party apparatus. But in the works of Lenin and Stalin which contain the principal message of Soviet communism we find little more than precepts for political strategy and tactics and in the best case explanations of certain sociological phenomena. Neither Lenin nor Stalin nor any of their disciples have attempted to create an all-embracing code of moral behaviour and to give a definition of permanent values that could rival any of the sacred books which originated in Asia, the Old and New Testaments, the Hindu Scriptures, the Avesta or the Koran. Consequently, through communism Asia would lose more in the spiritual field than it might gain in the material. Herein lies the chief weakness of the whole political and ideological communist system and of its nationalities policy.

*Some of the types and personalities
mentioned in the text*

186

1 The Yakut historian Georgy Basharin whose views on Yakut literature *Pravda* denounced as 'anti-Marxist'.
2 The Khakassian student N. S. Tenashev, of the teachers' training college of Abakan.
3 A Buryat – Mongol peasant, Bula-Tsyren Tugutov, who was awarded the title 'Hero of Socialist Toil'.
4 An actor of the former Chinese theatre of Vladivostok.
5 Valentina Khetagurova-Zarubina, a Russian, wife of a Red Army officer serving in the Far East. She appealed to Russia's girls to live and work in the Soviet Far Eastern territories.
6 Kim Penkhva, chairman of the Korean collective farm 'Polar Star' of the Tashkent Province (Uzbekistan), previously in the Soviet Far East.
7 A Nanai woman, Samar, accountant of a collective farm.
8 The Shorian miner Dmitry Pyzhlakov (Tashtagol iron-ore mines, Kemerovo Province).
9 Otke, a Chukcha, Chairman of the Executive Committee of the Chukcha National Area.
10 Sad Belbekov, an Oirot shepherd of the 'Paris Commune' collective farm (Autonomous Province of the High Altai).
11 Marshal Choibalsan (1895–1952), Premier and Commander-in-Chief of the Mongol People's Republic.
12 Dzhansi Kimonko (1905–1949), an Udege writer, hunter and village council chairman.
13 Mavra Mironova, a Tunguz student of the Leningrad Pedagogical Institute reading the *History of the Soviet Communist Party*.

187

INDEX